VOCES

Voices from the Hispanic Church

Other books by Justo L. González published by Abingdon Press:

Christian Thought Revisited: Three Types of Theology

(ed.) *Each in Our Own Tongue: A History of Hispanic United Methodism* (Spanish translation also available).

A History of Christian Thought: From the Beginnings to the Council of Chalcedon, Vol. I

A History of Christian Thought: From Saint Augustine to the Eve of the Reformation, Vol. II

A History of Christian Thought: From Saint Augustine to the Eve of the Reformation, Vol. III

(With Catherine Gunsalus González) *Liberation Preaching: The Pulpit and the Oppressed*

Mañana: Christian Theology from a Hispanic Perspective

(With Catherine Gunsalus González) *Vision at Patmos: Studies in the Book of Revelation*

Out of Every Tribe and Nation: Christian Theology at the Ethnic Roundtable

VOCES

Voices from the Hispanic Church

Edited by
Justo L. González

ABINGDON PRESS
Nashville

VOCES:
Voices From The Hispanic Church

This book is printed on recycled paper.

Library of Congress Cataloging-in-Publication Data

Voces: voices from the Hispanic church / Justo L. González, editor.
       p.   cm.
    Essays were originally published in Apuntes, a journal of Hispanic theology.
    ISBN 0-687-43810-1 (alk. paper)
    1. Hispanic American--Religion.   2. Theology.   I. González, Justo L.
BR563.H57V63   1992
277.3'0829'08968--dc20   91-42501
                                                    CIP

The cover illustration, furnished by Justo González, is a detail of a fresco by Diego Rivera in the Presidential Palace, Mexico City.

MANUFACTURED IN THE UNITED STATES OF AMERICA

CONTENTS

Rethinking Our Future

Preface

New voices are making themselves heard in the field of theology: Afro-American voices, Women's voices, Third World voices, Hispanic voices. In the traditional chorus of theology, such voices often sound a dissonant chord or a different rhythm. They speak of a new reading of Scripture and history, of new interpretations of traditional doctrines, and of the surreptitious inroads of class, race and gender into supposedly objective theological research. And they do so in a clipped rhythm of urgency seldom heard in modern theological inquiry.

The dissonance is jarring. As such, it may be too easily dismissed by the choir directors of theology as well as by audiences that expect theology to be soothing.

But listen again. Perhaps these voices are dissonant, not out of tone-deafness, but out of a keen hearing that perceives in the Gospel a different tune.

This book is a collection of such voices out of the Hispanic church in the U.S. and Puerto Rico. The essays in it were originally published in *Apuntes*, a journal of Hispanic theology published under the joint auspices of the Mexican-American Program at Perkins School of Theology and the United Methodist Publishing House. It began publication over ten years ago, in 1980, as the modest endeavor of a small group who saw the need for such a journal, and has gained a respected place among the many theological journals in the nation. Out of the first ten years of publication, we have selected the articles included in the present book as a representative sample of the work and concerns of Hispanic theologians. Many other articles were equally worthy of republication, but were not included in order to keep the representative character of the present volume.

The voices that speak in the pages that follow are varied, and their concerns are equally varied. Catholics and Protestants address concerns that cut across denominational and confessional lines. Women speak of issues and realities that male theologians often ignore or misinterpret. Puerto Ricans, Mexican Americans and others deal with a number of issues specific to their communities, as well as with others that are relevant to all Hispanics in the United States. Several discuss the urgent issues facing our communities or the world at large such as international migration, racism, ecology, militarism, etc. Others deal with biblical and historical research, with matters of church order and management, with counseling, music, etc. Thus the scope of the pages that follow is wide and far reaching.

Yet, if the scope is wide, the focus is sharp. We are not interested in idle speculation having nothing to do with our situation and our context. We are speaking in the midst of a people that has often been ignored and has long been oppressed, not only by society at large, but also by the church and by theology, and that is what gives our dissonant voices their staccato beat of urgency.

That we have often been ignored can easily be documented. How many standard text-books on American Church History begin with the South-West rather than with the Mayflower? And yet, there are in the U.S. today, in the formerly Mexican South-West, Christian churches that are much older than any in Massachusetts. How many such text-books pay significant attention to the Mexican-American war and its impact on the denominational composition of this country? Yet today it is becoming increasingly apparent that in terms of its impact on that denominational composition, the Mexican-American war is fully comparable to the Wesleyan revival.

That our people are oppressed even in the church and theology can be proven with equal ease. One glaring statistic should suffice: during the last decade, in a good year, the number of Hispanics graduating with a Ph.D. in religion or its equivalent from all institutions accredited by the Association of Theological Schools, Protestants and Catholics, reached the incredible total of four! To teach in all the seminaries and departments of religion in the U.S., Canada and Puerto Rico, the theological establishment produced and certified less than four Hispanic candidates per year! There are many reasons for this --lack of educational opportunities from the very first years of learning, insufficient funding, ecclesiastical indifference and academic insensitivity and snobbism. Whatever the reasons, the fact is that Hispanics are grossly underrepresented in the various fields of theology, and generally excluded from the centers of higher theological education.

It is this situation that gives our varied voices their sharp and common focus. We are all dealing with issues that are crucial and urgent to us, both as Christians and as Hispanics. As Christians, we believe that matters of faith, its meaning, and its significance for life today are of paramount importance. As Hispanics, we are dissatisfied with the manner in which the church in general, and its theology specifically, have dealt with such matters. Yet, we have made every attempt not to turn the pages of *Apuntes* or of this book into a forum to air our dissatisfactions. We have sought to move beyond that, grounding what we have to say on an alternative reading of Scripture and Christian tradition, and on a vision of what the church is called to be.

Thus we raise our dissonant voices. We raise them, not for the sake of dissonance, but in the hope that, like the jarring crow of a rooster long ago, our cry may awaken the church as well as each one of us to our betrayals, and call it to repentance and greater faithfulness.

Finally, a word of gratitude. Gratitude, first of all, to those who have made *Apuntes* possible during all these years: to Dr. Roy D. Barton, who caught the vision and secured funding and other forms of support; to Perkins School of Theology, for its backing; to the United Methodist Publishing House, which has printed and distributed the journal free of cost; and especially to our readers and authors, who have believed and supported our commitment to make this a truly ecumenical journal, and have thus made the entire enterprise eminently rewarding. Then, gratitude to those who have made this book possible: to Drs. Roberto Gómez and Roy D. Barton, who convinced others as well as myself that a volume such as this should be published; to the United Methodist Publishing House, and particularly within its staff to Ron Patterson and Richard Peck, who have provided technical and other support and guidance; and to Javier Quiñones-Ortiz, who has done all the clerical, administrative and transcribing work, as well as much of the design and typesetting.

Justo L. González
Decatur, Georgia
October 28, 1991

Note: For further information regarding *Apuntes*, please write to Dr. Roy D. Barton, Director, Mexican-American Program, Perkins School of Theology, Southern Methodist University, Dallas, TX 75275

Contributors

Cecilio Arrastía is a retired Presbyterian pastor and a preacher of international renown. He is currently Visiting Professor of Homiletics at St. Vincent de Paul Regional Seminary in Boynton Beach, Florida. He frequently leads national and international seminars and workshops on preaching. His article appeared in *Apuntes*, Vol. 1, No. 1, Spring, 1981, pp. 7-13.

Michael Candelaria is Assistant Professor of Religious Studies at California State University in Bakersfield. He is a participant in an ongoing dialogue between discourse ethics and the philosophy of liberation headed by Enrique Dussel. His most recent publication is *Popular Religion and Liberation: The Dilemma of Liberation Theology*. His article appeared in *Apuntes*, Year 3, No. 4, Winter, 1983, pp. 75-82.

Ignacio Castuera is the Senior Pastor of the First United Methodist Church of Hollywood. He has served as District Superintendent of the Pacific and Southwest Annual Conference of the United Methodist Church, as adjunct faculty of the School of Theology at Claremont, as Counseling Psychologist at UCLA, and many local and national boards in his denomination. His article appeared in *Apuntes*, Vol. 3, No. 2, Summer, 1983, pp. 33-45.

The late *Orlando E. Costas*, after a fruitful career as a pastor in the U.S. and Puerto Rico, and as a Professor at the Latin American Bible Seminary in Costa Rica, founded the Hispanic Program at Eastern Baptist Theological Seminary. He then served as Dean of Andover Newton Theological School, until his untimely death. He authored several books, including *Christ Outside the Gate* and *Liberating News*. His article appeared in *Apuntes*, Vol. 2, No. 4, Winter, 1982, pp. 75-84.

Francisco O. García-Treto is a Presbyterian who is Professor and Chair of the Religion Department of Trinity University in San Antonio. Educated in Cuba and the U.S., his main area of interest is Old Testament Narrative Theology. His article appeared in *Apuntes*, Vol. 1, No. 4, Winter, 1981, pp. 3-9.

Minerva Garza Carcaño is an United Methodist District Superintendent of the Western District of the Rio Grande Conference. She has served several pastorates in Texas and California, and also as a chaplain in a United Methodist secondary school. Her main interests are biblical studies and evangelization. Her article appeared in *Apuntes*, Year 10, No. 2, Summer, 1990, pp. 27-35.

Roberto L. Gómez, born in San Antonio and the son of a retired minister, is a United Methodist District Superintendent of the Rio Grande Conference. He is a Hispanic Instructor of the Mexican American Program at Perkins School of Theology, lectures in the M.Div. program, and teaches pastoral counseling in the Spanish Conference Course of Study Program. His article appeared in *Apuntes*, Vol. 2, No. 2, Summer, 1982, pp. 31-39.

Jorge A. González is Fuller E. Callaway Professor of Religion at Berry College. He is a United Methodist minister and a member of the North Georgia Annual Conference. His present research field involves the history of the Spanish Bible. His article appeared in *Apuntes*, Vol. 1, No. 4, Winter, 1981, pp. 10-15.

Justo L. González is the founding editor of *Apuntes* and Director of the Hispanic Summer Program of the Fund for Theological Education. After many years of teaching in theological institutions, he now devotes most of his time to writing. He is a member of the Rio Grande Conference of the United Methodist Church. His articles appeared in *Apuntes*, Vol. 1, No. 1, Spring, 1981, pp. 3-6, and in Year 10, No. 4, Winter, 1990, pp. 84-86.

Ada María Isasi-Díaz is Assistant Professor of Theology and Ethics at Drew University. Born and raised in Cuba, she is also a well-known speaker, preacher and process person. Her commitment is to develop a *Mujerista* theology --a Hispanic Women's Liberation Theology-- the beginnings of which she sketched in the article included in this book. Her article appeared in *Apuntes*, Year 6, No. 3, Fall, 1986, pp. 61-71.

Jorge Lara-Braud is a native of Mexico and a U.S. naturalized citizen, who has devoted his life to theological education, human rights and the promotion of Christian unity. He served as an ecumenical and denominational executive, as well as in theological institutions in both the U.S. and Mexico. His main interest is the relationship between theology and culture. His article appeared in *Apuntes*, Vol. 2, No. 1, Spring, 1982, pp. 3-7.

Jill Martínez is the Associate Executive Presbyter for Mission for the Presbytery of San Diego. She is responsible for liaisoning with 20 mission projects located within Imperial County, San Diego County and Baja California. As a D.Min. candidate, she is completing a dissertation on cross-cultural dynamics in strategic planning. Her article appeared in *Apuntes*, Year 9, No. 1, Spring, 1989, pp. 3-9.

Joel Martínez is pastor of Emanu-El United Methodist Church in Dallas. He has served as President of MARCHA (National Hispanic Caucus of the United Methodist Church). He is also serving as President of the Greater Dallas Community of Churches and Vice-President of the General Council of Ministries of the United Methodist Church. His article appeared in *Apuntes*, Vol. 1, No. 2, Summer, 1981, pp. 10-13.

Roberto W. Pazmiño is an ordained American Baptist minister, who is currently serving as Professor of Religious Studies at Andover Newton Theological School. He has special interest in the theory and practice of Christian education and multicultural education. His works include *Foundational Issues in Christian Education*. His article appeared in *Apuntes*, Year 8, No. 2, Summer, 1988, pp. 27-37.

Yolanda E. Pupo-Ortiz is currently the pastor of the Bethesda Hispanic United Methodist Church in the Baltimore Annual Conference. At the time of the writing of her article she was an Associate General Secretary of The General Commission on Religion and Race. Her article appeared, under the name Yolanda E. Rivas, in *Apuntes*, Vol. 2, No. 2, Summer, 1982, pp. 40-47.

Harold Recinos is an Associate Professor of Theology and Culture and Director of the Urban Ministry Track at Wesley Theological Seminary. As a Ph.D. candidate in Cultural Anthropology at American University, he is exploring globalization in terms of urban life. His forthcoming work *God's Sacred Place: The City*, will be published by Abingdon Press. His article appeared in *Apuntes*, Year 7, No. 4, Winter, 1987, pp. 86-95.

Luis N. Rivera-Pagán is a member of the Baptist Convention of Churches of Puerto Rico. He is an Associate Professor of Humanities, Humanities Department, General Studies School, University of Puerto Rico. His most recent publication, *Evangelización y violencia*, is a best seller which is in the process of translation and publication by Westminster/John Knox Press. His article appeared in *Apuntes*, Year 10, No. 3, Fall, 1990, pp. 59-69.

José David Rodríguez is a Lutheran minister from Puerto Rico. He has served pastorates in both the U.S. and Puerto Rico. He is an Assistant Professor of Hispanic Ministries and Theological Studies at the Lutheran School of Theology in Chicago, and Director of the Hispanic Ministries Program at the same institution. He is married, with two daughters and two sons. His article appeared in *Apuntes*, Year 10, No. 4, Winter, 1990, pp. 75-83.

Caleb Rosado, a Puerto Rican who holds degrees in theology and sociology, is an Associate Professor of Sociology at Humboldt State University. His publications explore race relations and religion. He regularly serves as consultant with corporations, universities and community organizations on issues of cultural diversity and multicultural education. His article appeared in *Apuntes*, Year 9, No. 2, Summer, 1989, pp. 27-35.

Carlos Rosas is a renown composer, hymnologist and liturgist, who currently serves as Liturgical Director of the San Juan de los Lagos parish in San Antonio. He was also Liturgical Director of the Mexican American Cultural Center in the same city. His article appeared in *Apuntes*, Year 6, No. 1, Spring, 1986, pp. 3-11.

María Luisa Santillán Baert is a United Methodist clergywoman from the Rio Grande Conference. She is presently the Managing Editor of *The Upper*

Room, and has also served in the faculty of Perkins School of Theology at Southern Methodist University. She is married to Mr. Simon Baert and has two children. Her article appeared in *Apuntes*, Vol. 1, No. 1, Spring, 1981, pp. 14-18.

Edwin E. Sylvest, Jr. is an Associate Professor of the History of Christianity at Perkins School of Theology at Southern Methodist University. He is a member of the Rio Grande Conference of the United Methodist Church. His article appeared in *Apuntes*, Vol. 1, No. 2, Summer, 1981, pp. 14-19.

David Traverzo is a Puerto Rican raised in the Bronx, who is an ordained minister of the Reformed Church in America. As a Ph.D. candidate in Social Ethics at Drew University, he is analyzing the concept of social ethics present in the thought of Orlando E. Costas. He is currently serving at an African-American Presbyterian Church. He is married, and has one daughter. His article appeared in *Apuntes*, Year 9, No. 3, Fall, 1989, pp. 51-57.

Note: An index of the first six years of publication in *Apuntes* was published in Year 6, No. 4, Winter 1986, pp. 84-94. The next index will be published in Year 12, No. 4, Winter 1992.

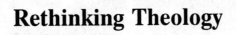

Rethinking Theology

Prophets in the King's Sanctuary

Justo L. González

> And Amaziah said to Amos, "O seer, go, flee away to the land of Judah,
> and eat bread there, and prophecy there; but never again prophesy at
> Bethel, for it is the king's sanctuary, and it is a temple of the kingdom."
>
> Amos 7:13

Apuntes, small though it may be, intends to be a serious journal of theology. But not any theology. *Our* theology. A theology which is *nuestra*, not simply because we have developed it, but because it has been born out of the painful encounter between the Word of God and our experiences and those of our people.

The very word, "apuntes," is ambiguous, and has been purposely chosen because of the ambiguity. On the one hand, it means jottings, notes, or marginal glosses. That is partly how we see ourselves. We do not deceive ourselves into believing that we are at the very heart of the theological enterprise. That enterprise reflects the structures of the society around it, and Hispanics are not by and large in the decision-making centers of that society. Hence the subtitle of our journal, "Reflections from the Hispanic Margin." We intend for the theology aired in this journal to be a marginal gloss to the dominant forms of Christian theology. And by this we mean both that it will be *on* the margin and that it will be *from* the margin.

But the word "apuntes" also means aimings. And that indicates that we do not intend simply to doodle at the margins of the theological enterprise. We are taking a bead on the very heart of theology, hoping --even against hope-- that our comments on and from the margin will help the Church at large to rediscover some forgotten dimensions of the biblical message. While still at the margin, and form the perspective of our Hispanic experience, we shall take a new look at Scripture, and at the entire theological enterprise. And we are convinced that this new look will be valuable, not only to us, but also to the Church as a whole.

Such presumptuousness has ample biblical foundation, for as we read Scripture we repeatedly see that God uses the margin to speak to the center. God did speak to Pharaoh; but spoke to him through the exiled Moses. God spoke to the mighty Roman Empire; but that Word came out of a despised corner of a distant province.

Such was the case with Amos, the lowly shepherd and dresser of sycamore trees from barren Tekoa in the underdeveloped kingdom of Judah who crossed the border to prophesy in the richer land of Israel. (Did that make him and illegal alien?) Out of the backwoods, where sycamores were considered fruit fit for human consumption, came the shepherd. And he did not speak the words of the learned, for he knew and spoke only of locusts,

3

and summer fruit, and plumb lines. But that was not what disturbed Amaziah. In the rich kingdom of Israel, where some slept in ivory beds and anointed themselves with the finest oils, there were many who were as poor as Amos. There were many who performed the hard and lowly tasks connected with the upkeep of life, so that the few could live in comfort. What disturbed Amaziah was that this immigrant, whose accent still rang of the southern wilderness, dared criticize what was going on in Israel. And that, not only in the small villages or quietly by the fires of the shepherds, but in Bethel, which was no less than the kings's sanctuary. And so Amaziah followed a two-pronged strategy. On the one hand, he sent word to King Jeroboam, accusing Amos of conspiring against him. On the other, he invited Amos to leave the country; to return to his homeland and prophesy there, where his words would spell trouble for neither Amos nor Amaziah.

Amaziah's words have a familiar ring to Hispanics. repeatedly, when we have spoken of the social evils of this country, we have been told --sometimes openly, and sometimes subtly-- to go prophesy in our own land. That is particularly puzzling for those of us whose ancestors were in this land generations before they were occupied by the United States. But in any case most of us are aware that there is a connection between such invitations to return to our poorer countries in the South and the threat which we pose to the Amaziahs and the Jeroboams of the Northern Kingdoms. Things would be safer and quieter were we to go and speak our radical word down south.

For some odd reason, God has told us to speak here. And speak we must. And speak we shall.

However, that "we" does not refer primarily to those of us who write in *Apuntes*. Most of us cannot say, like Amos, that we are not professional prophets. On the contrary, we have been trained in the official "schools of prophecy," and many of us "eat our bread" as prophets. The *we* that stands in the place of Amos today is that larger community of migrant laborers, vinedressers, garment workers and janitors whose truly prophetic word those of us who write in *Apuntes* simply try to articulate. Our word may be silenced. But theirs cannot be, for their very existence is in itself a prophetic word. In the harsh deeds that one sees and the harsh words that one hears in East Harlem, God speaks an even harsher word of judgement to this Northern Kingdom. As God lives --and because God lives-- a nation whose social and economic structures produce such evil cannot long remain unpunished. That is the word that we have heard. Most of us do not like it any more than Amos liked the news of the chastising of Israel by the hand of Assyria. But we have heard this word, and we must raise the cry.

This word is more radical than most of us would like. It speaks of evil and the need for reformation, not only in society at large, but also in the Church. Amaziah and Jeroboam are closely allied. That alliance has taught us to read Scripture in such a way that it does not threaten the privileges of the powerful. Quite unconsciously on the part of both teachers and students, that is what many of us learned in our "school of prophets." At best, we learned to challenge social evil, but did not see to what an extent that evil was reflected in our own theological formulations and ecclesiastical structures. What we have now leaned, from the Word of God crying out to us out of Harlem, Chicago, Miami, Crystal City and San Joaquin, is that we must look anew at the entire fabric of Christian theology and ecclesiastical organization. We must look at it from the margin, and from that margin we must both make comments and take aim at the core of the life of the Church.

That is what "apuntes" means. And that is what *Apuntes* means to do. We realize that this is not an easy task, nor one to be undertaken lightly. What is at stake is no less than a total rethinking of the entire corpus of Christian theology. This cannot be done by any single individual, for the task is too vast. Nor can it be done within the confines of denominational lines, for those lines often reflect concerns and experiences which are not those of the Hispanic community. For that reason we invite all who see the need for the development of a Hispanic perspective in Christian theology to join us in this undertaking, and to use *Apuntes* as their means of reflection and expression.

De "apuntes" a "esbozo": diez años de reflexión

José David Rodríguez

El surgimiento de una perspectiva teológica hispana en los Estados Unidos
En 1971 Gustavo Gutiérrez publicó su libro titulado *Teología de la liberación*. Esta obra que ha sido traducida a varios idiomas se convirtió en la presentación más abarcadora y conocida de la teología latinoamericana. A este libro le siguieron un gran número de estudios que le han dado a esta perspectiva teológica un lugar importante en la reflexión teológica internacional.

Para muchos de nosotros la teología latinoamericana de la liberación ha provisto valiosos elementos para la afirmación de nuestra fe cristiana. También nos ha ayudado a comprender la necesidad de formular una interpretación de la fe desde nuestra perspectiva para nuestro propio contexto histórico. Con la intención de ilustrar este asunto Justo L. González hace la siguiente historia. Unos años atras el presidente de un seminario prestigioso en una de las ciudades mas grandes de este país le comentaba con orgullo que casi la mitad de los profesores de su seminario habían mostrado tanto interés en la teología latinoamericana que estaban comenzando a tomar clases de español. González respondió que sin duda se sentía muy contento de saber que una teología latinoamericana había creado tanto entusiasmo en miembros de la facultad, pero que era realmente penoso que su decisión para aprender español se debía a que había tantos libros interesantes para leer y no al hecho de que este seminario se encontraba rodeado por miles de personas pobres de habla española y en necesidad del evangelio.[1]

Para responder a este urgente desafío gran número de líderes religiosos hispano-americanos en los Estados Unidos han comenzado a formular propuestas teológicas que surgen de su compromiso con las experiencias de esta comunidad. Estos esfuerzos que aparecen como artículos en revistas o libros que se publican surgen de personas que provienen de un diverso trasfondo con raíces en México, Cuba, Puerto Rico y otros países latinoamericanos y de afiliación religiosa tanto católica romana como protestante. Lo que es común a estas personas es que comparten una perspectiva que de manera profunda informa y distingue su teología. Tres de las personas mas importantes y originales que le han dado forma a esta perspectiva son Virgilio Elizondo, Justo L. González y Orlando Costas.

En la primavera de 1981 bajo la dirección editorial de Justo L. González y el respaldo institucional del Mexican American Program del Perkins School of Theology dirigido por Roy D. Barton, salió a la luz el

---

1. Justo L. González, "Hacia un redescubrimiento de nuestra misión", en *Apuntes* 7:3 (1987), pp. 51-60.

primer volumen de la revista *Apuntes*. Esta revista, producto modesto del interés de un creciente número de personas por fortalecer el desarrollo de recursos para la formación del liderato religioso de la comunidad hispana en los Estados Unidos, celebra este año diez años de publicación.

Desde su inicio, la revista se convirtió en un instrumento para fomentar el diálogo entre hispanos y otras personas interesadas en darle forma a una teología cristiana desde una perspectiva hispana. Se proponía además una reflexión desde el margen hispano con la intención de promover una relectura de la totalidad del quehacer teológico para ayudar a formular lo que significa ser una persona hispana cristiana en este país, entender el significado bíblico y teológico de nuestra situación, y establecer un mejor entendimiento de nuestra contribución teológica para el resto de la iglesia.

El título de la revista se adoptó intencionalmente para sugerir dos aspectos importantes que han de distinguir el carácter peculiar de esta teología. El primero tiene que ver con el hecho de que nuestra teología, al ser producto del penoso encuentro entre la palabra de Dios y la experiencia de nuestras comunidades, será necesariamente reflejo de la marginalidad a la cual está sometida esta experiencia en el contexto de la estructura social. Es en este sentido que nuestro pensamiento teológico surge de la periferia y se convierte en "apuntes", o notas marginales acerca da la vida y pensamiento de la iglesia. El segundo de estos aspectos indica que nuestros "apuntes" también señalan al corazón mismo de la tarea teológica, y por lo tanto nuestros comentarios sobre y desde el margen ayudarán a recuperar esas dimensiones olvidadas del mensaje bíblico que serán valiosas no solo para nuestras comunidades sino también para la iglesia en general. Esta es una referencia a la importante tarea profética de la fe a la cual están llamadas nuestras comunidades. Tal función tiene un amplio fundamento bíblico ya que al leer la Escritura notamos continuamente que Dios utiliza a quienes se encuentran en la periferia para confrontar a los sectores dominantes de la sociedad con aspectos centrales de la fe cristiana que han sido generalmente relegados.[2]

En este artículo haremos un breve examen del desarrollo de esta teología hispana en los Estados Unidos. En nuestro estudio utilizaremos como referencia la contribución de la revista *Apuntes* para la realización de esta tarea. Examinaremos aquellas etapas claves en el desarrollo de esta teología que han ayudado a adelantar sus metas. Estas etapas serán presentadas desde un punto de vista no estrictamente cronológico, sino desde una perspectiva que nos ayude a describir la maduración de la reflexión. En la sección final señalaremos algunos de los desafíos que se presentan en el futuro inmediato para continuar la labor importante que tenemos por delante para avanzar el desarrollo de esta tarea.

Sentando los cimientos

Aunque podríamos afirmar que desde el comienzo de la conquista

---

2. Estos propósitos generales de la revista fueron establecidos por el editor y el director del Mexican American Program del Perkins School of Theology en sus artículos publicados en el primer número de la revista. Véase, *Apuntes* 1:1 (1981), pp. 2-6.

española en 1513 en lo que era la Florida se pueden trazar los orígenes de una teología hispano-americana en estas tierras,[3] los primeros esfuerzos por darle forma a esta teología en los últimos diez años fueron dirigidos a sentar los cimientos de esta reflexión. Con este propósito se publicaron artículos que examinaban el contexto histórico-social, la interpretación bíblica, la afirmación teológica, y la experiencia pastoral propia de esta comunidad. Algunos de estos artículos fueron publicados en antologías,[4] y otros en revistas. Como complemento a estos escritos algunas revistas publicaron reseñas de libros y apuntes bibliográficos para ayudar a identificar aquella literatura disponible que estudia de manera más profunda y amplia estos asuntos. Esta etapa de fundamentación de caracterizó por el establecimiento de las líneas generales que habrían de darle forma a esta perspectiva teológica.

En su artículo para establecer los fundamentos de una relectura de la historia desde una perspectiva hispana Justo L. González proponía la definición de lo hispano a base de tres elementos diferentes pero a la vez complementarios: la raza, la cultura y la clase social. El primero sugiere la idea de que somos una raza en la cual se juntan las corrientes sanguíneas de Europa, Africa y la antigua América. El segundo alude en particular al lenguaje y a otros elementos culturales relacionados al común idioma. El tercero señala que la experiencia dominante de nuestras comunidades en este país es una de pobreza y explotación. Ninguno de estos elementos debe abandonarse si hemos de entender lo que significa ser hispano en los Estados Unidos. Es sobre estas bases que tenemos que volver a leer, a escribir, y a hacer la historia.[5]

El breve estudio de González sobre la vocación profética de Amós, tanto como la reflexión bíblica de Luis N. Rivera Pagán sobre la carta de Santiago, sugerían recobrar el recurrente tema bíblico de la opción preferencial de Dios por los marginados, unido a la exhortación de una militancia paciente pero activa del creyente en la historia.[6]

El examen de Edwin E. Sylvest, Jr. sobre el valor de tomar en

---

3. Lo que aquí queremos señalar es que en los Estados Unidos ya ha comenzado a surgir una relectura de la historia de la iglesia y una perspectiva teológica hispano-americana de esta historia desde sus orígenes en el siglo XVI. La primera obra que inicia estos estudios es *Fronteras: A History of the Latin American Church in the U.S.A Since 1513* (San Antonio: Mexican American Cultural Center, 1983). Este estudio escrito casi enteramente por autores hispanos en los Estados Unidos es también parte de la colección de CEHILA (Comisión para el Estudio de la Historia de la Iglesia en América Latina) que dirige el Dr. Enrique Dussel.

4. Antonio M. Stevens Arroyo, *Prophets Denied Honor: An Anthology on the Hispanic Church in the United States* (Maryknoll, N.Y.: Orbis Books, 1980).

5. Justo L. González, "Towards a New Reading of History," en *Apuntes* 1:3 (1981), pp. 4-14. Este artículo fue presentado originalmente por el autor en la reunión de teólogos hispanos auspiciada por el Fund for Theological Education radicado actualmente en la ciudad de New York, celebrada en abril de 1981 en la ciudad de San Antonio. Con el fin de dar a conocer el contenido de estas presentaciones a un público mayor, dos de las ponencias presentadas allí se publicaron en *Apuntes* 1:3 (1981), pp. 4-21.

6. Véase Justo L. González, "Prophets in the King's Sanctuary", en *Apuntes* 1:1 (1981), pp. 3-6; Luis N. Rivera-Pagán, "La paciencia de la espera", en *Apuntes* 1:2 (1981), pp. 3-9.

consideración algunos elementos de la teología de Juan Wesley,[7] el estudio de Cecilio Arrastía sobre la experiencia de nuestra pastoral como "comunidad hermenéutica",[8] el artículo de María Luisa Santillán Baert donde señala la necesidad de que nuestra comunidad de fe tome partido para responder al dolor de los desheredados y oprimidos,[9] y el artículo de Jorge Lara-Braud que describe la necesidad de promover una práctica eclesiástica en la cual los líderes desarrollen un compromiso con las luchas de nuestro pueblo[10] son ejemplos de las coincidencias importantes de estos autores en la lectura de la experiencia religiosa de nuestro pueblo.

Estos estudios, que fueron escritos por personas de diversa experiencia, trasfondo, y afiliación denominacional, apuntan nuevamente al carácter profético y periférico de esa perspectiva teológica en proceso de formación.

Articulación temática

Una segunda etapa en el desarrollo de esta perspectiva fue la que facilitó la discusión y el estudio de temas pertinentes a nuestra teología. El número y variedad de estos temas es bastante amplio como para hacer un listado completo en este trabajo. En la revista *Apuntes* se publica con regularida un índice para identificar muchos de estos temas y a los autores que han ofrecido estudios y reflexiones sobres estos asuntos.[11]

La manera de trabajar estos temas se ha caracterizado por la intención de descubrir la forma particular en la cual se establece una intersección entre la experiencia histórico-social de nuestras comunidades y su expresión religiosa.[12] Un ejemplo específico de esta articulación temática se puede ver en la manera en la que se trabaja el tema de la migración. Este asunto se examina desde sus dimensiones históricas,[13] sociales,[14] bíblicas,[15] y

---

7. Según el autor, Wesley no solo estudió español para emprender su tarea misionera en la colonia inglesa de Georgia en 1735, sino que también su doctrina de la santificación guarda estrecha relación con la perspectiva de la teología de la liberación. Véase E. Sylvest, Jr., "Wesley desde el margen hispano", en *Apuntes* 1:2 (1981), pp. 14-19. Vale la pena señalar que en publicaciones posteriores de la revista se vuelve a considerar este tema invitando a otros hispanos a estudiar sus respectivas tradiciones denominacionales para formular una recuperación crítica de aquellos temas que pueden ayudar en la formación de nuestra perspectiva hispana en el presente. Véase, Nora Quiroga Boots, "The Wesleyan Tradition and Latin American Theology", en *Apuntes* 5:1 (1985), pp. 9-15.

8. Cecilio Arrastía, "La iglesia como comunidad hemenéutica", en *Apuntes* 1:1 (1981), pp. 7-13.

9. María Luisa Santillán Baert, "The Church and Liberation", en *Apuntes* 1:1 (1981), pp. 14-18.

10. Jorge Lara-Braud, "Monseñor Romero: Model Pastor for the Hispanic Diaspora", en *Apuntes* 1:3 (1981), pp. 15-21.

11. El índice correspondiente a los primeros seis años lo preparó el Rev. Raúl Fernández-Calienes y se publicó en la edición de invierno de 1986.

12. John P. Rossing ha escrito un estudio muy importante sobre este asunto que ha de guiar nuestro análisis en esta sección. John P. Rossing, "Mestizaje And Marginality: A Hispanic American Theology," en *Theology Today* 45:3 (1988), pp. 293-304.

13. Marta Sotomayor-Chávez, "Latin American Migration", en *Apuntes* 2:1 (1982), pp. 8-14.

14. Rebeca Radillo, "The Migrant Family", en *Apuntes* 5:1 (1985), pp. 16-19.

teológicas[16] para formular un pronunciamiento creativo y pertinente, que reclama nuestra obediencia de fe. En este sentido, cuando se discute el tema de la migración no solo se presentan los problemas que desafían la presente pastoral como son los intereses económicos y políticos que condicionan la legislación federal sobre migración y nacionalidad en los Estados Unidos sin atender con el mismo interés el costoso sufrimiento y deterioro humano creado por esta legislación, o las consecuencias legales a las cuales están sujetas aquellas personas que ofrecen santuario a quienes se encuentran en este país sin la documentación requerida por el gobierno.

El tema se discute tomando también en consideración la experiencia bíblica y eclesiástica del pasado confrontándola con los retos del presente para descubrir aquellas dimensiones inherentes a esta experiencia de fe que permiten nuevas oportunidades de testimonio cristiano. Es en este sentido en que Francisco O. García-Treto sugiere que al tratar al emigrante en los Estados Unidos debemos seguir la tradición bíblica en la cual los extranjeros se consideraban bajo la protección divina y hacer lo posible por prestarles nuestros servicios.[17] Es también en esta línea de pensamiento que Justo L. González nos señala que tanto la Biblia como la iglesia cristiana primitiva nos llaman la atención a no prestar obediencia absoluta al estado y sus leyes, cuando estas se oponen a la voluntad divina.

Formulación teológica

Otra etapa importante en el desarrollo de nuestra teología hispano-americana es la que representa los esfuerzos por conferir contenidos doctrinales a la experiencia de fe de esta comunidad que experimenta un sentido de marginalización y mestizaje. El punto de referencia esencial para esta teología se da allí donde ocurre la suprema auto-revelación divina. Es decir, en la experiencia de su encarnación. Es allí donde según Justo L. González, se encuentra el fundamento, no solo de nuestra doctrina de la redención, sino también y sobre todo de nuestro entendimiento de Dios.[18]

De acuerdo a Orlando Costas la encarnación es la entrada de Dios a un contexto humano particular, la presencia de Dios en la historia. Lo verdaderamente espectacular de la realidad de la fe cristiana es que tiene su origen no simplemente con la encarnación del Hijo de Dios, sino con su venida como Jesús de Nazaret. El Hijo de Dios es enviado como un ser

---

15. Justo L. González, "Sanctuary: Historical, Legal and Biblical Considerations", en *Apuntes* 5:2 (1985), pp. 36-47. Francisco O. García-Treto, "El Señor guarda a los emigrantes", en *Apuntes* 1:4 (1981), pp. 3-9.

16. Justo L. González, "The Apostles' Creed and the Sanctuary Movement", en *Apuntes* 6:1 (1986), pp. 12-20. Jorge Lara-Braud, "Reflexiones teológicas sobre la migración", en *Apuntes* 2:1 (1982), pp. 3-7. Hugo L. López, "Toward a Theology of Migration", en *Apuntes* 2:3 (1982), pp. 68-71; "El Divino Migrante", en *Apuntes* 4:1 (1984), pp. 14-19.

17. Francisco O. García-Treto, *op. cit.*

18. Justo L. González, "Let the Dead Gods Bury their Dead", en *Apuntes* 4:4 (1984), p. 93. Para un estudio mas completo de la doctrina de Dios en esta teología véase González, *Mañana: Christian Theology from a Hispanic Perspective* (Nashville: Abingdon Press, 1990), pp. 89-167.

humano de carne y hueso para proclamar el evangelio del amor al mundo. Esto significa que Jesucristo realizó su evangelización como una persona común y corriente, que perteneció a un pueblo particular, que habló su idioma, y que vio la realidad desde la perspectiva de su misma situación socio-cultural.[19]

El que Dios entre a una historia y cultura particular nos fuerza a proclamar la presencia de Dios en la historia y cultura de toda persona en el mundo. Por lo tanto, es la doctrina de la encarnación lo que hace imperativa la teología contextual, y lo que provee la justificación a una teología desde la perspectiva hispano-americana.[20]

Para Virgilio Elizondo, todos los dogmas de nuestra tradición cristiana cobran un sentido más rico cuando reconocemos la realidad socio-cultural a través de la cual se llevan a cabo los eventos de nuestra salvación. El Nuevo Testamento no dice que en Jesús Dios se hizo carne y habitó entre nosotros para predicar y dar testimonio de las buenas nuevas de salvación universal. Es decir, se hizo una persona capaz de ser verdaderamente identificada de forma histórica, cultural y racial. La identidad galilea de Jesús y la de sus primeros seguidores es uno de los rasgos más prominentes del Nuevo Testamento. La realidad socio-cultural de Galilea en aquel tiempo era la de una región fronteriza entre los judíos y los griegos de Judea. Gentes de todas nacionalidades venían en las rutas de las caravanas en camino hacia y desde Egipto. Los judíos galileos, quienes eran minoría y fueron forzados a mezclarse con sus vecinos gentiles, hablaban con un marcado acento y seguramente mezclaron su idioma rápidamente con el griego de la cultura dominante y el latín del Imperio Romano. Como los judíos en Galilea eran muy judíos para ser aceptados por la población gentil, y muy contaminados con hábitos paganos para ser aceptados por los judíos puristas de Jerusalén, Jesús también tuvo que experimentar la experiencia de distancia y ridículo que caracteriza la historia de comunidades marginalizadas como la nuestra. Pero fue también desde las filas de los pobres y destituídos de la sociedad que uno de sus propios miembros vino a convertirse en el salvador del mundo. El desafío para nosotros consiste en dar testimonio de esta actividad divina creativa, redentora, y santificadora en el presente.[21]

Marginalidad y mestizaje como claves de interpretación

Toda perspectiva teológica se distingue por un tipo de énfasis o método peculiar de abordar su estudio de la realidad y la tradición de fe. Para la teología latinoamericana de la liberación este énfasis se hizo explícito en la

---

19. Orlando Costas, "Evangelism from the Periphery: A Galilean Model", en *Apuntes* 2:3 (1982), p. 51. También del mismo autor, *Christ Outside the Gate: Mission Beyond Christendom* (New York: Orbis Books, 1982), pp. 6, 12.

20. Rossing, *op. cit.*, p. 298.

21. Virgilio Elizondo, *The Future is Mestizo* (Bloomington: Meyer-Stone Books, 1988), pp. 76-81. Otros autores han estudiado diferentes temas doctrinales como la misión, la liturgia, y la espiritualidad cristiana en los mismos términos con que se define la doctrina de la encarnación. Un buen estudio de estos temas se encuentra en el artículo de Rossing, *ibid.*, pp. 298-304.

famosa expresión de Gutiérrez donde se describe la tarea teológica como "reflexión crítica de la praxis histórica a la luz de la fe".[22]

La teología hispana en los Estados Unidos tiene una clave de interpretación hermenéutica característica que podría describirse con los conceptos de *marginalidad* y *mestizaje*. Para Justo L. González estos términos apuntan primeramente al caracter marginal característico de la perspectiva hispana. La experiencia de ser parte de una minoría étnica puede llevarnos a entender la marginalización a la cual están sujetas nuestras comunidades y otros grupos sociales en los Estados Unidos; así como también a escuchar el clamor por la justicia que surge de estos grupos, muchas veces en nombre de la fe cristiana. Esta experiencia puede hacer posible un nuevo entendimiento de la autoridad de la Biblia como instrumento de Dios para proveer un correctivo necesario contra los prejuicios e injusticias presentes en la sociedad.[23]

Para González, esta perspectiva se acerca más a la de los protagonistas de la Biblia que la utilizada por los grupos dominantes para mantener su situación de privilegio al costo del sufrimiento de otros sectores humanos de la sociedad. Esta convicción le lleva a sugerir que nuestra perspectiva sobre la historia y la interpretación bíblica puede llegar a ser útil no solo a nuestras comunidades sino también a toda la iglesia en sus esfuerzos por ser fieles a la voluntad de Dios en el contexto social.[24]

El término *mestizaje*, que en primera instancia se usa para referirse al proceso que dio origen al pueblo méxico-americano cuyo producto es el resultado de la mezcla de la raza europea y la indígena-americana, lo utiliza también Virgilio Elizondo para referirse el tipo de cristianismo que se produjo en América Latina.[25] Ada María Isasi-Díaz señala que como fruto de este mestizaje es que la cultura hispano-americana desarrolla su entendimiento de lo divino, de lo humano, y que le encuentra el sentido a su existencia.[26]

Es importante señalar que lo que aquí se entiende por mestizaje es mucho más que la memoria cultural de un tipo de cristianismo específico. El término es más bien una metáfora que apunta al tipo específico de síntesis, o nueva creación que se produce como resultado de la interpretación de la fe desde esta perspectiva. El resultado es la fusión del mensaje cristiano con la experiencia del pueblo hispano-americano en un pronunciamiento de fe

---

22. Gustavo Gutiérrez, *A Theology of Liberation* (New York: Orbis Books, 1973), p. 15.

23. Justo L. González, "Reading the Bible in Spanish", en *Apuntes* 9:2 (1989), pp. 39-46.

24. Para un mejor entendimiento de este tema véase Justo L. González, *Mañana, op. cit.*, pp. 21-30, 75-87.

25. La tesis doctoral de Virgilio Elizondo fue sobre el tema del mestizaje y su relación con el anuncio del evangelio. Este estudio se publicó bajo el título: *Galilean Journey: The Mexican-American Promise* (New York: Orbis Books, 1983).

26. De hecho, la autora insiste en que aunque con frecuencia al formular su perspectiva teológica personas de extracción hispano-americana ignoran esta realidad cultural e histórica, la religiosidad popular demanda que la teología le dé la misma consideración a estas tres estratas culturales desde donde surge este mestizaje. Ada María Isasi-Díaz, "Apuntes for a Hispanic Women's Theology of Liberation", en *Apuntes* 6:3 (1986), p. 66.

original que hace posible otra vez la encarnación del evangelio en la situación particular de una comunidad marginada para luchar contra la opresión con el poder del amor divino, que al igual que en la experiencia de la resurrección, resulta invencible.[27]

Conclusión

Luego de haber hecho una breve descripción del desarrollo de la teología hispano-americana en los Estados Unidos durante los últimos diez años nos toca ahora hacer una evaluación de esta experiencia.

Mi primera impresión es que ha habido un progreso significativo en la producción y refinamiento de esta perspectiva durante los últimos años. La lista de publicaciones, el número de escritores, la variedad de temas, y la profundidad de la reflexión son muestra elocuente del crecimiento cualitativo en esta teología. En este sentido podemos hablar de una teología que va tomando forma, una teología que va en progreso de una etapa de "apuntes", es decir, de notas marginales, a un "esbozo", o mejor dicho, un borrador, una propuesta de trabajo con contenido específico pero que requiere mayor refinamiento y sistematización.

Sin embargo, es lamentable que gran número de los temas que se han presentado para la discusión no se han desarrollado con amplitud y que la tarea de sistematizar el pensamiento de esta teología se encuentra aún en etapas muy primarias. Uno de los temas que me parece necesario examinar más a fondo es el de la relectura de nuestras tradiciones denominacionales. Actualmente, la mayoría de los grupos denominacionales en los Estados Unidos están realizando grandes esfuerzos de evangelización entre grupos étnicos y sectores de la población tradicionalmente marginalizados. Para evitar que estos esfuerzos resulten en procesos conscientes o inconscientes de dominación, es imprescindible recuperar críticamente aquellos elementos de estas tradiciones que promuevan una expresión del testimonio de fe que ayude a corregir los errores del pasado, promuevan una obediencia de fe más evangélica en el presente, y fomenten una visión para el futuro más a tono con la promesa de vida del Reino.

Es interesante notar que revistas como *Apuntes* no solo prestan un servicio especial para la promoción y discusión de temas relacionados a esta perspectiva teológica a un público mas amplio; sino que también se convierten en foros donde algunas personas comienzan a someter hipótesis que desarrollan más ampliamente en publicaciones posteriores.

Cuatro obras recientes me llevan también a sugerir que esta teología hispana se encuentra en una etapa importante de desarrollo en la cual se estan haciendo esfuerzos por presentar un trabajo mas profundo y sistemático. Dos de estas publicaciones tienen como autor a Justo L. González. Estas sugieren formas de recuperar de manera crítica la tradición teológica proponiendo además una metodología mas pertinente para la reflexión

---

27. Rossing, *op. cit.*, pp. 295-302, 304.

teológica en el presente.[28] Las otras dos son un esfuerzo por abrir la discusión a temas que requieren mayor articulación. Una de ellas está escrita por Luis N. Rivera-Pagán y trata el tema del presente desafío nuclear.[29] La otra es una producción en sociedad de Ada María Isasi-Díaz y Yolanda Tarango sobre el papel profético de la mujer hispana en la iglesia.[30]

Por último quisiera mencionar que debido a la trayectoria que va tomando el incremento de la población hispana en los Estados Unidos, se está haciendo importante revisar la función social de nuestras comunidades y especialmente lo que hemos descrito anteriormente como la perspectiva desde el margen. Es posible que esta nueva situación requiera un mejor entendimiento de nuestra responsabilidad ya que nuestro papel social está cambiando pero a la misma vez cobrando mayor significado tanto político como religioso.

Creo que nuestra teología continuará cumpliendo una función profética importante. Como afirma González en su artículo que le dio comienzo a la revista *Apuntes*, por alguna razón extraña Dios nos ha llamado a proclamar y a dar testimonio de nuestra fe en este lugar. Y así lo habremos de hacer.[31] Dios nos dé fuerzas para realizarlo de la manera mas fiel y responsable.

Summary

This article provides a brief summary of the development and main features of the Hispanic/Latin theology emerging in the U.S. While the origin of this theological perspective can be traced back to the beginnings of the Spanish conquest in Florida (1513), the article covers roughly the last ten years of its development. It also focuses on this development as evidenced in the journal Apuntes.

The article starts by acknowledging the relation of this perspective with that of Latin American theologians. In response to the challenge posed by liberation theology, an increasing number of Hispanic religious leaders in the U.S. from Roman Catholic and Protestant backgrounds have begun to formulate an ecumenical interpretation and witness of faith in the context of the experience and commitment to the struggles of their community.

While the goal of Latin religious leaders in the U.S. is no less than a total rethinking of the entire corpus of Christian theology, their initial efforts in this task have contributed in establishing the distinctive character of this perspective. Its two most prominent and recurring features are those of marginality and mestizaje. The former refers to the experience of being a member

---

28. Justo L. González, *Christian Thought Revisited* (Nashville: Abingdon Press, 1989); *Mañana*, *op. cit.*

29. Luis N. Rivera-Pagán, *A la sombra del armagedón* (Río Piedras: Editorial Edil, 1988).

30. Ada María Isasi-Díaz y Yolanda Tarango, *Hispanic Women* (San Francisco: Harper & Row, 1988).

31. González, "Prophets in the King's Sanctuary", p. 5.

of an ethnic minority in the U.S. Within this experience Hispanics along with Afro Americans, Native Americans, and other marginalized groups have listened to the suffering and cry of justice of these communities, many times in the name of Christianity, recovering the important prophetic character of our common faith. The latter notion, building on the process that gave origin to the Mexican American people as the product of the mix between European and Mezo American cultures becomes a metaphor pointing to the specific synthesis or new creation that may be achieved by interpreting our faith from this experience.

These two hermeneutical keys point to both the prophetic and evangelical character of this perspective. With them in mind the most prominent Hispanic authors (Justo L. González, Virgilio Elizondo, Orlando Costas, Ada María Isasi-Díaz, and others) have reflected on a variety of issues that have confronted our community in their journey of faith and socio-historical experience. Thus when approaching the experience of migration, the problem of justice, and the role of women, as well as when reflecting on the doctrine of God, the meaning of the Incarnation, or the notion of Church, these and other Latin authors try to discover the particular way in which the socio-historical experience of our communities intersect with the religious expression of their obedience of faith. In this process the authority of the Scriptures and the experience of those who have preceded us in our witness of faith, critically examined, become a needed corrective to address the mores and prejudices of our society. And it is the conviction of Hispanic theologians that the product of this approach will be valuable, not only to the Latin community, but may also become the most significant contribution that out community can make to the church as a whole.

The article ends by noting some important challenges for the continuing development of this perspective. The issues that have been explored need further substantial development. New themes are being studied and a greater list of Hispanic authors is beginning to emerge. The political and religious role of Hispanic/Latin Americans needs to be reexamined given the trend of increasing growth of this ethnic community in the U.S. What stands out clearly is the prophetic role that this perspective will continue to perform in the future. Others are encouraged to contribute in this effort.

Evangelism from the Periphery:
The Universality of Galilee

Orlando E. Costas

In a previous article we noted the significance of Galilee for Mark's understanding and exposition of the person and work of Jesus Christ.[1] We also noted its correspondence in Paul's Corinthian Christology (cf. I Cor 1:18-31). For Paul as for Mark the Son of God was revealed in a "no-body" (cf. Phil 2:5-9). This assertion is reinforced by the other Synoptics (for whom Mark was a foundational source), the Fourth Gospel (cf. Jn 1:14, 43-49), and the Epistle to the Hebrews (Heb 2:9ff; 4:15; 5:7-8; 12:2; 13:12-13). In arguing thus, the New Testament writers were simply clinging onto, and appropriating, the servant of Yahweh tradition derived from the prophets of Israel, especially the Isaianic prophets. This tradition sees the messianic promises in connection with the sufferings of the servant of Yahweh. The one "who brings good tidings, who publishes peace and salvation" (Isa 52:7) is also the one who "poured out his soul to death, and was numbered with the transgressors," the same who "bore the sin of many, and made intercession for the transgressors" (Isa 53:12b).

Galilee not only has universal validity for New Testament Christology, but also for evangelism. The fact that mark locates Jesus' proclamation of the good news of the kingdom in the periphery is not simply a reflex of the Evangelist's own context, as some New Testament scholars have argued.[2]

Rather the location of Jesus' ministry in the periphery is consequential with the witness of the entire New Testament which sees Jesus as a poor man, who identified with the oppressed and died as one of them to liberate women and men from the power of sin and death, bringing into being the new order of life --of love, justice, freedom and well-being. If the good news is first and foremost for the poor and outcast (Mt 5:3; 11:4-6; 25:34; Lk 6:20b; 7:23; 12:32; Jas 2:5) and if they are the ones who best understand what its message is all about (Mt 6:25; I Cor 1:26-28), then it follows that Galilee, as a symbol of the periphery, is also an universal when it comes to the theology of evangelism. In this case, the particularity of the periphery is to inform each and all evangelistic contexts. From this premise, we can draw out three implications from Jesus' Galilean model for contextual evangelism today.

The Socio-Historical Ground of Evangelism: A Base in the Periphery

First of all, Jesus' Galilean model implies that contextual evangelism

---

1. "Evangelism from the Periphery: A Galilean Model," *Apuntes*, Vol. 2, No. 3, Otoño, 1982, pp. 51-59.

2. See Willi Marxsen, *Mark the Evangelist: Studies on the Redaction History of the Gospel* (Nashville: Abingdon, 1969).

should be grounded socio-historically in the periphery. Evangelism presupposes a base; it neither takes place in a vacuum nor originates out of nowhere. A base, however, is not simply the beginning point of an operation, or the place in which it is carried out. It is, especially, a fundamental association rooted in the lowest level or most marginated space of society. To say that evangelism should have a base in the periphery is to argue for the popular grass roots as its starting point and fundamental point of reference,[3] which in any society constitutes, by and large, the marginated in life and powerless in decision-making.

Only by starting in the periphery, or working from the bottom up, can the good news of God's kingdom be vividly demonstrated and credibly announced as a message of liberation, justice and peace. It is when the gospel makes "somebody" out of the "nobodies" of society, when it restores the self-worth of the marginated, when it enables the oppressed to have a reason for hope, when it empowers the poor to struggle and suffer for liberation and peace, that it is truly good news of a new order of life --the saving power of God (Rom 1:16). When evangelism begins in the center, working from the top down, its content ends up being an easy and cheap accommodation to the vested interests of the powerful and well-to-do. Indeed, evangelism turns out to be reductionistic since it truncates the content of the gospel by making it a privatistic white-wash, manipulated to soothe the conscience of those who by virtue of their "central" position control, economically, socially, politically and culturally, the destiny of the people in the fringes of society. Hence an evangelism that is geared in the first place to the "elite" of society will most likely end up being absorbed by their system.

Evangelism can only be prophetic, and thus liberating, if it has a communal base, a basic witnessing community. Such a base can only be built from the periphery, from outside the centers of power. Since the gospel seeks to set men and women free from all godless, de-humanizing, alienating and therefore, oppressive forces for the service of God's kingdom of justice and peace, enabling them to live freely and lovingly for God and humankind, it follows that evangelism should be able to challenge and transform such centralized, absolutist power-systems. The only way it can achieve this end is by building, as Jesus did, a sound base in the periphery, i.e., a community of lame, lepers, blind, poor and ignorant people transformed by the saving power of God's Messiah.

Here we must interject a note of criticism for contextual models of evangelism which concentrate on cultural, linguistic and psychological adaptation and fail to probe into the deeper and wider problem of social,

---

3. Cf. Jose Marins, "Basic Ecclesial Community," *The Community of Believers, UISG Bulletin*, No. 55 (Rome, Italy), p. 293.

economic and political relationships.[4] Such models may be anthropologically helpful, but they are socially and theologically deficient. For the kingdom of God is an all encompassing, transforming reality. Indeed, it is the power of the new creation (cf. I Cor 4:20; 2 Cor 5:17). An evangelism which is only interested in finding formal equivalences in a given culture or in discovering the felt needs of a people in order to make the gospel culturally, linguistically or psychologically relevant is contextually superficial and prophetically acritical. As a matter of fact, it smacks of a theological cop-out in the face of a planetary reality of evil, under the leadership of demonic principalities and powers which are present in every human situation. Only a prophetically critical and theologically radical contextual approach to evangelism can do justice to the cutting edge of the gospel, namely, its liberating and transforming message to the poor, the powerless and the oppressed and its consequential demand for conversion to their cause, which in turn makes it necessary to have a social base in their peripheric historical situation.

The Public Nature of Evangelism: Proclaiming the Kingdom Amidst the Multitudes

The contextual evangelistic approach of Jesus and its socio-historical grounding in Galilee implies, secondly, that evangelism is by its very nature public. It not only has a public message (the presence and promise of God's kingdom in Jesus Christ), but takes place amidst the multitudes. The gospel is not simply personal and public. It is rather a public message of ultimate concern for each and all human beings. Nor is the gospel public because it is personal; on the contrary, it is personal because it is public. The good news is for everyone, not for a chosen few. Accordingly, it needs to be proclaimed in the "circles of pagans" that comprise our human mosaic. Wherever there are people that do not have a knowledge of the God whose only Son was revealed in Jesus Christ; where people are trapped in structures of evil and death and are the powerless victims of injustice, suffering oppression and poverty, there the gospel is to be proclaimed, Jesus Christ exalted and the power of the kingdom demonstrated. Because it is there that the majority of human beings are to be found and there is the most overt need.

Evangelism should be geared to the multitudes because it is the communication of a message which is meant especially for them. It is only in the perspective of the multitude that so-called personal evangelism (one on one) can and does take place. Women and men can be evangelized to the extent that they share in the predicament and vulnerability of the multitudes. Evangelism presupposes the solidarity of all as far as the experience of sin and death is concerned. And it is this reality that best characterizes the multitudes of our world.

---

4. See, for example, Charles Kraft, *Christianity in Culture: A Study in Dynamic Biblical Theologizing in Cross-Cultural Perspective* (Maryknoll, N.Y.: Orbis Books, 1979); Edward Dayton and David Frazer, *Planning Strategies for World Evangelization* (Grand Rapids: Eerdmans, 1980); and David J. Hesselgrave, *Communicating Christ Cross-Culturally: An Interpretation to Missionary Communication* (Grand Rapids: Zondervan, 1978).

Jesus described the multitudes (ochlos) of his day as harassed and helpless, "like sheep without a shepherd" (Mt 9:37). That is, they were leaderless, without a goal, uncertain of the future. He evangelized them by announcing the dawning of a new age wherein their burdens would be lifted and their vulnerability be eliminated. He invited them to participate of that new reality by trusting in him (Mt 11:28ff.).

This is without question the evangelistic challenge that is before Christians today in the face of the multitudes of human beings around the world that find themselves harassed and helpless, threatened by the material and spiritual reality of sin and death. The fact that we all participate of the vulnerability of the multitudes does not mean that any human group is thereby a multitude in the theological sense in which we have been speaking. The multitudes are defined not by the sum total of individual human beings, but by the social reality of vulnerability. Of course, quantitatively speaking, it is not difficult to determine today who are the multitudes: they are the overwhelming majority of human beings who bear the brunt of injustice, powerlessness, oppression and poverty on planet earth. What qualifies them as multitudes, however, is not their overwhelming quantity, but rather their social condition. Even if they were not the majority, as in the case of oppressed minorities in the North Atlantic, they would still be the concrete referent of human alienation and vulnerability. In their material condition, we see the spiritual reality of sin and death.

To evangelize the multitudes is to announce the glad news of God's action in Jesus Christ to change radically the frail, unjust and death prone patterns of human existence by bringing into being a new world order. Such an announcement cannot but be public. To keep it private, announcing it to a select few, is to deny the very content of the gospel. Furthermore, it is to keep out of reach its privileged addressees. On the other hand, when the multitudes are evangelized everybody hears about it: the press, government authorities, the business community, the religious leadership, the army, the comfortable and secure individuals who usually remain aloof from the cry of the multitudes. Very often these various institutional and personal groupings become irritated and threatened, joining forces as a sort of "counter-multitude," to quench the hope and aspirations which come to the harassed multitudes as they hear the gospel and appropriate it by faith in Christ.

This in fact is what happened in the case of the crowds of Jerusalem that called for the crucifixion of Jesus. The Jerusalem establishment became offended and threatened at the way the Galilean multitudes that followed Jesus appropriated the messianic promise (Lk 19:37ff). Hence when Jesus entered the Holy City amidst the celebration of the Galilean multitudes, spreading their garments and leafy branches and singing praises to God, the Pharisees asked him to rebuke them (Lk 19:30). A few days later the chief priests, scribes and elders managed to form a counter-crowd based on a socio-religious coalition of those who could not accept a new era of freedom, fraternity and just peace where the uncultured and marginated could be on an

19

equal socio-religious footing with the privileged few (Mk 14:43). It was the counter-crowd of Jerusalem, not the Galileans, who angrily asked Pilate to release Barrabas and crucify Jesus (Mk 15:8ff; Mt 27:15ff; Lk 23:1-5, 13-21; Jn 19:6-7, 12, 14-16).

Something similar has occurred in Latin America. After centuries of massive popular harassment and marginalization, the gospel has begun to be preached and lived amidst the displaced multitudes. As a result, the "lame," the "blind," and the "lepers" are appropriating the messianic promises of the new age; the poor are at last receiving good news! Even a significant minority from the privileged sectors of society, including professionals, intellectuals, students, and religious, business and political leaders, have ceased to be scandalized at Jesus' identity with the poor and oppressed! Never before have so many Latin American "pagans" taken so much interest in the gospel, and never before have the powers and principalities that rule the countries of the region been so irritated and threatened. It is no wonder that they have unleashed a brutal and repressive offensive which has seen literally thousands follow in the path of martyrdom,[5] even as Jesus suffered outside the gates of Jerusalem (Heb 13:12).

When the multitudes are evangelized the whole creation hears about it! Indeed women, men and children have the opportunity to respond personally and collectively to the gospel and commit their lives to the Galilean Messiah who cast his lot with the wretched of the earth and thus made possible a new future for all.

This explains why it is so important that there be a strong base-community in the periphery. For only by building a strong community of women, men and children from the ochlos (the marginated multitude) can evangelism acquire the necessary credentials and spiritual strength to fulfill its general and specific objectives. Put succinctly, evangelism can only be prophetic, and thus liberating, if it has an engaged, witnessing base, and such a nucleus can only be built from the periphery.

The Global Scope of Evangelism: Into the Periphery of the Nations

In the third place, the contextual model we find in Jesus' Galilean-rooted ministry implies that evangelism has a global scope. The fact that in the Markan narrative Galilee became the launching pad for world evangelism should not be taken lightly. As has been noted, evangelism is not a ghetto affair; it takes place in the open-space of the multitudes. As an apostolic mandate, it can only be fulfilled in a worldwide pilgrimage. Evangelism is the outgrowth of the movement of Jesus' messianic community through the nations, even as New Testament scholars suggest that the Great Commission in Matthew's Gospel should be read: "Going therefore, disciple the nations" (Mt 28:18ff).

To evangelize is to communicate the good news to the multitudes near and far. No individual Christian, local congregation or denomination can

---

5. Cf. Penny Lernoux, *Cry of the People* (Garden City, N.Y.: Doubleday & Co., 1980), pp. 3ff.

be content simply with evangelizing the multitudes which lie geographically and/or culturally near. They should always seek to extend their evangelistic witness beyond their frontiers. To be evangelistically concerned with just those who are within one's geo-cultural context while remaining aloof from those who lie beyond one's frontiers, is selfish and hypocritical. If the gospel is important for those who are geo-culturally close, it should be equally valuable for those who are afar.

Contextual evangelism should not be limited, therefore, to local situations. Rather it should seek to be global in scope. It should be globally contextual, addressing women and men in their socio-historical reality everywhere on planet earth.

This does not mean, of course, a relativization of the Galilean principle: the perspective from the periphery. If that were the case, we would be wiping out in one stroke everything I have been arguing for in the previous subsections. Indeed it would mean a return to an uncritical and prophetically crippled contextuality.

In insisting that contextual evangelism be global in scope, however, I am building upon all that I have argued heretofore. The global scope of contextuality should be in congruence with the Galilean principle. This means, concretely, that evangelism should be geared, first and foremost, to the periphery of the nations wherein lie the multitudes and where the Christian faith has always had the best opportunity to build a strong base. Whenever the Christian faith has gone straight to the centers of power (as, for example, in those situations of mission history where the first to be evangelized has been the monarch, the head of state or ruling elite), usually it has resulted in a great massification of the faith. The gospel has been cheapened and devalued. Evangelism has become the propaganda arm of the ruling class, focusing on mandatory mass-conversions and losing thereby its critical, prophetic edge.

But when evangelism is done at the periphery of the nations the outcome is, by and large, much different. The critical, liberating thrust of the gospel is bound to come forth in one way or another, because of the similarities in historical situations. Indeed for the poor and the oppressed no "demythologizing" of the gospel is possible. The Christ of the gospel is Jesus of Nazareth, the poor and solitary Galilean who lived a just life and died for the salvation of the world. They have, therefore, no problem in understanding the cross and resurrection in their concrete reality because they have no other historical instruments to mediate the message of Christ than their experiences and situation. At the popular level, the theoretical postulates of religion are relativized. For people who live in the fringes of society, the fundamental theological question is: does religion have a liberating word to say to them? From the perspective of Jesus Christ and the gospel, the answer is affirmative, even if the answer given through the behavior of Christians and the church in history has often been negative.

This question was vividly articulated when I visited Sri Lanka. I participated, together with several colleagues from around the world, in an "immersion exposure" of urban Colombo from the perspective of the "shanty towns" where half of the population live. We saw Buddhists, Hindus, Muslims and Christians living side by side, suffering and experiencing together the effect of a de-humanized social, economic and political reality, as described in the following local song:

> Cardboard and tin cans all straightened out
> Patched up with these and blocked round about
> Everyman's junk we've built up our house
> That's one of many in old shanty town.
>
> A million mosquitoes, we wait for the rain
> To wash away all the dirt filled up drains
> The water we get comes down from the skies
> But the drought's going on and our homes full of flies.
>
> A slum is where the world forgets who you are
> They close their eyes, no time to care
> They pass you by, faces full of frowns
> Turned up noses at our shanty town.

The same song extends a moving invitation:

> Come take my hand
> Some time can you give
> To open your heart and see how we live
> Visit my home, I'll take you around
> The Forgotten People of old shanty town.

We visited the "forgotten people of old shanty town" and saw ourselves deeply interrogated from the very heart of the gospel. How is it that the ruling elite can be satisfied with the dehumanization that takes place in these slums? How have religious communities, in general, and Christians, in particular, allowed themselves to be so dehumanized that they can go on to sleep in spite of the millions around them who live and suffer in the shanty towns of the world? We discovered the shanty as the new universal, found almost everywhere in the world, including the Americas. (In the continental United States, for example, the shanty is our urban ghettoes; in Puerto Rico, arrabales; in Central America, tugurios; in Brazil, favelas; in Argentina, villas miserias, and so on.) Most importantly, however, we who as seminary and university professors from around the world came there to learn and reflect theologically on the problem and challenges of religious pluralism, left nevertheless feeling that we had been evangelized by the risen Christ hiding in the suffering faces of the residents of "old shanty town."

The shanties are without a doubt a fundamental point of reference in evangelism, being at the same time a disturbing sign of the dehumanizing effect of sin, and a liberating possibility for those who take the gospel sincerely. This experience reconfirmed the conviction, derived by me first of all from the evangelistic praxis of Jesus, that authentic, contextual evangelism should start from the periphery, with an immersion in the pains and agonies of the people in the fringes and bottom of society, and the disturbing effect which such an involvement has upon one's conscience. In such an experience, one encounters the risen Lord, enlarging and deepening one's limited vision of human reality, challenging one's presuppositions, renewing one's mind, liberating and empowering one's life for service as a channel of grace in the "Galilees of the nations" --the shanties and ghettoes, the marginal provinces and forgotten nuclei of the world.

If we take Jesus' Galilean evangelistic model seriously, our evangelistic practice will never be the same. For we will be forced to ask, *where* is our base, *who* is our target-audience and *what* is the scope of our evangelistic praxis? And when we start asking such questions in earnest and in the light of Jesus' own ministry, we are challenged to either conform our evangelistic witness to his model or close shop and go home. May we be led to follow in his steps!

"Apuntes" for a Hispanic Women's Theology of Liberation

Ada María Isasi-Díaz

Some time ago, I wrote:

> The academicians will excuse the almost total lack of academic footnotes. The activists will excuse the academic footnotes even if they are few. Those who struggle for liberation will know that as a sister-in-the-struggle, my organic understandings belong to all. They will accept my sense of gathering the knowledge of the people --of being a voice through which their voices and mine speak. I do not, however, relinquish responsibility for what I have here written . . .[1]

I have always considered myself first and foremost an activist. But for me reflection is intrinsic to being an activist and I see no split or contradiction between being an activist and being a theologian. This coming together of activism and theology will become clearer as I attempt to clarify my understanding of praxis and of organic theology and communal theologizing.

I do theology out of, because of, and for the community with which I participate in the struggle for liberation. That community is my primary community of accountability.[2] My theology has to make sense to that community; it has to be clear to it, to be valid for it. But the religious and theological understandings of the Hispanic Women's community are intrinsically linked to the Christian tradition. Classical theology can and does provide tools for understanding and proving the theology of Hispanic Women. At the same time, a Hispanic Women's Theology questions classical theology in regard to its source, process, etc. Neither can stand apart from the other if they are to bear fruit.

Because of this, I engage theologians who have enlightened my understanding, whose ideas challenge me or affirm what I think. I acknowledge their contribution and influence in what I call "academic footnotes." As important for me as these footnotes are what I call "experiential footnotes" --they document the experiences and conversations which are part of the theological understandings with which I am dealing. These experiences and conversations are central to my theology --they are the source of my theology, providing not only the content but in a large part also determining the process. Classical theology helps me with the methodology and provides the adequate terminology to express the theological understandings Hispanic Women are living.

---

1. "A Liberationist Perspective on Peace and Social Justice, in *Education for Peace and Justice*, ed. Padraic O'Hare (San Francisco: Harper & Row, 1983), p. 231.

2. David Tracy, *Blessed Rage for Order* (New York: Seabury, 1978), p. 7.

This leads me to say why I am involved in doing Hispanic Women's Theology. The reflective aspect of praxis is extremely important for the self-definition of a people. Hispanic Women's Theology is a praxis, and yet few have recognized it or understood it as such because the reflective aspect has not been explicated. Such explication is sorely needed if we are to gain momentum and focus in our struggle as Hispanic Women living in the USA. Secondly, unless explicated and written, we have but little hope of having our understandings and commitments --our lives-- taken seriously. Because we believe that we have a contribution to make and because struggling to make that contribution part of the norm is intrinsic to our liberation, we take time to write down the Hispanic Women's Theology we are always doing.[3]

Thirdly, I do not pretend to be nor would want to be objective. I do not believe that objectivity is possible; but even if it were, that is not an understanding that I value. I believe intellectual honesty requires that I identify my subjectivity and then open that subjectivity to the critique of others involved in the community of struggle.[4] Objectivity for me means "openness to other critical claims."[5] The only objectivity that I seek "is the one of an engagement, a militancy."[6] It is my hope that Hispanic Women's Theology will always be a "passionate language" because our survival is indeed at stake.[7]

Fourth, I believe that this theology and any theology can only be understood from a solidarity stance. That is why I ask those reading these pages to do so only after attempting to begin the process of standing with the struggle for liberation of Hispanic Women. A fair beginning seems to me to be a commitment to learn about us and to support us in our struggles even if the reader does not understand us fully. The specifics of such a support do, of course, depend on each individual.

Fifth, because of the shortness of this essay, it is to be understood only as a beginning sketch of some of the understandings that are becoming clearer as some of us Hispanic Women engage in the process of doing theology. Hispanic Women's Theology is a cultural theology --struggling against ethnic prejudice; it is a feminist theology --struggling against sexism; it is a liberation theology --struggling against classism. Hispanic Women's Theology is Christian Theology because it is grounded in Christian understandings and practices. We welcome questions which would lead us to clarify further our praxis. As a matter of fact, we understand questions and serious engagement as an affirmation of the task which we have set out to do.

---

3. Cf. Gustavo Gutiérrez, *A Theology of Liberation* (Maryknoll, N.Y.: Orbis, 1973), p. 14.

4. Dolly Pomerleau, co-founder and co-director of the Quixote Center, a justice center in Washington, D.C., has used and explicated this term for me.

5. Beverly Harrison in a lecture on the steps involved in liberation social ethics. Union Theological Seminary, N.Y., 1977.

6. Georges Casalis, *Las buenas ideas no caen del cielo* (San José, Costa Rica: Editorial Universitaria Centroamericana, 1979), p. 9.

7. James Cone, *A Black Theology of Liberation* (New York: Lippincott, 1970), p. 45.

Finally, I want to identify some of the basic presuppositions which ground my life and, therefore, my praxis. I believe that these presuppositions will help explain some of what is being said in this paper.

1.- When in doubt, I act; for if I do not, possibilities will never unfold.

2.- Risk is part of life. So I do not attempt to avoid it. I am afraid but not paralyzed.

3.- Divine revelation is always happening in the community and through the community because our Divine Friend is present when the community gathers.

4.- My goal, my hope, is the creation of the community and its common good: that is what the "reign of God" is all about. The common good is always being understood afresh and cannot fall under ideological control. Therefore, leadership belongs to the community, and to hold those who exercise it accountable is both the right and obligation of the community.

5.- Joy is an intrinsic part of the work for justice and peace. As a joyful community we express our belief in the presence of the divine among us and in us, a presence which pushes us on because in our being fulfilled, divinity is fully revealed.

Apuntes

Theology is a praxis --a critical, reflective process about questions of ultimate meaning[8] which is possible only through the existential engagement in a specific struggle.[9] Because praxis is a concrete reality, theology has to engage consciously and recognize the cultural/historical reality within which it is operating. This necessitates three very clear and concrete commitments: to *do* theology; to do theology from a *specific* perspective; to theology from a specific perspective *as a communal process*. To *do* theology is to free theology of the exclusive hold over it which the intellectual arena has had and to understand theology as a doing as much as it is a thinking. To do theology is to recognize that the source of theology is human existence, its questions and preoccupations as well as beliefs.

---

8. A phrase I have learned from Mary Hunt.

9. Cf. Gutiérrez, *A Theology* . . ., p. 11. I disagree with his understanding of theology as a "second step." My understanding of praxis as reflective, critical action sees theology in the action as well as in the reflection. My understanding is closer to Padma Gallup's when she says: "Doing theology . . . means monitoring development projects on the basis of full participation by women both in the planning and in the programme." And, "doing theology would be to be involved in the sort of demonstration a women's rights group in Madras undertook to remove a grossly offensive cinema poster form a main thoroughfare in the city." Padma Gallup, "Doing Theology: An Asian Perspective," *CTC Bulletin*, Vol. 4, No. 3 (December, 1983), pp. 24-25.

To do theology from a *specific perspective* requires a clear identification of the day to day life of those engaged in doing this theology, their needs and their struggles. Because of this it is presumptuous to speak of "theology" as if there were only one, as if theology were an objective science. Likewise, it is unacceptable to speak of Theology (with a capital T) as if it were the only true way to deal with questions of ultimate meaning. "Theology" or "theology" is therefore only acceptable as a heuristic device which provides a "space" in which the different theologies can meet to discuss their commonalities and differences in order to deepen their understandings. This conversation is an important one for the different theologies to engage in because the struggles they relate to are interconnected.

What are the questions of ultimate meaning in which theology engages through reflective practice? For Hispanic Women they are questions of survival. Survival has to do with more than barely living. Survival has to do with the struggle *to be* fully. In order to survive one has to have "the power to decide about one's history and one's vocation or historical mission."[10] This translates into two sets of questions: questions about physical survival and questions about cultural/historical survival. Though these two aspects of survival are closely linked in many situations, they are not identical. To keep these two different aspects of survival in mind is especially important for theologies of "remnant groups"[11] --groups excluded from participating in setting the norm and distributing the resources-- in first world countries where, strictly speaking, and specially in comparison with so-called Third World peoples, physical survival is not a constant preoccupation though it is not by any means too far removed. The questions of ultimate meaning which Hispanic Women's Theology engages have to do not only with the survival of Hispanic Women but also with the survival of their children, their families.

What also makes these questions, questions of ultimate meaning is the fact that they are the questions of Hispanic women and are asked by Hispanic women.

> Christian theology for centuries refused to attribute the fullness of the imago dei to women. . . men were thought to participate in the imago dei primarily and fully, while women participated in it secondarily and partially. . . .
> Not only could women not represent God to the Christian community, they could not represent the generically human --before God or before the community.[12]

---

10. Juan Carlos Scannone, "Teología cultural popular y descernimiento," in *Cultura popular y filosofía de la liberación* (Buenos Aires: Fernando García Cambeiro, 1975), pp. 253-54.

11. I refuse to use "minority" or "marginalized" since these labels communicate the way the dominant group sees us. The Biblical concept of the "remnant" seems to me better to describe us: a hermeneutically privileged group with a significant contribution to make.

12. Margaret Farley, "Moral Imperatives for the Ordination of Women," in *Women and Catholic Priesthood: An Expanded Vision*, ed. Anne Marie Gardiner (New York: Paulist Press, 1976), pp. 40-41.

Given this distorted but operative understanding about women, to ascertain that questions asked by women are questions of ultimate meaning constitutes in itself a most important theological statement. When these women belong to a "remnant" group, considered to be intellectually inferior because of its lack o accomplishments in the fields of academic and the published world --to claim that the questions of Hispanic women are questions of ultimate meaning becomes a threat to the dominant groups and a strategy for Hispanic Women.

Hispanic Women's Theology also denies the operative understanding which the above quotes so succinctly state. Hispanic Women can and do image God in so far as they engage in the lifelong process of becoming fully human which does not depend on gender, race, class, but on the willingness to be in relationship.[13] Relationship requires commitment to vulnerability, justice, honesty --love. No relationship is private, for all relationships contribute to the building up of the community. It is in this sense that the personal is political.

Hispanic Women's Theology is a process, it "both grows and, in a certain sense, changes."[14] This process is organic insofar as it is "vitally engaged in historical realities with specific times and places."[15] It is organic because it "arises spontaneously and inevitably in the believer . . ."[16] It is organic because it engages the whole person and does not necessitate sophisticated academic knowledge which is not available to most Hispanic Women. All that is needed is to believe in one's intrinsic value, the willingness to share openly, and to ask questions seriously.

The specificity of Hispanic Women's Theology has as its *locus theologicus* cultural/historical reality. This places the theological task in contact with three very different cultures and histories: the Amerindian, the African, and the Spanish. *La Raza*, the race, is the *mestizaje* that has resulted from the mixture of these races, cultures and histories.[17] Hispanics are *mestizos* belonging indeed to *la raza*. Therefore, the Hispanic understandings of the divine, the human, the meaning of life, emerge from this *mestizaje*. The theological task of any and every Hispanic cannot ignore this three pronged *mestizaje*. Though the Hispanic cultural/historical reality is often ignored in the doing of theology, the popular religiosity of the Hispanic community does call theology to give equal consideration to all three cultural strata out of which this *mestizaje* emerges. This means that religious understandings of the Amerindians are to be taken as seriously as the Catholicism of the Spaniards.

---

13. Isabel Carter Heyward, *The Redemption of God* (Washington, D.C.: University Press of America, 1982), pp. 1-18.

14. Gutiérrez, *A Theology* . . ., p. 12.

15. *Ibid.*, p. 13.

16. *Ibid.*, p. 3.

17. For a good history of this *mestizaje* and an explanation of how it functions see Virgilio Elizondo, *Galilean Journey: The Mexican-American Promise* (Maryknoll, N.Y.: Orbis, 1983), pp. 5-18.

28

Likewise, the cosmological, theological and anthropological understandings which the Africans brought to America are to be taken into consideration by Hispanic theologians. This has usually been called syncretism, and the attempt has been to purify the dominant religion and theology, the Christian one, of such elements. But if this is seen as a *mestizaje* and not syncretism,[18] if Hispanic Women's Theology has as its source the lived experience of Hispanic Women in which both Amerindian and African religious practices and understandings are present and active many times under the guise of Christian practice, then this theology has to take very seriously the popular religiosity in which these three strands converge.[19]

Besides culture and popular religiosity, Hispanic Women's Theology has to take into consideration the social sciences in order to include in its perspective an economic/political analysis and not to fall into a romantic attitude regarding culture.[20] Because of the very different economic/political backgrounds of Hispanic women in the USA, this could prove to be one of the most difficult variants with which Hispanic Women's Theology has to deal. Does culture prevail over economics and politics? Or are political ideology and economics more relevant or determining than culture when it comes to questions of ultimate meaning?

Hispanic Women's Theology is a *communal process*. There are three main reasons for this. First, the source of Hispanic Women's Theology is the lived experience, which has to include both personal and communal aspects.

---

18. I am always struck by the fact that Christianity denounces all syncretism except the one that gave it its original patterns and constructs for expressing what it proclaims and for designing its religious practices. The Graeco-Roman world of ideas and understandings plus the understandings of what Jesus preached, resulted in the syncretism that we call Christianity. For example, Christmas is celebrated at the time when the pagan Sun Feasts used to take place, pagan buildings such as the Pantheon were turned into churches, regular civil garbs and offices were turned into liturgical vestments and ecclesial offices, etc. Once that syncretism became official and controlled what was to be considered orthodox, it then refused to accept any other syncretism and instead attempted to "convert" all religious elements to Christianity. But operating in the hearts of Cubans who pray to Santa Bárbara is her identification with Changó, the African goddess; and the Peruvians who stop to pray before they start working in the field are asking Mama Pacha, the earth which for them is a divinity, pardon for having to hurt her, etc. A most important example if this is what happened and continues to happen with our Lady of Guadalupe. Compare Virgilio Elizondo, *La Morenita* (Liguori, Mo.: Liguori, 1981) with Jacques Lafaye, *Quetzalcoatl et Guadalupe* (Paris: Gallimard, 1974).

19. My problem with Elizondo's theologizing is that it does not take into account popular religiosity except in so far as it is in line with Catholic doctrine. He reinterprets popular religious practices according to Biblical and doctrinal understandings but does not allow the experience of the people to judge Biblical understandings and ecclesial doctrine which are indeed culturally determined.

20. Scannone sees these two lines, the cultural/popular religiosity one and the economic/political one, as two different lines being followed in Latin America. I believe that the bringing together of these two lines is most important for Hispanic Women's Theology.

Personal experience borders on solipsism if it is not mediated by community experience. Likewise the community's experience tends toward abstraction if it is not mediated by individual experiences.[21]

Second, the theological process is an intrinsic part of the liberation task because it is one of the ways in which the community becomes agent of its own history. Liberation is a personal process which takes place within a community and through a community. Liberation is at the very core "the unfolding of all of man's (sic) dimensions,"[22] and therefore has to do not only with an "interior liberation," but also with "liberation from exterior pressures which prevent his (sic) fulfillment as a member of a certain social class, country, or society."[23] Therefore, the link between liberation and theology points to the need for theology to be communal.

Third, one of the most pervading themes in Hispanic culture is the community. *La comunidad* is the immediate reality within which Hispanics find their personal identities and function. Among Hispanics the institutions that are "mentioned consistently in a positive way (are) the *family (familia)* and the *neighborhood (barrio, barriada)*."[24] Besides the cultural importance of the community, the "dynamics of mestizaje" include a need to "distinguish 'us' from 'them'."[25] Because of how important *la comunidad* is, the communal aspect should not be by-passed or suspended when it comes to theology.

The theological role of the community, then, it so explicate it own understandings and actions: why is the community believing, acting the way it does? What does that mean in terms of the liberation struggle? Where does the community find its inspiration and strength? Which cultural/religious traditions help and which ones hinder the process of liberation? Some in the group might have more skills in facilitating story telling; others might have a better understanding of the tools of analysis; while others will be best qualified to gather and write down the conclusions reached. The spiral process is always beginning anew, for the conclusions are always part of a praxis which then becomes the story of what the community has been doing. Those members who take upon themselves the job of synthesizing and writing have to be especially careful about their own presuppositions and understanding of what the theological task is.

Hispanic Women's Theology starts by renouncing "to the desire to inaugurate a world or historical project; instead it... respect(s) our peoples in their autonomous construction of history."[26] The Hispanic Women's theological task must insist on those questions of ultimate meaning which,

---

21. Mary Elizabeth Hunt, *Feminist Liberation Theology: The Development of Method in Construction* (Berkeley: Graduate Theological Union, 1980), p. 161.

22. Gutiérrez, *A Theology . . .*, p. 36.

23. *Ibid.*, p. 30.

24. Elizondo, *Galilean Journey*, p. 24.

25. *Ibid.*, pp. 16-18.

26. Scannone, p. 256.

together with this autonomous construction of history, put the community in touch with the ontological reality. These "religious" or "theological" questions do not detract or add but rather are an intrinsic part of the praxis of the community.

Hispanic Women's Theology is an organic theology because it is born of the experience of Hispanic Women and it is done by Hispanic Women. It is an intrinsic part of the liberationist praxis which enables Hispanic Women to proclaim proudly that *la vida es lucha* (life is the struggle) and *sí se puede* (yes, it can be done).

Epilogue

Of course, there is much that has not been said in this essay. For example, I have not mentioned Scripture and how it interrelates with experience in the life of Hispanic Women; I have not explicated how the Christian tradition of sacraments and spirituality comes into play mainly through the culture. I have dealt with the method of this theology very succinctly, and have not even mentioned how I would indeed apply David Tracy's categories of "adequacy" and "appropriateness" to evaluate this theology. I have given but a very sketchy presentation of the role and task of the theological community. I have not argued for this position but simply presented it, and yet I know that I need to rub these understandings against the traditional understandings regarding "the theologians," in order to clarify it further. I have not at all completed the explanation of the difference between theological *mestizaje* and syncretism.

Above all, the greatest shortcoming of this essay is that, because of the pressures of time, I have not submitted it to the theological community in which many of the ideas here presented have been shared. I hope that my synthesis and writing are faithful to *our* process. I present them here, not to indicate that Hispanic Women's Theology is unique, but that it is distinct and has an important contribution to make.

Rethinking Our Tradition

"El Señor guarda a los emigrantes" (Salmo 146:9)

Francisco O. García-Treto

El libro de Rut nos provee uno de los ejemplos bíblicos de la realidad de la migración por causas económicas en el mundo del antiguo Israel: "En tiempos de los jueces hubo hambre en el país, y un hombre emigró (*vayyelek... lagur*), con su mujer y sus dos hijos, desde Belén de Judá a la campiña de Moab".[1] Las tradiciones de los patriarcas de Israel los relacionan también al modo de vida del emigrante por pobreza. La primera vez que aparece la palabra hebrea *ger* (migrante, forastero) en el Antiguo Testamento es en referencia proléptica a esa tradición, es la promesa divina a Abrán en Gn 15:13: "Has de saber que tu descendencia vivirá como forastera (*ger*) en tierra ajena, tendrá que servir y sufrirá opresión durante cuatrocientos años"; es decir, que serán llevados por el hambre a emigrar de Canaán a Egipto. La historia de Moisés nos da un ejemplo del otro impulso a la migración, es decir, el escape de la opresión política. Moisés fue *ger* en Midián, donde encontró asilo de la persecución faraónica, y en memoria de tal hecho le da el nombre de Guersón a su primogéntio, diciendo "soy forastero (*ger*) en tierra extraña".[2] La palabra hebrea *ger*, que las versiones hispanas generalmente traducen "extranjero" (Reina y Valera, 1960), "forastero" o "emigrante" (NBE), es un término difícil de traducir por un simple vocablo. Así, Holladay lo define en estos términos: "*ger* es el hombre que, ya sea solo o con su familia, abandona su poblado y su tribu, por causa de guerra (2 S 4:2), de hambre (Rt 1:1), de pestilencia, de ser culpable de homicidio, etc., y busca otro amparo y estancia en otra parte, donde tiene restringidos los derechos a ser dueño de tierra, a casarse, y a tomar parte en la administración de la justicia, en el culto, y en la guerra".[3]

En este artículo trataré, en primer lugar, de resumir la situación del *ger* en las tradiciones legales y religiosas del Antiguo Testamento, y después, de bosquejar el sentido teológico que tales tradiciones sugieren.

Si quisiéramos resumir en una frase la clara tesis de esas tradiciones bíblicas, sería, simplemente, que el *ger* es protegido de Yahvé. La antigua tradición hebrea se destaca claramente de las actitudes xenofóbicas comunes en la antigüedad, y aún representadas en ocasión en la Biblia con referencia

---

1. Rut 1:1, *Nueva Biblia Española* (NBE), Luis Alonso Schökel y Juan Mateos, eds. (Madrid: Cristiandad, 1976).

2. Exodo 2:22 (NBE). También Exodo 18:3.

3. W.L. Holladay, *A Concise Hebrew and Aramaic Lexicon of the Old Testament, based upon the Lexical Work of Ludwig Koehler and Walter Baumgartner* (Grand Rapids: Eerdmans, 1971), p. 64 (traducción mía). Véanse también los artículos de T.M. Mauch, "Sojourner," *The Interpreter's Dictionary of the Bible*, R-Z (New York and Nashville: Abingdon), pp. 397-99, y de D. Kellermann, "gur, ger, geruth, meghurim," *Theological Dictionary of the Old Testament* (Grand Rapids: Eerdmans, 1975), II:439-449, ambos con buenas bibliografías.

al *nokhri*, es decir, al extranjero como tal, al extraño. El *ger*, el emigrante que reside entre el pueblo de Israel, pudo ser completamente privado de la dignidad y del más elemental derecho a la justicia, ya que carecía de los dos elementos consuetudinarios en que se fundaban la dignidad y el derecho, en cuanto a lo humano, en Israel: la propiedad hereditaria de la tierra y la protección de la familia y parentela de sangre. Sin embargo, la tradición bíblica sorprende al presentar al *ger* como el objeto de una predisposición por parte de Yahvé para incluirlo, junto al nativo, en los ritos que daban expresión a la solidaridad del grupo, y en la categoría de los protegidos por la ley. Un solo principio parece encontrar expresión en ambos casos, es decir, el principio de la igualdad ante la ley entre el *ger* y el nativo. El rito de la Pascua, por ejemplo, dice: "Y si el emigrante (*ger*) que vive (*yagur*) contigo quiere celebrar la Pascua del Señor, hará circuncidar a todos los varones, y solo entonces podrá tomar parte en ella: será como un indígena... La misma ley vale para el indígena y para el emigrante que vive con ustedes" (Ex 12:48,49; véase también Nm 9:14). En forma semejante, se incluyen los *gerim* en los ritos de la Fiesta de la Expiación (Lv 16:29), de la Fiesta de las Semanas (Dt 16:11), de la Fiesta de las Chozas (Dt 16:14 y 31:12), y en el descanso del Sábado (Ex 23:12 y Dt 5:14). El emigrante tendrá también derecho a ofrecer toda clase de sacrificios, ya sean holocaustos de animales (Lv 22:18) o libaciones y otros tipos de ofrenda, como por ejemplo lo prescribe Nm 15:13-16, reiterando el principio de la igualdad: "El mismo rito observarán ustedes y el emigrante residente entre ustedes. Es ley perpetua para todas sus generaciones. Ante el Señor el emigrante es igual que ustedes. El mismo ritual y ceremonia observarán ustedes y el emigrante residente entre ustedes."

La protección del emigrante se extiende también en forma positiva al ámbito económico y social. Es de notarse que se le incluye entre las categorías sociales de los que, carentes de medios económicos, pueden contar con que el grupo se hará responsable de darles asistencia social: la viuda, el huérfano y el levita, además del *ger*, constituyen esas categorías, es decir, los desposeídos de tierra. Tal ayuda no era simple acción caritativa dependiente de la piedad personal del pudiente --véase, por ejemplo, Job 31:32-- sino un requisito legal, una especie de impuesto sobre el usufructo de la tierra. Así, las cosechas de productos agrícolas, tanto los cereales como las frutas, estaban sujetas al requisito de dejar en el campo suficiente para que los pobres pudieran tomar parte (Lv 19:10, 23:22; Dt 24:19,20). Se dedicaba, además, el diezmo de cada tercer año (Dt 26:12,13) a la distribución entre los mismos. En Lv 25:35, se resuelve el problema de la situación del israelita "hermano tuyo" que se arruina, al aplicarle la misma regla que al *ger*, y hacer provisión para que reciba préstamos sin interés ni recargo.

El emigrante estaba en Israel para trabajar y, aunque una ley como la de Lv 25:47 reconoce la posibilidad de que se haga rico, tal caso debe de haber sido raro. Muchas más son las amonestaciones contra la opresión legal o el defraude del pobre emigrante jornalero, como por ejemplo la que sigue, dada a los jueces en Dt 1:16-17: "Escuchen y resuelvan según justicia los pleitos de sus hermanos, entre sí o con emigrantes. No sean parciales en la sentencia. Oigan por igual a pequeños y grandes. No se dejen intimidar por nadie, que la sentencia es de Dios." O, como dice Dt 24:14: "No explotarás al jornalero, pobre y necesitado, sea hermano tuyo o emigrante que vive en tu tierra... si no, apelará al Señor, y serás culpable." Y en forma de maldición ritual, en Dt 27:19: "Maldito quien defraude de sus derechos al emigrante, al huérfano o a la viuda."

La igualdad del *ger* ante la ley de Israel tenía por supuesto también la implicación de igual responsabilidad y culpabilidad en caso de transgresión, ya fuera de la ley religiosa, civil o criminal. La máxima legal es en todo caso la de Lv 24:22: "Aplicarán la misma sentencia al emigrante y al indígena. Yo soy el Señor, su Dios."

Es de recalcarse en todo lo que hasta este punto queda dicho que en la estructura religiosa y legal de Israel la protección del emigrante deriva directamente del insólito interés que evidencia Yahvé por su bienestar. Bien lo resume el Salmo 146, ese gran himno de alabanza a Yahvé como protector de los débiles, que después de decir "no confíen en los nobles, en hombres que no pueden salvar" (verso 3), dice que "el Señor guarda (*shomer*) a los emigrantes" (verso 9). Si hacemos el experimento de aplicarle a ese verso el significado "socioeconómicamente desmitologizado" que ha sugerido Gottwald para Yahvé, es decir, "el poder primordial, pero hecho concreto históricamente, que establece y mantiene la igualdad social en oposición a la contraopresión externa y en contra a tendencias provincialistas y antiigualitarias procedentes de dentro de la sociedad,"[4] vemos claramente que la legislación de Israel con referencia al *ger* y a los otros "pobres y débiles" de la sociedad encaja perfectamente en la lucha contra esas "tendencias provincialistas y antiigualitarias". Como ha dicho Enzo Bianchi, "presenciamos la elevación del extranjero al estado de persona en una serie de estatutos meticulosos que no se atestiguan en ningún otro lugar del Oriente antiguo".[5]

En una importante obra, se estudia el significado teológico de la posesión de la tierra por el pueblo de Israel, tierra que para que no se convierta en fuente de tentación destructiva debe siempre ser vista como "tierra de pacto", es decir, concedida por Yahvé, que es el verdadero dueño, bajo ciertas condiciones. En la frontera, es decir, como preludio y preliminar a la ocupación de la "tierra del pacto", Yahvé le presenta a Israel tres tareas que simbolizan y resumen esas condiciones. Las dos primeras son "no tener imágenes que nos aparten de la historia" y "guardar el Sábado para que la vida no se haga coercitiva". La tercera tarea, que es la que aquí nos interesa, es la de "honrar a los hermanos y hermanas en el pacto que aunque carezcan de poder no carecen de dignidad".[6] En su cuidadoso análisis, Bruggemann incluye al *ger* en este grupo, al que describe como "los que no tienen base de sostén

---

4. Norman K. Gottwald, *The Tribes of Yahweh: A Sociology of the Religion of Liberated Israel, 1250-1050 B.C.E.* (Maryknoll: Orbis Books, 1979), p. 692 (traducción. mía).

5. Enzo Bianchi, "The Status of Those without Dignity in the Old Testament," en J. Pohier y D. Metz, eds., *The Dignity of the Despised of the Earth, Concilium*, 1979, 3-12, p. 7 (traducción mía).

6. Walter Bruggemann, *The Land* (Philadelphia: Fortress Press, 1977), p. 67 (traducción mía).

en la comunidad. Al carecer de tierra, y por consiguiente de dignidad. No tienen 'porción ni herencia con ustedes' (Dt 14:27). A los poseedores de la tierra se les da como tarea en la frontera el cuidado de éstos cuando vengan a la tierra. Es una de las tareas que pertenecen a la tierra del pacto, y que la mantienen como realidad pactada; que a los que aparentan carecer de derecho se los tiene que honrar y cuidar."[7] La tierra, o más precisamente, la posesión de la tierra, se convierte en peligrosa oportunidad de pervertir la justicia. Así dice Bruggemann que tal posesión "tiende a disminuir el valor, y aún la presencia, del hermano y de la hermana. Israel supo que la única defensa contra tal autodecepción es un sentido de que los hermanos y las hermanas están dentro de la misma historia con nosotros. Ellos constituyen los límites impuestos a nuestra codicia."[8]

La tradición bíblica toma el paso que le sigue lógicamente a tal actitud cuando reitera el concepto de que Israel mismo no sólo fue, sino continúa siendo, un pueblo "emigrante". La solidaridad con los desposeídos no es solamente una actitud externa, sino la más profunda realidad de la existencia de Israel como pueblo de Yahvé. Tales citas como Dt 28:8 le recuerdan a Israel que fue emigrante en Egipto, pero más al caso vienen muchas otras como Lv 25:23, donde Yahvé amonesta a su pueblo: "La tierra no se venderá sin derecho a retracto, porque es mía, y en lo mío ustedes son emigrantes y sirvientes." Es bien claro que este paradójico concepto, es decir, la comprensión de que el pueblo de Yahvé es un pueblo emigrante aún en su posesión de la tierra, fue una de las claves para la sobrevivencia de Israel como entidad nacional y religiosa cuando Babilonia y Roma le arrebataron la tierra. Y, como ha dicho en resumen Enzo Bianchi, "En realidad, después del exilio babilónico, cuando Israel se encontraba como imigrante en tierra extraña, los profetas identifican a los creyentes y piadosos, los *hasidim*, con los pobres (*anawim*) y también con los extranjeros. Así es como preparó el judaísmo el camino para el Nuevo Testamento, donde frecuentemente se les llama extranjeros y peregrinos a los cristianos (Ef 2:19, I P 1:1, 2:11, Heb 11:3, etc.)."[9] Adumbrado ya en el Antiguo Testamento, pero claramente presentado como tesis central del Nuevo, llegamos al paso final de este proceso de comprensión del *ger*, al ver al Señor que lleva su identificación con todos los desposeídos hasta el punto más íntimo, desde un nacimiento en un establo, seguido de una vida entre los más pobres de la sociedad, hasta la muerte oprobiosa de una ejecución pública.

La realidad del emigrante, es decir, del refugiado político, del fugitivo económico, del que tiene que cruzar fronteras --con papeles o sin ellos-- para escapar de la violencia o del hambre (que también es violencia) no se ha convertido, como otras realidades del mundo del Antiguo Testamento, en polvo. Para nosotros, el *ger* del Israel histórico, más que desaparecer, se replica en múltiples epifanías: vivimos en la edad del refugiado, del bracero,

---

7. *Ibid.*, 65, 66 (traducción mía).

8. *Ibid.*, 66 (traducción mía).

9. Bianchi, *op. cit.*, 7,8 (traducción mía).

del emigrante, del indocumentado. Si queremos ser fieles a nuestras tareas de frontera, a nuestro carácter como pueblo del pacto, es decir, como iglesia, nos toca oír claramente la voz de nuestro Señor, "el que guarda a los emigrantes", para alzar la nuestra a favor de ellos. El derecho a la emigración, la igualdad de trato, la asistencia social, la protección legal del *ger* de hoy en día, todas son causas que nos conminan. Un vivo ejemplo de esta actualidad se nos presenta en el caso del derecho de niños de padres indocumentados a la educación pública en el Estado de Tejas, derecho que muchos en esta sociedad --y aún en sus iglesias-- quieren negar que existe.[10]

Y el Israel de que somos ciudadanos, como el antiguo, puede ser fiel a su naturaleza y llamamiento solamente cuando no se deja engañar, por la propiedad o por la tierra, hasta olvidar que es también un pueblo peregrino y emigrante, que espera una tierra mejor. El hermano y la hermana emigrantes nos recuerdan quiénes somos, y a quién servimos.

Summary

In the biblical tradition, the emigrant alien (ger) is under the special protection of God. They are among those who receive that protection because they do not have land: the widow, the orphan and, the Levite. Without the economic strength which rights to the land provided in ancient Israelite society, and without the protection of a extended family who could be expected to come to the emigrant alien's aid, or even to avenge his death, the situation of the ger would be untenable, were it not for the Lord who, "watches over the emigrant aliens."

This means that the alien is to be dealt with in the same manner as the native. This is true both of religious and civil rights. Indeed, once circumcised, the alien can fully join alongside the native Israelites in the religious rites decreed in the Torah. Besides, that which is set aside for the alien, the widow and the orphan is not the result of an act of optional charity, but of an obligation on the part of Israel, who in truth is herself an alien dwelling in God's land. Individual models, such as Moses or Ruth, and above all the collective model of the sojourn in Egypt, identify Israel as a ger, a fortunate one who has been given the right to their land as an unmerited and conditional grant, as what Walter Brueggemann calls "covenant land." Both the Babylonian Exile and the experience of the New Testament church gave occasion for new expansions of the idea of the People of God as the poor, the strangers, the dispossessed whose trust is in a God who supremely cares for those in their circumstances.

The traditions of divine favor towards the emigrant alien, and of identification of God's people with them, should be taken into account by Christians and others as they deal with the issues of the rights of refugees, of the poor, of the dispossessed today, and particularly in the American Southwest with the plight of economic refugees whose rights some would seek to deny.

---

10. Véase Elena R. González y Linda B. Team, *Por los niños: Education of Undocumented Children* (Austin: Texas IMPACT and Texas Conference of Churches, 1980).

Justice: Extrapolations from the Concept Mishpat in the Book of Micah

Michael Candelaria

The eighth century Hebrew prophets were exegetes of history and existence.[1] They were filled with the *ruach Yahweh* (spirit of God). Their utterances and oracles unveil the interpretative word of God's redemptive acts in history. This is not naive biblicism, but an acknowledgment that the apex of the political consciousness of God's historical activity was reached by the Hebrew prophets and the Christian apostles, and their interpretation of reality should serve as the starting point for hermeneutical methodology and give direction to critical reflection on the historical praxis of human liberation.

Critical reflection on justice, then, should begin with the ethical preaching of Israel's eighth century prophets. The theme of justice (*mishpat*) played a key role in their prophetic proclamations and denunciations. Western and Greek conceptions of justice fall short of the depth, the scope, and the value of the prophetic preaching of *mishpat*. Amos, the sheepherder from Tekoa, petitioned for justice (*mishpat*) to "roll down like waters and righteousness like an everflowing stream" (5:24). He gave charge that *mishpat* be established in the gates, the provincial courts (5:15). Hosea, the son of Beeri, admonished Ephraim and Judah to "observe kindness and justice" (12:6). Isaiah, the son of Amoz, defined justice in concrete terms as the reproving of the ruthless, the defending of the orphan, and the pleading for the widow (1:17). He portrayed justice as an attribute of Yahweh (30:18). Micah insisted on the doing of justice as the center of the cultus (6:8).

Micah was primarily a prophet of judgment and justice. He came from the village outpost of Moresath, a satellite village of Gath located about twenty miles southwest of Jerusalem in the western foothills. Micah is a type of the Hispanic American religious spokesperson. He lived outside of the political-economic center of Jerusalem, on the periphery of the system, in the margin of society. Yet, he challenged the totality (to use Enrique Dussel's terminology). He denounced the oppressive structures of sin headed by the political, economic, and religious dominators. He condemned the status quo as a system of injustice and violence directed against the working class, the poor of the land, the people of God.

Micah prophesied judgment and destruction to the cities of Israel and Judah (ch. 1). He pronounced woe upon the rich and powerful who robbed the poor of their homes and fields (2:1,2). He denounced the political heads of Judah for failing in the public administration of justice (3:1). He portrayed the false prophets as corrupt and greedy, while he claimed to have the *ruach Yahweh* and the sense of justice (3:8). He gave the classic expression of the

---

1. Abraham J. Heschel, *The Prophets* (New York: Harper and Row, 1962), p. xviii.

eighth century prophetic conception of religion with justice at the center of the cultus rather than the sacrifices (6:8). Finally, he portrayed justice salvifically as an eschatological hope (7:9).

Three extrapolations can be drawn from the use of *mishpat* (justice) in the book of Micah to serve as theologico-ethical points of departure for the Hispanic community's *kerygma* (prophetic proclamation of God's redemptive acts), *koinonia* (fellowship of the people of God), *diakonia* (service to the world), *didache* (redemptive education and "conscientization"), and *leitourgia* (adoration and cultus). First of all, the prophetic denunciation of injustice arises from a charismatic sense of justice. Secondly, the ethical praxis of justice is ontologically grounded in love. Finally, justice can be anticipated as the eschatological hope of liberation.

A charismatic sense of justice

The term *mishpat* occurs first, in the book of Micah, in chapter three. This chapter contains three strophes of four verses each (vv. 1-4, 5-8, 9-12). *Mishpat* is the key word in each strophe (vv. 1, 8, and 9). Micah denounced the public leaders for disregarding the implementation of justice:

> And I said,
> Hear now, heads of Jacob
> And rulers of the house of Israel.
> Is it not for you to know justice (*mishpat*)? (3:1)

The duty of the public officials was to know the right juridical decision and to implement justice. Leslie Allen says that the leaders were to be the "watchdogs of public welfare and the guardians of the old morality."[2] It was incumbent upon them to know and to practice *mishpat*.

Mishpat is a polymorphic term widely used throughout the Old Testament. The primary meaning of *mishpat* is "judgement." *Mishpat* refers to the decision of a judge (*sophet*). The judgment of Yahweh is his *mishpat* (Zeph 2:3). *Mishpat* may be used to refer to the law in a general sense (Lev 24:22). In Ps 1:5 *mishpat* refers to the place where judgment is administered. The word can mean "conformity" with the resultant meaning of "mode of life" (Jer 13:12).

Interestingly, Hertzberg claims that in the eighth century literature *mishpat* acquired a new meaning.[3] It lost its juridical sense of an ethical tone and took on a distinct relationship to the poor. Allen calls *mishpat* "a sense of responsibility toward weaker members of society lest they go to the wall."[4] Wolff concurs by saying that justice to Micah means "rescue for those who are

---

2. Leslie C. Allen, "The Books of Joel, Obadiah, Jonah, and Micah," *The New International Commentary on the Old Testament*, edited by R.K. Harrison, (Grand Rapids: Wm. B. Eerdmans, 1976), p. 309.

3. H.W. Hertzberg, "Die Entwicklung des Begriffes *mishpat* im Alten Testament," *Zeitschrift für die alttestamentliche Wissenschaft*, (14 Mai 1923): 274.

4. *Op. cit.*, p. 273.

endangered, help for those who have been hurt, surcease to those who have suffered violence."[5]

The verb "to know" (*lada'ath*) means knowledge manifesting itself in praxis. The public officials were denounced for failing to uphold the rights of the innocent, the poor, the oppressed, and weaker members of society. The heads of Israel knew the right judgment but purposely perverted it for their own gain.

Years earlier, Amos admonished the leaders to "hate the evil and love the good" (5:15). The leaders, on the contrary, perverted justice, hating good and loving evil (Mic 3:2). Using the metaphorical language of cannibalism Micah accused the leaders of tearing the flesh of the people, stripping their skin, breaking their bones, and chopping their meat for the kettle (3:2, 3). In Allen's words the leaders participate in a "tyranny of evil."[6] Wolff conjectures that the mode of economic production was not "adjusted according to what is right for the protection of the weak but according to the financial calculation of the powerful."[7] Miranda claims that injustice is based on the differentiating property acquired by just such violence and spoliation.[8]

In the second strophe, Micah accused the cultic prophets of leading the people astray and divining for money (vv. 5-7). In contrast to the corrupt prophets, Micah proclaimed:

> On the other hand I am filled with power--
> With the spirit of the Lord--
> And with justice (*mishpat*) and courage
> To make known to Jacob his rebellious act,
> Even to Israel his sin. (3:8)

Mays observes that *mishpat* in this context refers to a sense for what is just according to the will of Yahweh.[9] Wolff says that it was the sense of justice that gave Micah orientation to his work.[10] Von Rad says that the preaching of the prophets, their proclamation of God's law, became "charismatic."[11] This charismatic sense of justice characterized Micah as a true prophet in contrast to the false prophets. The prophet called sin sin. Micah showed that justice consisted in calling the good good and evil evil. Herzberg points out that *mishpat* was the orientation of the will to good rather

---

5. Hans Walter Wolff, *Micah the Prophet*, translated by Ralph D. Gehrkee, (Philadelphia: Fortress, 1981), p. 75.

6. *Op. cit.*, p. 317.

7. *Op. cit.*, p. 77.

8. *Marx and the Bible* (Maryknoll, New York: Orbis, 1974), p. 19. Quoted by Andrew J. Kirk in *Liberation Theology: An Evangelical View from the Third World* (Atlanta: John Knox, 1979), p. 84.

9. "Micah: A Commentary," *The Old Testament Library*, edited by Bernhard W. Anderson (Philadelphia: Westminster, 1976), p. 85.

10. *Op. cit.*, p. 75.

11. *Old Testament Theology*, vol. I, translated by D.M.G. Stalker, (Edinburgh: Oliver and Boyd, 1962), p. 94.

than evil.[12] Micah focused on the sin of the nation and the judgment that would follow.

Micah prophesied the inevitable judgment that would come upon the nation because of its political graft, economic oppression, and religious hypocrisy. The heads of Jacob abhorred justice (3:9), and built Zion with bloodshed (v. 10). The priests instructed for a price and the prophets prostituted their ministry (v. 11). Hence Zion was doomed to be plowed into a heap of ruins (v. 12).

Micah proclaimed *mishpat* as justice on the side of the poor, the innocent, and the oppressed. The prophets demanded justice out of a concern for those oppressed, not merely for justice's sake. Berkovits says that justice is done not that justice prevail but that life prevail.[13] Western power structures follow the dictum of Thrasymachos in Book One of the *Republic*, that justice is whatever is advantageous to the stronger. The biblical demand for justice, on the other hand, denounces the oppressor and takes the side of the oppressed. In the dialectic of the oppressor/oppressed, biblical justice may be said to be whatever is advantageous to the oppressed. Yet, the oppressed must be guided by a sense of justice in order to struggle for a just society.

Micah was empowered by a sense of justice, a discernment for what is right engendered by the infilling of the Holy Spirit. The sense of justice enabled the prophet to make known the sins of the nation's political leaders. Likewise, Hispanic Americans, empowered by a sense for what is just, will be able to develop a political consciousness and take political action to institute reforms, and denounce the wicked power structures that discriminate against the Spanish speaking people and do not give them a voice in the decision-making process. Marxist ideologies and the socio-economic sciences may provide the Hispanic community with descriptive-analytic tools, but not with a sense of justice, without which the prophetic denouncement of injustice cannot proceed.

Ontological grounding in love

In a dialogical context, reminiscent of the case-suit or lawsuit, Micah summed up the essence of true ethical religion:

> He has told you O man, what is good;
> And what does the Lord require of you
> But to do justice (*mishpat*), to love kindness (*hesed*)
> And to walk humbly with your God. (6:8)

Yahweh brought forth a case-suit against the people (vv. 1, 2) and recounted to them the great saving act in their history --the exodus (v. 4). He instructed them to remember the "righteous acts of Yahweh" (v. 5). The sacrifices they offered to present to Yahweh revealed that they had no true knowledge of God (vv. 6, 7). Therefore, the prophet directed them to the true

---

12. *Op. cit.*, p. 276.

13. *Op. cit.*, p. 204.

cultus demanded by Yahweh (v. 8). Allen says that it would be unfair to conclude that Micah replaced the cultus with social ethics.[14] Miranda, on the other hand, thinks that it is clear the Yahweh requires justice in the place of religious rites.[15] Von Rad states that what took place in the cult could be the *mishpat* of God. "The *mishpat* of God in human life was the foundation stone of the cult."[16]

Mays says that to do *mishpat* is to uphold the right according to the tradition given by Yahweh "both in legal proceedings and in the conduct of life."[17] Wolff interprets the passage in terms of praxis: "putting into effect a just social order."[18] Jeremiah insisted that the praxis of justice consisted in the concrete historical realities of protecting the alien, the orphan, and the widow (7:5, 6). Deuteronomy emphasized God's insistence upon justice (1:17; 10:18; 32:4). Amos equated justice with seeking the good and not the evil (5:14, 15). Micah rooted the praxis of justice in lovingkindness (*hesed*) (6:8).

Tillich based justice ontologically on the principle of love. He also suggested that justice in the Old Testament is "expressed in the divine grace which forgives in order to reunite."[19] Justice based upon love recognizes the needy and acts upon the condition of the poor "as an obligation upon conduct which is meant in the expression 'to love mercy' (*hesed*)."[20] Acting in love to the fatherless and the widow also means debilitating the power of the oppressor. Berkovits asks, "But how else is the oppressed to be relieved if not by judging the oppressor and his ability to oppress."[21] The biblical demand for justice is rooted in love for the other. Justice in Scripture is not an idealistic notion nor is it ahistorical or apolitical (Western conceptions of justice are to be criticized for their idealistic nature). Biblical justice is to be manifested in concrete, historical, political realities --maintaining the rights of the dispossessed people of society, upholding a just wage and a just price, denouncing the sins of the political leaders, and struggling for a just society. But these acts are not to be performed out of hatred for the oppressor or out of zeal for ideological conceptions of justice; rather, the praxis of justice arises out of love for the other. The struggle for justice working out of love can overcome the dialectic of the oppressor/oppressed.

The eschatological hope of liberation

In a passage not considered Micah's, hope is expressed for the liberating execution of justice (*mishpat*) from God:

14. *Op. cit.*, p. 374.

15. Cited by Andrew J. Kirk, *op. cit.*, p. 84.

16. *Op. cit.*, p. 242.

17. *Op. cit.*, p. 125.

18. *Op. cit.*, p. 106.

19. *Love, Power, and Justice: Ontological Analysis and Ethical Applications* (New York: Oxford, 1970), pp. 55, 57.

20. *Ibid.*, p. 125.

21. "The Biblical Meaning of Justice," *Judaism*, vol. 18, no. 2, (Spring 1969), 192.

I will bear the indignation of the Lord
Because I have sinned against Him,
Until he pleads my case and executes justice (*mishpat*)
  for me.
He will bring me out to light,
And I will see his righteousness (*tsedaqah*) (7:9).

Jacob understands *mishpat* in this text as a manifestation of Yahweh's righteousness that will put an end to sin.[22] This passage reveals the true salvific nature of justice in the Old Testament --justice is to save the unfortunate from injustice. Justice and salvation are equated in the Old Testament. Justice (*mishpat*) and salvation (*y'shuah*) are used synonymously in a parallelism in Trito-Isaiah: "We look for *mishpat* but there is none, for *y'shuah* but it is far from us" (59:11). *Mishpat* is justice that does not break but liberates, "and if it breaks it is in order to deliver."[23] The blindfolded maiden holding a balance does not symbolize the *mishpat* of Yahweh. The justice of Yahweh, Jacob points out, extends an arm of salvation to help the "wretched stretched out on the ground, while with the other arm he pushes away the one who causes the oppression."[24] Justice, then, saves the poor from the corporate structures of technologically developed nations --delivers the oppressed from the cruel hand of the oppressor. Yet, God's justice will reveal itself eschatologically.

The believer expressed hope for the final execution of justice that would put an end to the oppressing conditions of injustice. He realized that justice was in the making but not yet consummated (already but not yet). He hoped for his vindication and deliverance. Yet, in his hope he possessed liberation as anticipation. God's *mishpat* is present in hope. It is present in the dialectic process of history. The *mishpat* awaited for was no mere utopian dream; on the contrary, *mishpat* contains a historical-political content as its core, a justice that will deliver the body politic from differentiating class structures and plead the case of the innocent historically at the eschaton. The just society, to be revealed eschatologically, will be established and governed on the basis of God's *mishpat*.

Rejecting Western conceptions of justice --treating equals equally and unequals unequally (Aristotle), might is right (Thrasymachos), natural law theory (Aquinas), that which works the greatest good for the greatest number of people (Bentham), and the pragmatism of the consumer society-- and appropriating the biblical concept of *mishpat*, "el pueblo de Dios" can confidently take up the struggle to set up a just society, knowing that it will be eschatologically vindicated.

---

22. *Theology of the Old Testament*, translated by Arthur W. Heathcote and Philip J. Allcock (New York: Harper and Row, 1958), p. 101.

23. *Op. cit.*, p. 206.

24. *Op. cit.*, p. 99, 100.

The Reina-Valera Bible: From Dream to Reality

Jorge A. González

The Spanish Bible most frequently used in Hispanic Protestant churches, the classic Reina-Valera version, owes its name to Casiodoro de Reina and Cipriano de Valera, two sixteenth century Spanish reformers.[1] It was Reina who published the "Bear Bible" in Basel in 1569. Valera edited a revised New Testament in London in 1596, and six years later, in Amsterdam in 1602, the complete Bible. Without detracting from the recognition which these men deserve, this article points out that the Reina-Valera Bible is in fact the end product of the collective efforts of a larger group of people who were obsessed by a dream: to provide Spain with the Scriptures in its vernacular.

Both Casiodoro de Reina and Cipriano de Valera were part of a group of twelve monks from the Monastery of San Isidoro del Campo, in Santiponce near Seville, who fled to Geneva in 1557, when the Inquisition unleashed its wrath against the "Lutherans" of Seville. Others had preceded them. Among them was Doctor Juan Pérez de Pineda, headmaster of the Colegio de los Niños de la Doctrina in Seville, who later became a member of the company of pastors of Calvin's Geneva. From 1556 through 1560, Juan Pérez published in Geneva, at the press of Jean Crispin, a number of works designed to introduce Protestant ideas in Spain. Among them were his *El Testamento Nuevo de Nuestro Señor y Salvador Jesu Christo* (1556) and *Los Psalmos de David* (1557). These works were first steps toward an eventual publication of the Bible in Spanish. Pérez did not see most of his works through the press himself, for it was during this period that he was absent from Geneva for almost two years, due to problems which arose in 1554 in the French Church of Frankfurt-am-Main regarding the manner of the observance of Holy Communion. By September 1556, the crisis had reached the point where it became necessary for John Calvin and a group of notables of the Genevan Church to go to Frankfurt to arbitrate in the dispute between the minister, Valerand Poullain, and the Consistory which was led by the French merchant Augustin Legrand. Pérez was a member of the delegation, and when the others returned to Geneva he remained at Frankfurt through June, 1558. It was during his stay there that he established a fund to be used for the publication of the projected Spanish Bible. The money was deposited with Augustin Legrand, who served as its administrator and chief trustee.

The Isidorean monks arrived in Geneva while Juan Pérez was away in Frankfurt. In his absence Casiodoro de Reina became the spiritual guide

---

1. For full bibliographical information on the sources used in this article, see my monograph *Casiodoro de Reina: Traductor de la Biblia en español* (Mexico, 1969). In the Summer of 1980, I traveled extensively in Europe collecting and copying thousands of pages of manuscripts related to the lives of Casiodoro de Reina and other Spanish reformers of the sixteenth century. This will serve as the basis for further research in this area of our history.

of the small community of exiled Spaniards. His leadership was so much felt among the group that he became known as "The Moses of the Spaniards." But he soon ran into trouble because of his commitment to conciliatory, irenic principles, which were not very much appreciated in the sixteenth century. From the moment of his arrival he had lifted a voice of protest and censure against Geneva's justice for having condemned Servetus to be burnt at the stake. In 1558, Reina declared that Geneva had become "a new Rome" and, followed by several of his fellow monks from San Isidoro, left for Frankfurt. At about this same time John Calvin called Juan Pérez back to Geneva, probably to help calm the Spaniards who had been roused up by Reina. It is not certain whether Reina and Pérez met at this time in Frankfurt or in Geneva. It is most probable, however, that the two discussed some time during this period the possibility of publishing the Bible in Spanish, for it is from this time that Reina dates de beginning of his work on the Scriptures, as can be seen from the preface of his "Bear Bible" and from the autograph dedicatory of the copy which he donated to the University of Basel.

Upon the accession of Elizabeth to the throne of England, Casiodoro went on to London, where he continued work on the Bible translation. There is ample evidence that by this time the plans for publishing the Bible were some kind of a group project. For example, in the letter which Bishop Alvaro de Quadra, the Spanish Ambassador to England, wrote to King Philip II on June 26, 1563, he reports the arrival in London of Don Francisco Zapata, who was living in Reina's house, and who had come to England for the purpose of working with Casiodoro de Reina "and others" on the Spanish Bible.[2]

A manuscript found at the Bodleian Library gives further evidence of the fact that the Spanish Bible was a community project. This manuscript consists of 613 folios written on both sides, two columns to the page. The left-hand column, written by several hands, has the text of the "Ferrara" Bible from Gen 1 through I Kings 15:22, where it abruptly ends before the last word of the verse. The right column, also the product of several different handwritings, which are not the same as those in the other column, is evidently the draft for a new version of the Bible. The right-hand column appears only from Gen 1 through Ex 23, is blank from there through the end of Lev, and at that point the text reappears again from Num 1 through 27. This manuscript has been identified as "an early draft of the Bible which Valera published in 1602, quite different from the finished product." While a definitive statement of fact must await a complete study of this manuscript, it should be

---

2. This letter of the Spanish ambassador to the King of Spain (Archivo General de Simancas: Estado 816:166) has four sections of varying length written in cipher. About half of the paragraph quoted above, which is frequently cited by writers dealing with Reina, is written in cipher. The deciphered text of that portion of the letter has been lost, as is also the key to the secret code of the Quadra-Phillip correspondence. Recently, I have been able to reconstruct and recover the key to this correspondence, and it is presently in preparation for publication. This will give scholars access for the first time to a hitherto unavailable portion of this important diplomatic correspondence.

noted that Valera's Bible was a revision of Reina's and not a piece of original work. But this manuscript with its several different handwritings may be representative of the type of collective work to which Quadra referred in his letter.[3]

A third piece of evidence for the thesis of the Bible as a communal project comes from the letter which Antonio del Corro wrote to Casiodoro de Reina from Théobon, in Aquitaine, on Christmas Eve, 1563. Corro was an Isidorean monk who became a minister in France, and who appears in the records of the French church under the name "Bellerive." In this letter he advises Reina that he has made arrangements for the printing of the Bible with a printer who has offered to print 1,200 copies with verse divisions, in folio size, for four and a half reales each if they provide the paper, or six reales if this is to be the printer's responsibility. He assures Reina that there will be no difficulty in securing the paper, for there are three or four paper mills nearby and, as to a place to set up the printing press, the Queen of Navarra has offered one of her castles. The only difficulty will be, he says, with the proofreading of the text, and to that end he suggests that Reina bring Cipriano de Valera with him to work as proofreader.

Reina never received the letter. It arrived in London after he had fled England under accusations of heresy and sodomy. With a price placed on his head by Spanish authorities, Casiodoro sought refuge in Antwerp, Frankfurt, Orleans, and finally in Bergerac, where his friend Corro was a pastor.

Later, when Princess Renée de France took Corro to her castle at Montargis to serve as her chaplain, Reina accompanied him. There the two has ample time to talk about the plans for the Spanish Bible with Juan Pérez, who at the time was also serving as Renée's chaplain. Perhaps the Princess expressed some interest in the project, since the "Ferrara Bible," published eleven years before by the crypto-Jews Yom Tob Leví Atías (Jerónimo de Vargas) and Abraham Ben Salomón Usque (Duarte Pinel), was dedicated to her husband, Ercole II d'Este, Duke of Ferrara. When Reina published his own Bible in 1569, he used as one of his main sources this Jewish Bible which he called "the ancient Spanish translation of the Old Testament provided in Ferrara." Reina would not have called "ancient" a book printed barely four years before he began his own translation unless he was referring, not to the time when it was printed, but to the antiquity of the translation itself. In fact, this version is one which had long circulated among the Jews of Spain and of which we can find earlier evidence in the Polyglot Pentateuch published by Eliezer B. Gerson Soncino in Constantinople in 1547. This Pentateuch includes a text in Spanish printed in Hebrew characters, as was the custom of the Sephardic Jews. Comparison of this ladino text with the Ferrara Bible convinces me that both are representatives of the same textual tradition.

Reina's own work was concentrated on the Old Testament. His plans were to use Pérez's New Testament which was then being reprinted in Paris.

---

3. This is the Manuscript Bodley 386 of the Bodleian Library in Oxford, England. I am currently preparing a descriptive analysis of this text.

On the morning of October 20, 1566, Juan Pérez died in the arms of his friend Antonio del Corro. Corro left the matter of publication of the New Testament in the hands of Pérez's assistants, Bartolomé Gómez and Diego López. According to Corro, Pérez died without leaving a will, but in his death bed he made known his wishes that Renée was to be his universal heir. She was to see that the New Testament was published using the funds derived from the sale of his belongings. Gómez and López objected to such an arrangement. They wanted that the money which Pérez had left deposited with Augustin Legrand be also applied to their project. Corro was opposed to such a use of the funds, since they were to be used for the publication of the entire Bible. The Consistory of Paris was called to intervene in the rather nasty quarrel which ensued, and it decreed that the sum of 300 crowns was to be given from the Frankfurt fund to Gómez and López for the publication of the New Testament, while the balance of the one thousand "escudos" which Legrand held in trust were to be used in the publication of the Bible.

The Paris New Testament was never published. On April 6, 1568, Phillip II wrote to his ambassador in France, Don Francisco de Avala, instructing him to confiscate the original draft and to burn the portions which had been printed. Thus Reina had to prepare his own translation of the New Testament. The Pérez fund, however, was made available to him for the publication of the Bible, and it was with this money that he contracted with the famous printer Oparino for the printing of the work of so many for so many years. Unfortunately Oparino died after he had collected the money but before he had been able to deliver on the contract. The money was lost. But again the friends and funds from Frankfurt came to the rescue, and the first edition of the Spanish Bible, the culmination of the dreams, hopes and aspirations of a wandering group of Spanish exiles, saw the light in Basel, Switzerland, in 1569.

Wesley desde el margen hispano

Edwin E. Sylvest, Jr.

Es bien interesante pensar en las relaciones entre la tradición wesleyana y la hispana. ¿Qué tiene que ver una tradición anglicana con una hispana? ¿Hay razones más profundas que las meramente históricas y accidentales para que parte de la comunidad cristiana hispana se interese en el pensamiento de un sacerdote inglés del siglo décimooctavo? ¿No es la tradición wesleyana misma señal de un imperialismo cultural y religioso?

En verdad, es necesario reconocer que en gran parte un ensayo acerca de "Wesley desde el margen hispano" tiene sus raíces en la época del expansionismo estadounidense del siglo pasado. En cierto sentido la pregunta misma refleja los resultados de la ideología del "destino manifiesto", en su dimensión eclesiástica. Pero, a la vez, es igualmente necesario reconocer que, después de un siglo, la tradición wesleyana ya se fija entre el pueblo hispano y forma parte de un nuevo mestizaje; ya es algo indígena. Tenemos que recordar que hay gente hispanoparlante que es wesleyana por lo menos de la tercera generación. Esto sería razón suficiente para tratar del tema. Pero hay dos razones más, una histórica y otra teológica.

La razón histórica es que Wesley mismo tenía interés en lo hispano. En el año 1735 los hermanos Wesley y dos compañeros del "Club Santo" llegaron a la colonia inglesa de Georgia. Tenían dos metas: profundizar su espiritualidad y emprender una misión a los indios y a los colonos.

Para llevar a cabo la tarea misionera, Juan Wesley empezó el estudio del español, para poder hablar con los indios, algunos de los cuales ya hablaban la lengua de los conquistadores y de los misioneros franciscanos y jesuitas. Empezó sus estudios el 28 de junio de 1736, y los mencionó varias veces durante ese año y el siguiente.[1]

Aunque Wesley estudiaba para prepararse a servir a los indios, el gobernador Oglethorpe no se lo permitía. Oglethorpe no quería que Wesley fuera a los indios, sino que permaneciera en Savannah como párroco. Sin embargo, Wesley siguió sus estudios porque había algunos judíos españoles en el pueblo y él quería hablarles. De hecho, era uno de estos judíos, un Señor Moses Nunes (sic) quien le enseñaba a Wesley el idioma. En cambio Wesley le enseñaba el inglés a la hija del Señor Nunes.[2]

Wesley tenía mucho respeto para los judíos españoles. Dijo: "I began learning Spanish, in order to converse with my Jewish parishioners; some of whom seem nearer to the Mind that was in Christ than many of those who call him Lord".[3] Es interesante señalar que el interés de Wesley en el estudio

---

1. Juan Wesley, *Journal* (Nehemiah Curnock, ed.: London, 1909-17, 8 vols.), 1:237.

2. *Ibid.*, 1:361.

3. *Ibid.*, 1:346.

de las lenguas se manifestaba en aquel entonces en el estudio del hebreo con el Señor Nuñes (mientras tanto estaba aprendiendo el alemán con los colonos alemanes moravos, y estudiaba francés por sí mismo).[4]

Wesley tenía gran aprecio hacia la lengua española. Después de muchos años dejó una nota que revela también su prejuicio contra el francés: "...French is the poorest, meanest language in Europe... it is no more comparable to the German or Spanish than a bag-pipe is to an organ".[5]

No sabemos mucho de sus estudios lingüísticos, pero unos años después de su experiencia en Georgia, Wesley publicó gramáticas sobre el alemán, el francés, el inglés, el griego, el latín y el hebreo. Es notable que Wesley no publicó una gramática española. Su interés en este idioma fue primeramente utilitario en cuanto a una misión particular, y por lo visto se le olvidó debido a la falta de oportunidad de usarlo. Es cierto que en enero de 1763 Wesley necesitó un intérprete para hablar con dos "turcos" --judíos españoles que habían engañado a Wesley, y él les bautizó.[6]

Aunque a la postre se le olvidó el idioma español, durante el tiempo en que lo usaba Wesley se mostró muy impresionado por la literatura española. Mientras estudiaba la gramática, leía y cantaba poemas e himnos españoles. No sabemos qué poemas leía, pero tenemos el texto en inglés de un poema místico, quizá por Miguel de Molinos, que Wesley tradujo después de sólo cuatro días de estudio:[7]

> O God, my God, my all thou art;
> Ere shines the dawn of rising day,
> Thy sovereign light within my heart,
> Thy all-enlivening power display...

Las estrofas de este poema, basadas en el Salmo 63, reflejan la lucha personal de Wesley por la seguridad de la presencia del amor divino en su propia vida, y nos revelan una razón de su interés en la obra de los místicos, incluyendo al famoso Miguel de Molinos.

Molinos, sacerdote español del siglo decimoséptimo, fue condenado como quietista. Su obra más importante, que lleva el título de *Guía espiritual*, fue un libro muy popular entre algunos protestantes, y se ha traducido al inglés y al francés. La versión inglesa se publicó en 1688, y es probable que Wesley la haya leído por primera vez en esa traducción en 1736, durante su lucha personal.[8]

Lo interesante es que Wesley incluyó parte de la *Guía* de Molinos en su "Biblioteca cristiana", una colección de "the choicest pieces of practical

---

4. *Ibid.*, 1:361, 363.

5. *Ibid.*, 4:188.

6. *Ibid.*, 5:3.

7. *Ibid.*, 1:240, 299; G. Osborn, *The Poetical Works of John and Charles Wesley* (London: Wesleyan Methodist Conference Office, 1868), 1:174.

8. John Wesley, *Letters* (John Telford, ed.: 1931, 8 vols.), 1:207.

divinity which have been published in the English tongue".[9] La selección escogida por Wesley consiste en dos partes que tratan de "las tentaciones por las cuales Dios limpia las almas" y "los martirios espirituales; de contemplación, resignación perfecta y paz interna." Al leer estas páginas se descubren los rasgos característicos de la tradición wesleyana: las disciplinas de una vida santa, y la santidad que el amor de Dios crea en tal vida.

Ese énfasis en la santidad de vida quizás sea el rasgo más distintivo de la enseñanza wesleyana, y nos conduce a la segunda razón para tratar la tradición wesleyana "desde el margen hispano", la razón teológica.

Muchos han apuntado un sentido espiritual como elemento intrínseco del pueblo hispano. No es necesario estar de acuerdo en que los hispanos son más espirituales que cualquier otro pueblo para reconocer que la espiritualidad es algo importante en la vida humana, y que es algo que interesa tanto a hispanos como a otros. En verdad, la tradición mística es aspecto de suma importancia en la historia religiosa de los españoles, y acabamos de mencionar la influencia de Molinos en la vida y pensamiento wesleyanos.

Pero más allá de una supuesta razón cultural, la santidad de la vida tiene mucho que ver con la situación actual de muchos hispanos en los Estados Unidos y, de hecho, en todo el mundo.

No es algo intrínseco a la personalidad hispana, en lo individual o en lo cultural, sino un hecho socio-histórico, el que muchos hispanos, por razones de un imperialismo cultural o económico, viven como personas marginadas. La onda teológica contemporánea de muchos hispanos tanto en los Estados Unidos como en la América Latina es precisamente darse cuenta de esa situación de marginalización, y reflexionar sobre la praxis de la fe cristiana en tales circunstancias. El resultado ha sido una "teología de liberación", una recuperación del mensaje escriturario: el eterno amor de Dios se expresa en su obra creadora-liberadora (Salmo 136). Quienes conocen a Dios, aman a sus prójimos y participan en la obra creadora-liberadora de Dios mismo (Jer 22:15-16; I Jn 4:16, 19-21). Amar a Dios es amar al prójimo. Amar a Dios es hacer *justicia*, liberar a los cautivos.

Hacer que el amor sea eficaz en las vidas marginadas es participar en la obra creadora-liberadora de Dios mismo. Tal participación, tal obra, significa una espiritualidad liberadora. Es una espiritualidad mundana que lleva al amor de Dios precisamente en la carne.

Desde el margen hispano se descubre la verdadera perfección de que hablaba Wesley. La santidad de la vida no es solamente algo místico, una vida desencarnada, sino que pertenece a la vida cotidiana, actual. Las disciplinas de la santidad no son solamente obras de piedad, sino también de misericordia. A muchos wesleyanos se les ha olvidado la doble dimensión del amor a Dios. No hay amor a Dios sin amor al prójimo. El amor *a* Dios es una participación en el amor *de* Dios para nosotros, para el mundo. Nuestra perfección es la perfección del amor de Dios mismo, es un don que recibimos

---

9. John Wesley, *Christian Library* (Bristol, 1749-55), página de título.

cuando encontramos a Dios en la carne sufriente de nuestros prójimos pobres (Mt 25:40).

En la conclusión de su *Plain Account of Christian Perfection*, Wesley mantiene que la perfección es "darle a Dios todo nuestro corazón, es decir, el permitir que El gobierne nuestra vida. Es, además, dedicar no sólo una parte, sino toda nuestra alma, cuerpo y bienes a Dios. ...Por otra parte es amar a Dios con todo nuestro corazón, y a nuestro prójimo como a nosotros mismos".[10]

El mismo punto se expone aún más claramente en el sermón "La vía escrituraria de la salvación":

> En segundo lugar, son necesarias a la santificación todas las obras de misericordia --ya sea que tengan por objeto los cuerpos de los hombres, o bien sus almas-- tales como dar de comer al hambriento, vestir al desnudo, hospedar al extraño, visitar al preso, al enfermo o al afligido, procurar enseñar al que no sabe, despertar al pecador adormecido, vivificar al frío, fortalecer al débil, consolar al triste, socorrer al que siente la tentación, o contribuir de cualquier modo a salvar almas de la muerte. Tales son el arrepentimiento y las "obras dignas de arrepentimiento" que se necesitan para la plena santificación. Esta es la vía en la que Dios quiere que sus hijos aguarden la completa salvación.[11]

En conclusión, un sacerdote anglicano del siglo décimooctavo les ofrece mucho a los que trabajan en la iglesia desde el margen hispano. Juan Wesley nos da un buen ejemplo de la necesidad de tomar en serio el idioma y la tradición cultural al servir a los hispanoparlantes; pero también su doctrina de la perfección cristiana tiene mucho que ver con los que luchan por liberarse y reconquistar la dignidad de la plena humanidad. Más bien que señal de un imperialismo cultural y religioso, la tradición wesleyana tiene relaciones históricas y teológicas con las praxis de la fe en el medio ambiente hispano actual.

Summary

Although it might appear that the connection between the Wesleyan heritage and Hispanic peoples is primarily an expression of British and North American cultural imperialism, there are actually historical and theological grounds for viewing it otherwise. Historically, John Wesley had great interest in the Spanish language that he studied while in Georgia in order to communicate with Native Americans, earlier evangelized by Spanish missionaries, and to minister to a group of Spanish-speaking Jews who lived in his parish. He became especially interested in the work of the mystic Miguel de Molinos and translated one of his poems. Theologically, the Wesleyan tradition understands the Christian life as a journey toward perfection in love. That journey is realized in the twin process of loving God and the neighbor and is expressed in performing

---

10. Juan Wesley, *Perfección cristiana* (Medellín: Tipografía Unión, s.f.), pp. 122-23.

11. Juan Wesley, *Sermones*, trad. por Primitivo Rodríguez (Kansas City, Missiouri: Beacon Hill Press, s.f., 2 vols.), 2:274.

works of piety --participating in the means of grace, and in works of mercy-- meeting physical as well as spiritual needs of the neighbor. Through those works Christians participate in God's active loving of persons living on the margins. It is precisely God's active loving of the marginated that is expressed in the theology of liberation articulated by Hispanics who are historically marginated in the political and economic structures of the Americas. Rather than a reflection of cultural and religious imperialism, the Wesleyan tradition manifests intrinsic historical and theological relationships with the praxis of Christian faith in the present Hispanic context.

Surviving: The Prelude

Joel N. Martínez

The starting point for the Chicano theological task is our acknowledgment (in Spanish, *re-conocimiento*, re-knowing) of our historical particularity as a people. What is the history of the Chicanos? In spite of all the dangers of such attempts, what follows is an outline of an answer to that question.

For the inhabitants of Aztlán, the treatise of Guadalupe Hidalgo (1848) was in essence a passing from the hands of one empire to another. This was so because the northern lands of New Spain (up to 1821) and Mexico (up to 1848) were of marginal interest to the central government in Mexico City. In passing to the hands of the United States of America, the same people continued to be a marginal colony to the federal government in Washington. The people of Aztlán were subject to neglect by their new master, and then to a second class citizenship. They were also dispossessed of their lands, forced to accept alien cultural patterns, and became the main source of hard labor in the development of the great mining, railroading and agricultural enterprises of the Southwest.

If we believe, with professor James Cone, that we can only know God in the struggles and sufferings of our people, then our theological reflection as Chicanos must begin there. It is within that history and on the basis of that history that our own theological reflection emerges. It is in the field of the sad history of exploitation and bondage that I discover Christ both emotionally and intellectually. If I do not see the work of his hand in the words and events of my people, my own vocation as a subject of history becomes impossible. I become an object in a history that is not my own.

The Chicano people are now beginning to write their own version of the events and personalities that constitute their past. Until now the history of the Chicanos has been documented and interpreted by "writers-observers." The only authentic voice is the interpretation that comes from within the people. The very fact of writing our own history is in itself an act of resistance to slavery --to being defined and controlled by others. The presence of God in the events of the Exodus turns the slaves into a people that makes its own history. The Exodus infuses political significance into Israel's history. Likewise, that version of history written and proclaimed by the slaves (the Chicanos-defined-by-others) will underscore how a people transforms the world. The new reading of our past re-locates the focus of the historical drama. What is now decisive is no longer the treatises, nor the pronouncements of emperors or oligarchies, nor the battles of the generals. The main characters of Chicano history turn out to be those who survived economic, cultural and spiritual exploitation.

As a people whose history has been submerged in, or absent from the historical documents and even oral tradition, the Chicano people have suffered the psychological and political shock of having been severed from their roots.

Without that communitary memory it is impossible to appreciate the action of God among our people. And without reflecting on that history, and on the present reality, it is impossible to endow the church with a vital theology. This particularity is the door through which the church among the Chicano must go if it is to participate in the global mission of God with all peoples. This is so, because in "the struggles and sufferings of the people" the Christ of the Gospels is living and revealing himself. Each people has a particular mission. Ours is to deepen our understanding and reflection among the people in such a way that our gift to humanity in Christ may be illumined and made explicit.

The Chicano community has resisted the imperialistic assault on its mother tongue. At the same time it has offered a higher vision of a bi-/multilingual society where no language is rejected. In passing, one may note the theological significance of this view in connection with a humanity which receives the Spirit, "all in their own tongues." What is most important there is that the people turn the handicap of a rejected language into a path which opens up participation in a wider world. The Chicano people take a step toward universality using as a highway what others consider an obstacle. An indication of human capacity for survival is the ability to integrate the basic elements of our culture with the demands of a new situation.

The main affirmation of this essay is that the Chicano have survived as a people. But this is a prelude. To what?

It is a prelude to a questioning regarding our "place" in the world. This question, somewhat subversive, must be posed within the widest and most diverse contexts. In the context of the institutional church, for instance, what is the impact of the question regarding the historic role of the Chicano? This questioning in turn leads us to further inquiry and research into the alliances between the existing ruling powers, and their "use" of religion. In order to discuss this matter one must define a number of crucial terms: Who are the powerful, both in the institutional church and in society at large

The Chicano people can also pose the question within the geo-political context. Could today be the prelude to a questioning of the border itself? Every national border is provisional. Its power to continue basically depends on the relative military and economic strength of neighboring nations. The border between the United States of Mexico and the United States of America is not established by divine decree, but rather subsists for as long as the relative strengths of Mexico and the United States follow the pattern of the last 132 years. For our people, who had little say in the manner in which the original political arrangements took place, the question of the provisionality of the border is not an idle one. This very question implies that the people of the border intend to be part of any future arrangements.

There is also room to question the socio-economic arrangements. Is the "destiny" of the Southwest simply to produce "poor people" to supply the economic system of the United States? Is it the "place" of the farm laborers to be hungry while the invisible masters grow fat on the result of their labor? Is it the "destiny" of the Chicanos to have to leave their own barrios and cities in order to make room for the more recent arrivals from the North?

This series of questions will certainly be asked as the Chicano people accept the good news that no "place" in society is fixed. As we hear and understand that God is the One who calls us from the security of Egypt to the greater dangers of the desert, we shall grow in our capacity to question, and thus to become a people that makes history.

Rethinking Our Mission

In Search of an Inclusive Community

Jill Martínez

One of the most difficult tasks facing the Christian Church in the next decade is in understanding the make-up and work of the inclusive church. The issues confronting us will cause us to embark on a journey of tremendous significance that will gain great momentum once it is begun. As we begin to journey forward into new terrain, the land of full participation of the whole people of God, we will be faced with difficult decisions, fear and in some cases extreme danger. The journey will not be easy and it will not be just difficult. It will be tumultuous. Even so, we will not be the first of the Children of God chosen to begin such a journey.

In Scripture we are continually reminded that God calls the people out from where they are to a new land, a new terrain and a new life. The land to which they were called (or, in some cases, sent) was not always of the "milk and honey" variety, but it was rather of "dust and dry crust." Many had years of trial and pain on their journeys. Adam and Eve were "sent out" from their safe, comfortable, fruitful home. Abraham was forced into a nomadic existence. He was sent from Haran to Canaan, then to Egypt and finally back to Canaan. Joseph as a youth found his way to Pharaoh's court via a period of slavery and then a prison term. Similarly, Moses, born a Hebrew, raised as an Egyptian, labeled a murderer, becomes a fugitive, then finally returns to his people as Liberator. The Exodus event is probably one of the more dramatic examples of this kind of movement: a people of God called out from where they were to new terrain experiencing pain and death in a vast desert. After a full generation passes these chosen ones, a small meager band of refugees, finally reached the Promised Land.

Today, we are on a journey of our own to new ground. We come in support of the uniqueness and commonality of our traditions not only for men, but for women; not only for White, but for the Black, Brown, Red and Yellow. Let us take off our shoes for we are truly standing on holy ground. We hope to see a glimpse of the Promised Land, the inclusive church in the Kingdom of God where full participation is not just a dream, but a reality. We seek unity without sacrificing diversity, and we seek inclusiveness, not a bland form of acculturation where all people become the same. We seek a pluralism that affirms many ways of being, seeing, hearing and doing. As God's people we shudder and groan at the long process that takes us across what appears to be a vast and unproductive desert. The journey is so slow as we move step-by-slow-step. At the same time, however, we find ourselves elated by the hope that propels us as we come upon the "new land."

I begin by presenting a context for discussion by focusing on the identifiable, United States, Anglo-American Culture.[1] This culture permeates our traditions and institutions. It is essential that we examine some elements of mainstream culture in order to identify significant obstacles toward understanding and the development of the inclusive Church community. These obstacles inhibit efficient, effective movement of the underrepresented, racial ethnics and women, within traditionally White male systems. Let us peel back some layers of this acculturated reality by using examples from the Hispanic and White communities that have caused the two cultures to come into conflict. In order to be specific, I will identify a few culturally related issues and then move on to examine some aspects of Reformed theological thought which address the cultural values identified in the White and Hispanic communities. A concluding statement will deal with aspects of worship that can act as a vehicle for building bridges across vast cultural chasms. These chasms once crossed can bring about understanding and lead to healing in a broken community.

Culture and the Anglo-American Community

It has been my experience that most Anglo-Americans do not know that they have a culture. I was visiting with some Asian friends of mine and we began to discuss culture and the "Mestizaje" process,[2] when a young, Anglo-American, college educated man proposed that the issues being discussed had more to do with class than with culture. Having heard this before, I asked the young man to explain further. As he spoke, I began to realize that he did not know he had a culture. I finally asked him: "Do you have a culture?" His answer was definitive, "No! Not like you; I don't have a culture!" My Asian friends and I were astonished as some of us had spent many years, and others most of their lives, identifying the culture and people who dominate the United States. We all had been confronted with issues and obstacles throughout our lives that had put us into direct conflict with the dominant culture that was not our own. Many of us had worked hard at being artful in dodging some obstacles and in climbing over and around others as we worked our way toward "success" in the system. We were surprised to hear that such a young man was totally unaware of the struggle.

La Familia/Comunidad

An example of cultural conflict can be found in the value system of la "familia/la comunidad." Understanding the community as family has been

---

1. I bring particular attention to the work completed by Bellah, *et. al.*, in *Habits of the Heart*. This research covers a number of communities throughout the United States identifying a distinct culture. The book consists of the summation of a number of interviews admitting that the racial ethnic American community was not reached.

2. The "Mestizaje" process was first coined by Virgilio Elizondo in his book, *Mestizaje: the Dialectic of Cultural Birth and the Gospel*. This is a process with historical roots in Mexico where people of differing cultures intermingle, marry and participate in extended family relationships causing new cultures and new people to emerge who have never existed before.

a way of life for the Hispanic. The Hispanic has traditionally understood this reality of la comunidad y la familia; they are interchangeable where service and work are tied together. Each person is brought into the close circle of friends and family as he/she serves in the community for the good of the whole family. As the bonds of trust are established through those relationships, the person becomes a part of the family fully sharing in the work and in the celebrations of the community. In this way, the system of "compadres" is born.

Compadres are those who can always be depended upon, trusted with the deepest thoughts, feelings and family concerns. The religious sacrament of infant Baptism provides for a reaffirmation of this relationship, bonding the person to the family as true Godparents, full-fledged members of the family with all rights and privileges. In this sense, the sacrament of Baptism is not only for the infant, but for the participants as well.

Affirmed within a familial context, these relationships begin to expand out into the community. Within this context competition has a negative connotation because it is known that no one person can make it alone and no one person can take the credit for his/her work. The community has worked together in service for the good of the whole. When one member of the family suffers all suffer. This value is in direct conflict with the Anglo-American value or rugged individualism and independence.

This became quite clear to me when I worked as a migrant school teacher near my home in an economically depressed area. I was playing a game with two groups of young children, one group all Anglo-American, the other, first generation Mexicans. I played the same game with both groups. It was the same school, same socio-economic backgrounds and same teacher, myself. However, I noticed one distinct difference in their behavior as they played: both groups of children were cheating, but the English speaking, Anglo-Americans were each cheating for themselves; The Spanish-speaking children were cheating for each other. For the Spanish-speaking, their sense of family responsibility taught them if the youngest one or the one furthest behind was not having fun then none of them could have fun playing. The English speaking children had been taught that winning was the most important value. Both were living examples of their own cultures and traditions.

What happens to these young men and women as they move into a community that praises individualism and competition tearing them away from "la comunidad, la familia"? It is understood that some come form displaced homes and destructive environments. Many do not experience the expected and necessary extended family rituals. Many very often find their compadres in the streets, in gangs and thus participating in deadly games.

Who can understand the mind of such a young soul? Who can understand, forgive and know that God loves even the unlovely? Who will stand before the murderer and the fugitive and say "I love you, on behalf of the loving God, I love you!"? These youngsters are not confronted by love; they are confronted by a forceful, violent power that is oppressive. These youngsters grow into adults and finally end up in a system designed to control, constrain and discipline. How can the power and sovereignty of God be found and understood here?

Power and sovereignty are understood particularly within prison systems in the sense that he who is most powerful is most sovereign. Yet, these are words used to describe the loving Creator, the eternal God. Many of us come from religious traditions and cultures where power and sovereignty are valued commodities. Both are desired as objects to be possessed. Power is falsely seen as a commodity that only a few may own and then becomes closely related to sovereignty as the goal of the acquisition of power. The most powerful becomes the most sovereign. And there will continue to be a struggle for it as it shifts from person to person and place to place. Change will occur in this process only when power is understood in terms of love. It may seem that a prison is not the place where such a concept can be easily grasped and understood. Nevertheless, power is like love: the more it is shared, the more there is of it to share.

I remember counseling a young Anglo-American man who had a five year old daughter whom he loved very much, but he expressed to me his apprehension about having more children. After several conversations, it was discovered that he did not believe he would, or could ever, love any more children because as far as he knew all his love was focused on this one child. He worried about this a great deal because it was causing difficulty in his home with his wife who wanted more children. After a period of internal struggle, he came to understand that love does not divide, it multiplies. This is already understood in the Hispanic family; love cannot be limited or confined.

For the Hispanic, the family is a treasure, a heritage, much as it is in the Hebrew family. There is shared grief when one member dies or moves away. This makes it difficult for members of the family, male or female, who want to move away to get an education or a better job.

As a Hispanic, I understand what these relationships mean and why they are so strong. We live in a reality that says we are inter-related and powerful as we stand together. We are weak and powerless if we stand alone. We are interdependent and cannot survive without the other. Very often large families live together because of economic necessity, but others do so by choice.

On the other hand, we are being raised in an Anglo-American culture that honors rugged individualism dramatized by folk heroes such as Davy Crocket, Daniel Boone, and Horatio Alger, all of whom are revered for "doing it on their own" or "pulling themselves up by their bootstraps." Our history books celebrate the conquering mentality of "Manifest Destiny" that embodies mistrust of people and a disregard of existing indigenous cultures. The early pioneers were filled with the challenge of the hunt and the kill and with the blasphemy that says God honors one person over another.[3]

---

3. Albert K. Weinberg, *Manifest Destiny: A Study of Nationalist Expansion in American History* (Chicago: Quadrangle Books, 1963).

In the Anglo-American culture, the Hispanic is exposed to family units that act autonomously, separate from grandparents, uncles, aunts and cousins; families that have no understanding of or parallel to the compadre system. The Hispanic is exposed to families that seem to be annoyed whenever they are approached to help another family member financially or emotionally. Even in the homes that are visited, the Hispanic finds children living in their own rooms apart from the rest of the family.

Internal conflicts begin to fester as Hispanics move onto such terrain. Somehow our history is not recorded as we have known it to be; our folk heroes are not listed along with the others. Somehow it does not sit well with us that the Native Americans were the only hostile ones, violently attacking innocent pioneers. Somehow we know our people are not as they are stereotypically described, as lazy and ignorant. Somehow we know we, too, are to be included in the Family of God.

Reformed Theological Considerations

As we consider some Reformed theological foundations in the search for an inclusive community, I bring forward three concerns, or to return to our metaphor of the journey, three movements:

1. The movement from an understanding of community as the careful formation of a foundation for competition among other community bases, to understanding community as a primary element in building relationships that are cooperative.

2. The movement from understanding the glory of God as cold power and sovereignty to an understanding of the glory of God as God's grace revealed in the world.

3. To explore the worship experience as one of sharing the power and grace of life which God provides through the community of believers.

Dr. Edward Huenemann, Director of Theology and Research, Presbyterian Church (U.S.A.), states in his paper, "Worship and the Search for Community in the Reformed Tradition," presented for the Racial Ethnic Theological Colloquium, "for Calvin the adoration, the worship, the celebration of the grace of God's glory is the movement of the Holy Spirit which constitutes the church and creates human community." With the basic vision that gracious power produces shared joy and community, for Calvin all life can become an act of worship. Real community is a way of being together where all members have a sense of belonging. Each individual is provided opportunity to be a meaningful part of a larger body. A key toward health for the worshipping community is providing an arena within which people are freed to share this journey, their struggles and their gifts. This can be true even for those who are in confinement.

Toward an Inclusive Worshipping Community

At this point we should begin to understand that culture does make a difference. We are affected by our cultures, the one in our home and the one in the dominant society. We have so far discussed a variety of examples showing that there is a chasm between Anglo-Dominant and Mexican-American cultures. At this point I would like to bring forward three gifts the Hispanic brings to the community that can be celebrated in worship to cross over this chasm. The Hispanic brings: (1) the strength of the heart; (2) an acceptance of the mystery of silence; (3) language.

(1) The Hispanic understands and lives the deep emotions of the heart. This is one of our strengths, not a weakness. Out heart makes us courageous and we are filled with the power to love, care and risk and very often even the worst situations are changed into a gift of grace. It is this courage and strength that make some of us migrants. Even so, we can say we stand in the presence of God with our mind in our heart. Prayer for us is not just an intelligent exercise of our mind, or like Henry Nouwen has said, "we would soon become stranded in fruitless and trivial inner debates with God." Nor are we dependent on having only good feelings.

The gift of the heart enables even the weakest to embrace all of life, its horror as demonstrated in the violence done to us and that we do to one another, and its joy as lived out in our festive occasions, our fiestas. This is the experience that we bring to worship to be affirmed and shared, not to be trampled upon or trivialized as sentimentality. This gift can make our worship services spontaneous and at times long; but all participants have the experience of belonging.

(2) The Hispanic is comfortable with the mystery of silence. We listen to more than the words coming from a person's mouth. We have been taught by our Mothers to listen to the word spoken in silence. We are not taught to compete for attention with loud words, but instead are asked to wait for the appropriate time to speak if necessary. Very often though, we are conditioned to say nothing at all. We have through the years learned to deal with our frustration in not having the opportunity to speak. We therefore begin to find value in silence. In worship, we may have periods of silence that are natural and refreshing that return us to the comfort of our homes and very often to our Mother's presence. It is for us then not a moment of intimidation and oppression, but instead it becomes a true experience of liberation.

(3) Our language provides the opportunity for the church to experience Pentecost weekly. Some who were once apprehensive about attending bi-lingual services, soon found fulfillment and wholeness as they discovered they could understand and share in an experience beyond the sense where every word is heard and understood. This is the experience of Pentecost, hearing the Word of the Living God in an unknown tongue, a humbling experience indeed. This spirit lives today.

In summary, we must accept that the journey toward an inclusive community is going to be a long one. However, we might address one step on the journey that can make a difference for us all. We can begin to examine the worship experience, which by its very nature can either empower or dehumanize. We must be careful, in such a community as this where so many have experienced and continue to experience dehumanizing situations, to affirm, encourage, and empower the living. I was speaking with a group of Hispanic women as they explained the events in their lives that caused them to be silent when they should have spoken, immobilized when they should have acted. They explained that their experience in church was a major factor that kept them obedient and inactive, which filled them with a sense of inferiority and insignificance. It had taken a great deal of work on their part to break out of those bonds. In the same way, we today have the opportunity to empower. Worship can be an avenue of empowerment.

Worship should be an enabling opportunity for sharing the power and glory of God when:

(1) we listen to the heart, not blindly but intelligently;

(2) we embrace silence and enter into a timeless eternity where communication is not direct and God speaks in quiet tones;

(3) we experience Pentecost by sharing the presence of God and the Holy Spirit in unknown tongues.

In this way, we begin by participating with another community and then come closer to understanding the nature of the whole Body.

Conclusion

We are coming onto new land as we stand here hand-in-hand. Yet we can glimpse the future: Red, Brown, Black, White and Yellow, full participants in the Kingdom of God, accepting that we are together the Body of Christ, interdependent. As we acknowledge that no one is complete without the other, we are forced to live in the faith that says, when one part of the body is not fully becoming, the whole body suffers. The Kingdom of God is found here in people who are on the road, on the journey, on the Way coming out from where they are to a new land. The Kingdom of God is found here in our struggle as we unite the Body of Christ. Like Abraham, Moses and Joseph, we live between worlds. Our homes celebrate one tradition, our education another, our work another. For some of us our work appears foreign because of the culture of paper, information and computers. We groan with travail as we are being reborn, but somehow we know there is a God and that Christ lives in us and that we are being called to become whole into the new land of full participation of the whole people of God. The road is dangerous and the Way will not be easy, but we are propelled by the faith that guides us and the hope that tells us we will see the Promised Land.

The Church and Liberation

María Luisa Santillán Baert

In a technological and polluted age, in a secular and sacramental world, in a power-structured and poverty-stricken situation, redemptive movements rise and fall overnight. They whirl by in an effort to be the answer to humanity's plight and identity crisis.

The institutional Church finds itself in the midst of this confusion confronted by misery, corruption, injustice, violence, and millions of poor people --the "wretched of the earth," the powerless, the weak, the alienated. Should the Church become involved in society's problems? Should the Church force change, yea, even violent change? Should the Church take sides?

The place where Christ is present is the place where bread is broken, where bodies are also broken. And where wine is poured, where blood is shed, that is the place where Christ is present. The Eucharist affirms the real presence of Christ, not exclusively at a Communion table, but in every place where life is being squeezed out. "To share the bread and the cup around the table of the Lord becomes an act of political commitment to the doing of justice, rather than a retreat from a world where injustice is rampant."[1]

Sharing food around the table of the Lord implies that food must be shared around other tables. We cannot accept food at His table and remain unconcerned at the emptiness of other tables.

The meal around a common table is a sign of human community. As we break the bread and drink from the common cup our eyes are opened, our minds are illumined, our hearts are touched to know that God is the God of all persons, a God who offers life to all abundantly --everyone accepted, no one excepted, for in Jesus Christ, the Incarnate, Crucified and Risen Lord, all things hold together.

A Christian committed to liberation sees the oppressive efforts to preserve the status quo in the way power and authority are exercised, and therefore becomes involved in the struggle for the reformation of the Church. Míguez Bonino has put it more drastically by saying that a Christian committed to liberation becomes involved in the struggle "for the reconstitution of a Christianity in which all forms of organization and expression will be humanized and liberating."[2]

Traditionally, the institutional Church has sided with the forces of power and privilege. The Church has a long record of failing to support the poor and the weak. When it has been sensitive, it has often tried to act and make decisions for the outcasts of society rather than with them, and not always in their best interests.

---

1. Robert McAfee Brown, *Theology in a New Key* (Philadelphia: Westminster, 1978), p. 183.
2. *Ibid.*, p. 180.

The nonpoor are called to repentance. Repentance implies the restoration of goods. Without the restoration of goods, there is no repentance, for the retaining of goods that the poor need for their survival is sin.

Miranda says that early Christian thinkers saw almsgiving as a restitution that someone made for something that belonged to another, and he supports this assertion with a series of quotes.[3] Jerome declared that all riches come from injustice: "I believe the popular proverb to be very true: 'The rich person is either an unjust person or the heir of one'." Basil said that "the bread in your cupboard belongs to the hungry . . . the money which you hoard up belongs to the poor." And Ambrose agrees: "You are not making a gift of your possessions to the poor person. You are handing over what belongs to the poor." Ambrose clarifies this by asserting that "God willed that this earth should be the common possession of all, and he offered its fruits to all. But avarice distributed the rights of possession."

A theology of liberation implies a theology of relinquishment, of diminishment, of "letting go" of "our" possessions, of releasing what belongs to the poor. It is impossible to take liberation theology seriously without willingly making drastic changes in our own personal lifestyle and in our businesses, government and churches. We need to find the best way to challenge a system that allows a few to have so much at the expense of the many, so that our country will not usurp the largest possible portion of the world's resources, but will share them with those in need. We must also look for a better plan, one which does not allow inequities to build up so easily. People have the right to the resources of the land, whether that land is deeded to them or not. No matter who possesses food, it belongs to the hungry. And the Church is called upon to support the poor "as they reach out to take what is rightfully theirs."[4]

Segundo says that the Church is part of the problem. He is convinced that the present ecclesiastical structures, and their vested interests, resist liberation theology. At this point the Christian is faced by various possibilities:[5]

1. To leave the Church, since it "has become a thermometer rather than a thermostat, recording the climate around it, rather than changing it." The true community of believers, living in costly obedience and discipleship to Jesus Christ, does not need bishops or buildings or boards or budgets, for it can exist wherever two or three are gathered in Christ's name. This may well mean that the "Church" is more likely to be found outside official structures than within.

2. To accept the Church as it is, "warts and all," on the basis that, if it cannot improve the situation, at least it will not make it any worse.

---

3. José Porfirio Miranda, *Marx and the Bible* (New York: Orbis, 1974), pp. 15-16.

4. Brown, *op. cit.*, p. 182.

5. *Ibid.*, p. 158.

3. To affirm unashamedly that the Church has misunderstood its mission, and should not be concerned with changing society and its structures. Even if it takes the entire budget, the sounds of pain must be shut out. Christians must be cut off from the majority of humanity, who cannot afford "the luxury of a privatized faith," and who need material as well as spiritual food. It is about Christians who hold these views that Leo Nieto has said: "To be afraid and 'to play it safe' is to lack freedom and to choose slavery instead."[6]

4. The only possibility left to us in such a situation is becoming "the remnant within the remnant," becoming the self-conscious minority *in* the world who decides not to get out or to sit by serenely with folded hands. This "handful within the handful" seeks to discover what the church ought to be in spite of what it is.

Those who embrace the remnant concept today will live in two spheres: within the institutionalized church with all its complacency, culture of silence and "baños de pureza," in all its complicity with the ongoingness of evil; and in the world of the downtrodden, the abused, the pariahs. There they will denounce the dehumanization of the poor and the oppressed, and announce that all are called into full personhood. These acts of annunciation and denunciation must not be empty words, but strong and valid historical commitments. To denounce will involve speaking and acting. It may mean refusal to pay taxes to an unjust regime. Or it may mean to denounce an exploitative economy by becoming "the poor church," and refusing to become rich from that economy.

But this "handful within the handful" must not only speak for those who cannot speak themselves. They must also commit themselves to listen, really to hear the "voice of the voiceless" on *their* own terms. We must struggle to make the church the place where the only credential to gain a hearing is a cry of agony, and not power, or savoir faire, or position, or items with which to bargain. Once the church has truly heard that penetrating, agonizing cry, then it must transmit that cry elsewhere for all to hear and be moved with compassion into action. It will not be an easy or comfortable task, because those tormenting and disquieting cries of affliction will indict us as well as those beyond us.

We shall have to take sides politically. We take sides all the time. Our very refusal to become politically involved lends support to the status quo. Political commitment forces us to come clean as to whether we are for change or for keeping things as they are. Love forces us to act on behalf of those in need and to find ways to empower the weak so they can act on their own behalf.

If we are on the wrong side, then we must change sides. This is

---

6. Leo D. Nieto, "The Chicano Movement and the Churches in the United States," *Perkins Journal*, Fall, 1975, p. 41.

difficult and costly, for it means seeing things from a new perspective. Soon we discover that human concerns are also political concerns, and that those evils which we simply condone we really sponsor --torture, starvation, etc.

To know God is to work for justice. The church is called, not to guarantee "heaven," but to liberate the poor and the rich alike for the freedom of the Kingdom. We must not be the ones that say, "Lord, Lord," but do not do the will of God.

The Church, the City, and the Compassionate Christ

Caleb Rosado

Introduction

"And when he drew near and saw the city he wept over it" (Lk 19:41).

Tears, the temple, and the tearing masses. The picture is one of Jesus, at the beginning of the last week of his earthly ministry. Here at the beginning of this most momentous week, we find Jesus at the summit of the Mount of Olives and of his earthly career, about to descend into the valley of divine-human struggle, out of which the only exit is through death. God's Grain of Wheat is about to fall into the furrowed valley of earthly human existence at its lowest level, and die in order to bear much fruit.

Because he knows what awaits him down in that valley, Jesus lingers at the summit to reflect on the events that led him to this point and on what lies ahead. It is a contrasting scene, however, Jesus and the multitude with him. Those pressing around him cannot contain the joy they feel in their hearts, and with waving palm branches and spreading garments they shout praises to God with loud hosannas, for their long-awaited king is about to be crowned. In stark contrast, Jesus sits there pensively on the back of a colt, surrounded by the tumultuous masses, yet all alone within his own world of thought, weeping the tears of God.

There is something about coming to the end of one's ministry that always brings on moments of thoughtful and even tearful reflection. Have I accomplished all that I set out to do? Have people responded as expected? What has hindered people from reaching their full potential? What can I do in these last moments left as a final attempt to alter conditions hindering human response? Questions like these must have gone through Jesus' mind as he reflected over the city, from the brow of the hill, one last time.

The Tears of God

The text draws a picture of Jesus weeping over the city. "When he saw the city," the Bible declares, "he wept over it." Why did Jesus weep? What is there about the city that moves God to tears? The answer may lie in the nature of the city.

A city is "a dense concentration of people in a relatively small geographic area and engaged in nonagricultural pursuits," whose activities "are specialized and functionally interrelated and governed by a formalized political system."[1] Essentially a city is comprised of two components: people and a network of institutions which give meaning to their collective existence. A city is people and institutions, which define their place and proper behavior in society.

We are all surrounded by institutions. Collective group life is not possible without the many social institutions that impact and govern our lives from the moment of birth. Institutions --these interrelated systems of social roles and norms-- exist for the satisfaction of human needs. When institutions, however, turn inward and focus primarily or exclusively on their own needs for survival or quest for power, the strewn wreckage of human life whose needs are laid waste is the visible result.

In Mt 9:35-36, the writer declares:

> And Jesus went about all the cities and villages, teaching in their synagogues and preaching the gospel of the kingdom, and healing every disease and every infirmity. When he saw the crowds, he had compassion for them because they were harassed and helpless, like sheep without a shepherd.

For Jesus, the city was the masses of humanity, harassed, hopeless and helpless, for whom the institutions of society had failed to provide their basic needs and meaning for their lives. The city is people, people struggling for a meaningful existence, whether they are among the rich and surrounded by goods in exclusive suburbs or among the wretched poor and socially naked in the barrios and ghettos.

Why did Jesus weep? One reason could have been because of his identification with humanity, especially with suffering, oppressed and rejected humanity. Jesus realized that the vast majority of the population, as in Third World cities, is comprised of the poor, the lowly, the oppressed and rejected ones. Especially was this true of those living in Galilee. For Galilee, as the northernmost district of Palestine surrounded on all sides by gentile nations separating it from Judea to the south, was symbolic of that which the world rejects and regards as unimportant. It was a multicultural, multiracial region, biologically and culturally mixed, and its people were, in every sense of the word, a *mestizo* people --mixed humanity.

Galilee was the land of the rejected, the despised, the outcasts, the revolutionaries and the foreigners. Their racial and cultural *mestizaje*, their constant contact with gentiles and heathens, resulted in the Galileans being despised by the "pure" Jews of Jerusalem to the south, who saw themselves as the sole heirs of cultural, racial and religious purity.

We cannot begin to understand the feelings of Judean Jews towards Galileans, unless we understand the Jewish insistence on ancestral and racial purity.[2] The Jews held that only Israelites of pure ancestry made up the pure

---

1. George A. Theodorson and Achilles G. Theodorson, *A Modern Dictionary of Sociology* (New York: Barnes & Noble Books, 1979), p. 46.

2. This section on ancestral and racial purity is taken from Joachim Jeremias', *Jerusalem in the Time of Jesus* (Philadelphia: Fortress Press, 1969), pp. 275-302.

Israel. Thus, "even the simple Israelite knew his immediate ancestors and could point to which of the twelve tribes he belonged." After the exile, genealogies became important in order to separate pure families from those racially mixed, as a result of the racial-mixing practices of the Assyrians. The books of Ezra, Nehemiah, and 1 and 2 Chronicles, written after the exile, are all filled with genealogical lists. We often wonder why all the fuss over genealogies. In the post-exilic period, these lists were important in order to determine who was pure Israelite. A person could not be a priest unless they could prove their ancestral purity to at least five generations. No person could hold a public office who was not of pure ancestry, nor would they associate in court or in public office with a person whose ancestry was of doubt. Proof of pure ancestry was important for a woman to marry into a priestly family.

The most important reason for proof of ancestral purity, however, had to do with religion and salvation. If one came up short of merits in the judgment, the merits of Abraham could be added to one's account, so as to assure salvation. However, only those who could trace their lineage to Abraham would have access to his merits. Thus a person's salvation depended on the ancestral purity. Then too, prophecy had declared that before the coming of the end of the age, the prophet Elijah would return "to turn the hearts of the children to their fathers, and the hearts of the fathers to their children" (Mal 4:5-6). In other words, Elijah would restore the family to its ancestral purity so that people would be ready for the final salvation.

Joachim Jeremias declares:[3]

> Only families of pure Israelite descent could be assured of a share in the messianic salvation, for only they were assisted by the 'merit of their legitimate ancestry.' Here we have the most profound reason for the behaviour of these pure Israelite families --why they examined the genealogies of their future sons-- and daughters-in-law before marriage. For on this question of racial purity hung not only the social position of their descendants, but indeed their final assurance of salvation, their share in the future redemption of Israel.

This meant that Galileans, by virtue of their racial and cultural *mestizaje*, were prevented from holding any position of social merit; and of worse consequence, they had no share in the final salvation of Israel, but were despised and rejected, even by God! Thus they had no chance of being saved, none whatsoever . . . until Jesus came along!

In identifying with lost, suffering, oppressed, dejected and rejected, multiracial humanity, Jesus was putting into effect what Virgilio Elizondo calls, "the Galilean Principle": "What human beings reject, God chooses as his very own."[4] The apostle Paul proclaims this principle in 1 Cor 1:26-29, where he says:

> For consider your call, brethren; not many of you were wise according to worldly standards, not many were powerful, not many were of noble birth;

---

3. *Ibid.*, pp. 301-302.

4. Virgilio Elizondo, *Galilean Journey: The Mexican-American Promise* (Maryknoll, NY: Orbis Books, 1983), p. 91.

> but God chose what is foolish in the world to shame the wise, God chose
> what is weak in the world to shame the strong, God chose what is low and
> despised in the world, even things that are not, to bring to nothing things that
> are, so that no human being might boast in the presence of God.

A second reason why Jesus wept, and closely related with the first, was because the proclaimers of truth, the spiritual leaders of the nation, had become the ones that barred people from God. The reason why the people suffered and were "like sheep without a shepherd," was because the spiritual shepherds of Israel had sold them out for gain. "Woe to you, scribes and Pharisees, hypocrites! Because you shut the kingdom of heaven against people; for you neither enter yourselves, nor allow those who would enter to go in" (Mt 23:13).

This helps explain Jesus' words in Mt 23:38, "Behold your house is left to you desolate." Since you would not accept the One of whom Isaiah the prophet wrote: 'He was despised and rejected by men; a man of sorrows, and acquainted with grief; and as one from whom men hide their faces, he was despised and we esteemed him not,' therefore, your house, your beautiful temple, is left desolate, empty and forsaken. I'd rather be born in a stable where the shepherds, the rejected one; where the magi; the foreigners, are all welcome to visit and worship me.

One of the challenges facing the centers of ministerial training in the nation is how to respond to the newest comers to society (who have actually been here all along but relegated to an invisible status). People who come from predominantly Roman Catholic Latin American countries to the urban centers of America do not always feel welcomed by their Irish Catholic counterparts, and Protestantism, because of its strong individualism, leads many to lose their sense of group identity.

Let me explain: Spain's conquest of the New World was through the joint effort of church and state. The two were inseparable; it marked all aspects of life, including the layout of cities, the *pueblos*, around the central plaza, with the state house at one end and the church at the other, for "no community could exist unless God were a member of it."[5] In the center, communal life took place --the fiestas, the market, the religious celebrations, the gathering of people to play, to converse, to experience community-- all within the shadow of both church and state. In Spanish, the word *pueblo* means more than just living in the city or town, it means to belong to a community, to experience peoplehood, and the community was Catholic. "When a Latin American said he was *católico*, or, more commonly, *muy católico*, very Catholic, he did not necessarily mean he had been at Mass or the sacraments; he simply meant that he was a member of a people, a *people*, which was Catholic."[6] When Latino Catholics come to the United States, where religion is more of a private matter, they discover the presence of the

5. Joseph P. Fitzpatrick, *Puerto Rican Americans: The Meaning of Migration to the Mainland* (Englewood Cliffs, NJ: Prentice Hall, Inc., 1971), p. 116.

6. *Ibid.*

Church, but not the presence of the *pueblo*. That sense of community and peoplehood is missing. They thus experience alienation and rejection, even in their own church. Protestantism gives them a rediscovery of a personal God, but divorced from the sense of community, *el pueblo*. And the result is a loss of identity and a loss of a sense of peoplehood, and a ceasing to be Latino.

Historic Catholic centers, such as Boston, Chicago, and Los Angeles, are "communal living rooms," which do not always make the newcomers feel at home, nor desire to share the same living space with them. This sense of loss of community results in much of the negative social behavior impacting Latino barrios in our large urban centers. An alternative behavior, however, is that in their quest for community, as a consequence of experiencing alienation and anomie in the cities, a large number of Latinos, especially Puerto Ricans and Dominicans, are turning to Pentecostalism --the religion of the urban poor in America-- which has become the substitute for *el pueblo*.[7]

Our centers of theological training must strive, in their ministry to Latinos, to give them not only a proper understanding of God, but seek to connect them back to their community, their *pueblo*. For a person can only experience a genuine sense of human dignity and pride in who they are as an integral member of a community, and not in isolation from it.

This means that the church and its educational establishments must be sensitive to the needs of society, and like its Master, take on "human flesh" and identify with lost humanity. Like Christ, it must come "down" from its holy, sanitized and antiseptic environment, and become one with the people it is trying to reach. The church must know their needs, hear their cries, and understand all the factors that make up their situation of despair, distance and distress.

Blacks and Chicanos use expressions in reference to members of their own ethnic groups which are descriptive of their closeness to each other. Male Blacks refer to each other as "brothers," while male Chicanos address each other as "carnales" (of the same flesh). The Bible tells us that Jesus is our brother, and by taking on human flesh he became our *carnal*. That is the meaning of the incarnation, becoming one "flesh" and identifying with the needs of humanity. We need to stop kidding ourselves that we are doing ministry, when all along our moral hangups and leprous attitudes towards others who differ from us whether by religion, race or class, are keeping us from doing genuine, Christ-like, incarnational ministry. Such detachment is more reminiscent of the Pharisees in Jesus' day.

A third reason why Jesus wept was because the people --both the masses and the religious leaders-- did not fully understand the power and the purposes of God for humankind. Thus, in the end he was rejected by all, both Galilean and Judean, for they both misunderstood his intent and mission of creating a new humanity unto himself.

---

7. Renato Poblete and Thomas F. O'Dea, "Anomie and the 'Quest for Community': The Formation of Sects Among the Puerto Ricans of New York," *The American Catholic Sociological Review* 21, No. 1 (1960), pp. 18-36.

Why did God select Galilee, that mestisized, despised region of the earth as the place that would mark the identity of God's son for life? The answer is found in Heb 2:17: "He had to be made like His brethren in all things, that He might become a merciful and faithful high priest."

A new Christ is beginning to be experienced in the church today --Jesus the Galilean. He is replacing the "Generic Christ," the Christ of the universal pulpit, which has prevailed for too long in the church. This is the Christ similar to generic foods, with no market-specific identity, just a universal label stating what he is. As a result the quality of the goods tends to be inferior. You are not always too sure what you are getting --just general fodder to appease the masses. The high quality of the Divine Product, based on the market-specific needs of the different people, is missing.

For this reason the Apostle Paul never preached a "Generic Christ," but a market-specific one:

> For though I am free from all, I have made myself a slave to all, that I might win the more. To the Jews I became as a Jew, that I might win Jews; to those who are under the law, as under the law, . . . that I might win those who are under the law; to those who are without law, as without law, . . . that I might win those who are without law. To the weak I became weak, that I might win the weak; I have become all things to all people, that I might by all means save some. And I do all things for the sake of the gospel, that I may become a fellow-partaker of it (I Cor 9:19-23).

What does it mean to be Black to reach Blacks? What does it mean to be a Latino to reach Latinos? What does it mean to be a woman to reach women for Christ? That is preaching! Genuine contextual preaching! And the Christ that is being preached is a market-specific one --Jesus the Galilean. And to this Christ, who has identified with their specific needs, women, Asians, Blacks, Latinos and Whites are responding with a resounding "Yes." As for the "Generic Christ" of the colonial, ethnocentric, Western Church, concerned with homogeneity and uniformity, he is no longer acceptable to the needs of a multicultural world, but is a product of a by-gone age.

As a nation we have moved from an agrarian society concerned with conformity, through an industrial society, concerned with uniformity, to the new information society concerned with diversity in a global context. Yet in this information age of cultural diversity and pluralism, the church is still pushing the outmoded industrial society's assembly-line model of uniformity, as a methodology for mission. The current "English only" movement in education and the Homogeneous Unit Principle of the church growth movement, are both examples of nostalgic methodologies of a by-gone age.

In a multicultural society where the focus is on diversity, the church must develop a model of multicultural ministry based on unity in diversity in Christ. A new age demands new methods! Therefore, in order to stay relevant, our schools of theology must not only respond to change, they must also *anticipate* it!

A Compassionate Christ

What is this character trait of Christ that moves him to tears in view of the human condition? It is *compassion*, the compassion of God. Compassion is a rare commodity in the world today for it can only be generated by God. Compassion is a divine character quality that only comes from God and not from human hearts. Throughout the Four Gospels compassion is only found with reference to Jesus or mentioned by him. It is a divine plant of heavenly origin, and its source is heaven not earth. Whenever it is manifested by human beings, it is because God has moved upon the heart, whether or not they declare themselves to be children of God.

This is the declaration of John in 3 Jn 11: "Beloved, do not imitate evil but imitate good. He who does good is of God; he who does evil has not seen God." This text does not judge people on the basis of their beliefs, but on the basis of their behavior. Nothing is said of their beliefs. It is their behavior that determines whether they are of God, and not what they believe.

The tears of God, therefore, as seen in Jesus' behavior while overlooking the city of Jerusalem, reflect that aspect of character which motivated God to identify with suffering and separated humanity --his compassion!

Confronting the Structures of Oppression

But tears are not enough. All the emoting in the world does not remove suffering. Definitive action needs to take place. Jesus does not let it rest at mere weeping, but moves to relieve the suffering. This is the difference between sympathy and compassion. Sympathy looks down with teary-eyed pity and says, "Oh, I am so sorry." Compassion *comes down* with caring concern and says, "Can I be of help?" Compassion always moves from affection to action.

Thus, as his one last act, Jesus, like Jeremiah of old, takes on the single most important yet oppressive institutional structure of his day --the temple in Jerusalem-- and cleanses it (Mt 21:12-16). Paulo Freire declares: It is an "illusion that the hearts of men and women can be transformed while the social structure which make those hearts 'sick' are left intact and unchanged."[8]

The time for healing the sick, and preaching good news to the poor, and proclaiming release to the captives, and recovering of sight to the blind, and setting at liberty those who are oppressed, is over! The day of the Lord has arrived; the day of vengeance of our God. This is Judgment Day! People, it is closing time! And no deceptive theology of institutionalism based on "this is the temple of the Lord, therefore we are safe!" can alter the verdict.

The central purpose of this act and the meaning behind its significance, was Jesus' desire to give the people and the religious leaders of his day, and every day since, a new understanding of the nature of God, and that all peoples, no matter their race, class or gender, have equal access to him.

It must be understood that the reason why all this legalized exploitation

---

8. Paulo Freire, "Education, Liberation and the Church," *Risk*, 9:3, 1973, p. 34.

was permitted in the temple, was because of the understanding of God of the chief priests' and scribes --the theologians.

God, therefore, became the biggest exploiter. Because Jewish society in Jesus' day was a religio-political society, structured by and centered around the temple and the worship of a God who sanctioned this exploitation, the entire nation and its social structures were organized in harmony with this domineering, patriarchal concept of God. Jesus, by cleaning the temple, was putting an end to this socially constructed God, who benefitted the powerful, and replaced it with the God of compassion, who came to serve humanity.

In declaring, "My house shall be called a house of prayer for all nations" (Mk 11:17), Jesus was announcing the new universalism of God and an end to exclusivisms --no one would be excluded from the presence of God.[9] The temple officials had so structured the layout of the temple so as to exclude people from entry into the temple. There was the Court of Women, beyond which women could not go; then there was the Court of Israel, the men's court, beyond which men could not enter; and finally there was the Court of Priests, where only priests were allowed. In his declaration of universalism, Jesus, by breaking down the dividing wall of hostility that created social barriers in people's access to God (Eph 2:14-16), was proclaiming a new redemptive social order: *That all of God's children are one and have equal access to God.* "There is neither Jew nor Greek (no division based on racial and ethnic differences), there is neither slave nor free (no division based on social class), there is neither male nor female (no division based on sex and gender); for you are all one in Christ Jesus" (Gal 3:28). Therefore, the keeping out of women and ethnic minorities from full access to the temple is a human construction that flies in the face of the aim of God for all humankind.

And just to make sure that this new truth was not misunderstood as to God's intention, when Jesus expired his last on the cross, "the curtain of the temple was torn in two, from top to bottom" (Mk 15:38). This final act made it clear that the very presence of God, symbolized by the Holy of Holies, is now accessible to all, bar none. Women, gentiles and the laity had been excluded; now they all have free access to the temple. There are now no more holy places, for Jesus himself is the Temple. And where two or three are gathered in his name, Jesus promised he would be in their midst (Mt 18:20).

Matthew tells us that after driving out the money-changers, the blind, the lame and the children came to Jesus and he healed and blessed them. By this action Jesus showed what God was like, a God of compassion; and what true worship was all about, serving humanity at their deepest level of need.

This must be the mission of our centers of theological training.

God wants to convert our elaborate, expensive and exclusive temples, where often there is no room for people who might be different from us, into stables where all of humanity can come and worship him freely in open, loving oneness, without distinction.

---

9. Elizondo, *op. cit.*, p. 73.

Therein lies the significance of Jesus the Galilean, for Galilee, the "stables" of the world, has become the dwelling place of God. The end result will be the turning of stables into temples --his Holy Temple-- and the turning of temples, the human constructions of exclusiveness, into forsaken, desolate stables. For Jesus is first born in a stable, and then converts that stable into the Temple of the living God.

Confrontación y reconciliación

Yolanda E. Pupo-Ortiz

En julio del 1981 llegué a la Comisión de Religión y Raza de la Iglesia Metodista Unida, y desde entonces he tenido la maravillosa oportunidad de ampliar mi visión sobre el pueblo hipano. He estado en pueblos grandes y chicos, en cultos, comidas, reuniones y celebraciones. En cada lugar donde he estado he podido confirmar lo que ya sabía. Pero antes era un conocimiento al que le faltaba la dimensión total que da la visión que se concretiza y que se sale por tanto de la vivencia que es tan solo intelectual.

Al convertirse ese conocimiento, a través de estos encuentros, en rasgos definidos y personalidades propias con rostros sonrientes, cuerpos activos y mentes despiertas a todo lo largo y ancho del país, se me presenta en su confirmación como algo vivísimo en su realidad: Somos un pueblo grande y rico en pleno proceso de crecimiento y liberación. Elemento vital de esa riqueza es la casi increíble gama de diversidad que tenemos. Somos diversos en talento y en cultura, como es diversa y rica la lengua que nos une, como es rico y diverso nuestro folklore, y como son ricos, difrentes y profundos nuestros sentimientos. Es en esta visión de la grandeza de nuestro pueblo donde también he encontrado la razón mayor para la crítica de aquellos que al mirarla desde afuera la confunden, y llaman entonces a nuestra diversidad "división".

Por esta diversidad presentamos al ojo ajeno un grupo de personas que se llaman colectivamente hispanas, pero que reclaman también la propiedad de sus diferentes países de origen. Hablan la misma lengua, pero recogidos en ella se encuentran los matices del acento del altiplano boliviano, las pampas argentinas, los campos mexicanos, los llanos venezolanos o las islas del Caribe. Van a comprar a una misma tienda o pulpería en el barrio hispano, pero allí en su comida se aúnan el maíz con el chile, el plátano con los guineos, los frijoles con las habichuelas. Casi se siente el olor de las tortillas, tamales y pasteles. Rasgan las notas de su música, y el oído extraño se sorprende con las notas tristes del indio, el ritmo africano y la jota española, amalgamado todo en lo que llamamos música criolla.

Es en esta diversidad que confunde al que sólo quiere conocernos dándonos un vistazo a la ligera, donde está nuestra riqueza. Porque podemos encontrar inicios comunes, nos hermanamos en el nombre de "hispanos". Dentro de este lazo común la historia y la geografía nos han dado el espacio necesario para crecer dentro de la cultura propia de cada región y grupo, somos ricos, diferentes y únicos. Porque nos sentimos hermanos en nuestra hispanidad, iguales dentro de nuestra diversidad, somos un pueblo grande.

Entender esa diversidad es la clave de empezar a conocernos como pueblo. Cuando el anglo deja de sentirse perplejo al descubrir que el dueño del restaurante cubano es salvadoreño, que en el grupo que canta tangos en el teatro no son todos argentinos, y la preocupación por la educación bilingüe en Nueva York no es tan sólo de puertorriqueños, entonces ha empezado a entender y adentrarse en los complejos lazos de nuestra cultura.

No somos una cultura fácil, no. No se nos puede abreviar siguiendo la línea del menor esfuerzo, ni se nos puede simplificar en fórmulas de ABC. Hay que prestarnos atención colectiva e individualmente. Conociendo a uno no se nos conoce a todos, aunque en cada uno haya un pedacito de todos. Y es precisamente esta complejidad la que nos hace también grandes y ricos.

Pero la confusión de los de afuera no es el problema mayor. La tragedia verdadera está cuando la confusión no viene de afuera, sino cuando viene de adentro, producida en y por nosotros mismos --cuando permitimos que esta confusión externa se inmiscuya en nuestros asuntos convirtiendo entonces la riqueza y diversidad que nos caracterizan en símbolo de división.

Parte de la grandeza del pueblo hispano es precisamente la unidad que logramos en nuestra hispanidad. Un pueblo que persiste con la tenacidad con que lo hacemos en mantener su lengua, su cultura, su identidad propia en medio de una cultura que por ser mayoría exige asimilación, es un pueblo unido. Un pueblo que se busca con el afán con que lo hacemos en medio de climas diferentes y regiones extrañas, y que siente reverberar en él con dolor unísono el dolor del continente, es un pueblo unido. Es pues confusión de nuestra diversidad el epíteto de división que nos dan los de afuera y el sentimiento que a veces nos permea a lo de adentro de creernos desunidos.

Según el diccionario, "confusión" es una reunión de cosas inconexas, falta de orden, acción de tomar una cosa por otra, falta de claridad. Es posible que en medio del inmenso espacio geográfico que ocupamos y de la gama increíble de nuestra diversidad, perdamos a veces la debida perspectiva, y que la imagen que vemos y proyectamos sea distorsionada, fuera del orden correcto, y que por lo tanto se derive de ella esta confusión.

Toda confusión sin embargo tiene que ser aclarada, tiene que volverse a poner en el lugar establecido. Para un pueblo que está creciendo de una manera tan acelerada como el nuestro, que se predice llegará a ser la mayor minoría del país a finales de la presente década, esta necesidad es urgente. Pero más importante, para un pueblo que junto ha despertado a la necesidad no sólo de escribir sino de determinar su historia, un pueblo que está redescubriendo y haciendo redescubrir el significado de la liberación total, de alma y de cuerpo, de estructuras de opresión y de miseria, que está en un proceso de crecimiento no sólo físico o numérico sino también intelectual, político, espiritual y cultural, es imprescindible esclarecer esta confusión y volver a recuperar la visión que le corresponde.

Dos palabras acuden a mi mente martilleantes y persistentes en relación con la recuperación de nuestra total visión: Confrontación y Reconciliación. La completa realización de nuestra grandeza creo que se alcanzará cuando nos lancemos al acto de una Confrontación dentro de un marco de Reconciliación.

Confrontación

A veces le tenemos miedo a esta palabra. Primero porque tenemos demasiado metida en la cabeza la idea de que para ser cristianos hay que ser sumisos. Hemos confundido el concepto de humildad y de amor de Jesús con el de sumisión. La sumisión y el conformismo sin embargo estaban muy lejos de su evangelio. La humildad que Jesús enseñó no era en modo alguno sumisa o conformista. El Jesús humilde que lavaba los pies a sus discípulos era el mismo que "enseñaba como quien tiene autoridad", y que se levantaba en toda la hidalguía de su dignidad para afirmarse en el "YO SOY". El Jesús que trataba de ayudar a sus discípulos a vivir en el día presente en toda su extensión y en toda su potencia al exhortarles a dejar el mañana para mañana y dedicar sus fuerzas al afán de hoy, era el mismo Jesús que no vacilaba en resolver los problemas urgentes del momento que repercutían lo mismo en las tradiciones del pasado que en las consecuencias del mañana. No se conformaba en esperar por un día mejor. Empezaba a actuar en el Hoy. Siendo sábado no titubeó para curar al hombre de la mano seca, y las horas no eran límite para hablar y enseñar a la multitud que le seguía aunque el sol anunciaba que era la hora de comer. Denunciaba Jesús su carácter no conformista y revolucionario cuando arrojaba a los mercaderes del templo, cuando acusaba a los religiosos de su época de hipócritas, y cuando hablaba sin reparos con la mujer samaritana arriesgándose a la crítica y censura de sus contemporáneos.

La confrontación es el inicio de todo cambio, de todo proceso de recuperación. Aun en el plano personal no realizamos grandes cosas, no podemos hacerlo, hasta que no nos confrontamos cara a cara con el paso que queremos dar, con la pena que nos aflige, con el problema que nos paraliza, con nosotros mismos. Aun la experiencia de la salvación no comienza hasta que no pasamos por el proceso de una confrontación.

Esta confrontación que es necesaria para esclarecer la confusión de nuestra imagen se aplica a nosotros primero como una confrontación personal e íntima. Confrontación de cada uno como persona, como persona que lleva como uno de sus elementos más distinguibles y esenciales la naturaleza de ser hispana. Confrontación donde cada hispano se enfrente consigo mismo, a ese nivel de conocimiento donde se produce reconocimiento de lo que se es, y con ese reconocimiento se alcanza un sentimiento de orgullo y de satisfacción que hacen completa a una persona. No es hasta que una persona logra encontrarse en ese nivel de aceptación propia que se produce la realización de toda su capacidad. Es cuando ha logrado esto que una persona está preparada para de una manera positiva dar de sí misma y recibir.

Otro nivel de esta confrontación es la que se sale de lo personal para encontrarse al otro nivel esencial que hace a un pueblo, pueblo. Este es el nivel donde traemos nombres diferents, ideas afines o contradictorias, rostros blancos, trigueños y negros, toda esa nuestra diversidad fuertemente permeada por el sentido de un lazo común, del cual no nos podemos desatar ni queremos hacerlo, pues son nuestras raíces mismas, que nos hacen ser iguales pero diferentes en el amplio contexto de lo que llamamos "La Raza". Es el nivel donde traemos nuestras diferencias y descubrimos que aun ellas provienen de las mismas heridas y el mismo dolor, y nos atan ya no sólo por la comunidad de nuestras raíces sino por la conciencia de que juntos podemos alcanzar la total liberación. Es el nivel de hispano a hispano. Esta es la confrontación donde hispanos de distintas procedencias se encontrarán para ir desnudando confusiones, erróneas interpretaciones, rencores y prejuicios mal fundados, porque han sido fundados en la confusión de una visión desordenada, fuera de su perspectiva correcta. ¿Que pudiera haber elementos de ira en esta confrontación? Sí, probablemente los habría. Pero quizá son necesarios para llevar a cabo una verdadera confrontación --aquella confrontación que cansa y fatiga porque se lucha de cuerpo a cuerpo y hasta el mismo meollo del alma, como la lucha de Jacob al rayar el alba con el ángel lo convirtió en Israel "porque has peleado con Dios y con los hombres y has vencido". La verdadera confrontación conlleva lucha, ira, rebeldía, cansancio; pero es siempre positiva, trae resultados transformadores. No hay transformación verdadera sin antes haber pasado por ese proceso de confrontación donde están incluídos todos esos elementos, para culminar después con el sentimiento único de la gozosa realización de la victoria que con nuestras propias fuerzas hemos logrado.

De esta confrontación desnuda yo imagino como resultado un reconocimiento mayor de lo que somos, una apreciación más real del valor de nuestra diversidad, y una solidaridad más profunda en nuestra hispanidad. Un impacto mucho más revolucionario como pueblo que se ha confrontado para afirmarse a sí mismo y encontrar liberación.

El tercer nivel de esta confrontación que estoy visualizando es aquella donde lo que se realiza adentro se vuelca hacia fuera. De la misma manera que yo como persona no puedo dar ni recibir hasta que no me haya encontrado a mí misma, esté contenta y orgullosa de lo que soy, y esté en paz conmigo misma, tampoco como pueblo somos capaces de dar ni recibir hasta que no nos hayamos encontrado inmediatamente después del umbral de esta conjunta confrontación. Una vez hecho esto estamos preparados para salirnos fuera y, purificados y vigorizados por el esfuerzo de la lucha conjunta, hacer nuestra contribución comenzando con una confrontación. Esta confrontación es la que tenemos que hacer al barrio, a la ciudad, al estado y a la nación donde vivimos, a las estructuras y organizaciones a que pertenecemos, y a la iglesia de la cual somos miembros.

Esta confrontación es la que está sucediendo ya en algunos lugares, pero que quizás no ha pasado por esas confrontaciones iniciales y se está produciendo de manera aislada. Mediante esta confrontación marcaríamos nuestras huellas de una manera inconfundible en el proceso histórico y político de esta nación, y al mismo tiempo estaríamos dando espacio para recibir positivamente de su cultura. Es la confrontación que demanda el lugar que nos corresponde como hispanos --el lugar donde seamos nosotros los que estemos determinando el camino a seguir, donde el deber y la responsabilidad del ciudadano se unan a la participación del poder de manera que nuestra voz y actuación estén presentes en el proceso de las decisiones que van a afectarnos como parte de esta sociedad. El lugar donde la aceptación de nuestra diversidad como pueblo, pueblo que se crece en el concepto más amplio de "La Raza", sea totalmente inclusiva, sin tener que amarrarnos a patrones preconcebidos o a moldes delineados por otros.

Esta sería la confrontación final donde, afirmados ya en lo que somos, damos de nosotros, ofrecemos la contribución que como pueblo debemos dar y al hacer esto, al mismo tiempo, afirmamos a los demás. Decía Unamuno que "gran poquedad de alma arguye tener que negar al prójimo para afirmarse". Nosotros como gran pueblo que somos afirmamos de la única manera que se puede afirmar: Crecidos en nuestro encuentro y seguros de nuestra identidad y valor, incluímos entonces al prójimo, nos abrimos a él, le encontramos en medio del diálogo de la confrontación, y en ese plano de igualdad lo afirmamos.

Reconciliación

No se puede hablar de confrontación sin hablar de reconciliación, porque sería algo inconcluso. El Jesús transformador que confrontaba lo hacía con el propósito específico de reconciliar. Reconciliar al humano con Dios, al humano consigo mismo, al rico con el pobre, al fariseo con el publicano. Nuestra acción de confrontación, confrontación que como pueblo cristiano hacemos a la luz de Jesús, trae como consecuencia irremediable la reconciliación.

Así como hablaba de la confrontación en tres niveles, creo en la reconciliación que se produce en esos niveles inmediatamente después de la confrontación. Reconciliación personal, clave de tantos problemas aún no resueltos en las salas psiquiátricas; reconciliación como pueblo que dialoga, vive y actúa, inclusivo e igualitario, dentro de su diversidad; reconciliación creadora y transformadora que lleva a una mayor reconciliación dentro de la sociedad donde nos movemos.

Comencé este escrito diciendo que el pueblo hispano es un pueblo grande y rico en pleno proceso de crecimiento y liberación. "Por mí conoceréis la verdad y la verdad os libertará", dijo Jesús. La libertad es el resultado o la consecuencia última de conocer íntimamente a Jesús. Esta libertad de Jesús, este mensaje de liberación, conlleva estos dos elementos de los que he hablado aquí: Confrontación y Reconciliación. No puede haber libertad sin confrontación; no hay verdadera libertad sin reconciliación.

El pueblo hispano es un pueblo grande y rico. Un pueblo que en su diversidad busca como elemento final el de su liberación total. No en balde fue en el seno de nuestro pueblo y nuestro continente, herido por las masas adoloridas, que surgió la teología de la liberación.

Es a esa liberación total que debemos seguir apuntando, la que se produce de adentro hacia afuera, pero que por eso mismo, porque libera desde las mismas raíces, tiene resultados concretos en lo que pasa en la periferia. Es la liberación que, como Jesús, al mismo tiempo que sana al enfermo azuza, interroga, remueve las mismas bases para que la renovación sea total y permanente. Esta es la liberación que esclarece la confusión de que hablábamos, y la confusión mucho más amplia del propósito y sentido de la vida. Es la liberación de temores, miseria, prejuicios, racismo y opresión. Es la que aclara confusiones de valores, de prioridades, de principios y bases fundamentales.

Es nuestra responsabilidad no sólo luchar por mantener lo grande y rico que es nuestro, sino asegurarnos de que el proceso de crecimiento hacia esta liberación no se detenga, altere o desvíe por el camino. Acrecentarlo y acelerarlo mediante el esfuerzo conjunto e inclusivo de nuestro pueblo es el llamado y la tarea que se nos presentan cada día.

Al inicio de ese camino, camino de crecimiento y total liberación, veo todavía, persistentes en su pertinencia, estas dos palabras que se convierten al mismo tiempo en base y en ciclo perenne, necesarias para iniciar, proseguir y alcanzar la meta: Confrontación y Reconciliación. La Confrontación honesta y única se produce dentro del marco de la Reconciliación.

Summary

The growing Hispanic population in this country is in a process of self-determination and liberation. In that process, understanding the diversity that makes up the Hispanic people is a key factor not only for non-Hispanic persons but for the Hispanic population as well.

The Hispanic culture cannot be quickly simplified in formulas. In order to understand us, all groups cannot be lumped together under a label. On the contrary specific efforts must be made to thoroughly get to know each one with their own distinctiveness, uniqueness and "self". We are many and yet we are "One" in the larger context of history, tradition, and language. These forces have brought us together, thus intertwining our beings in such a way that a new race "La Raza" has been born.

However this diversity in the Hispanic people has been misunderstood by both non-Hispanics and Hispanics. It has bee called incorrectly "divisiveness". I believe that in order to fulfill the process of total liberation, liberation of body and spirit, liberation of misery and oppression, we need as a people to correct this misunderstanding or confusion. We need to claim back the vision of "One of Many", because that is what makes us rich. That is what enables us to become an instrument of inclusiveness and justice wherever we are.

As we move towards this kind of liberation, the Hispanic people need to go through two crucial elements: Confrontation and Reconciliation. On this road of confrontation and reconciliation there are three main stages, First, confrontation with oneself is necessary in order to be reconciled with what we are as persons. Secondly, as Hispanics, we must confront each other in the midst of our diversity, giving space to each group to be and to bring its won contribution, identifying with each others so that we can then become reconciled with one another, and consequently be stronger in our solidarity. Finally, we must confront society at large, confront systems and structures in order to obtain the place that is rightly ours, not to control and oppress but to make our contribution, to shape with others our destiny. This confrontation is central to our identity as people. Without it, we should lose our identity and our process of liberation would be stifled. As we do this, we experience the wholeness of total reconciliation. Reconciliation is the ultimate goal of confrontation. That was Jesus' method in his ministry and it must be ours in a constant cycle of honest confrontation which leads to reconciliation.

Reflexiones teológicas sobre la migración

Jorge Lara-Braud

De la sociología del conocimiento he aprendido que no se llega a temas como éste sin la huella profunda del lugar que uno ocupa en la sociedad. Por tanto, lo que he de decir aquí llevará necesariamente el sello de mi propia experiencia.

Soy uno de los inmigrantes afortunados. Y eso se lo debo principalmente a la Iglesia Presbiteriana. Tras estos apuntes sobre la inmigración hay una serie de experiencias que me causaron gran desilusión cuando por primera vez vine a los Estados Unidos. Nací en Mexicali, a sólo seis cuadras al sur de la frontera. Y sin embargo, a pesar de casi haber nacido en la "tierra prometida", no fue sino a los diecisiete años de edad que crucé la frontera. Vine a Texas a estudiar en una escuela presbiteriana, que entonces se llamaba Texan Mexican Industrial Institute ("TexMex"), y después se llamó Pan American School.

Mientras los mexicanos estábamos bajo la protección de la escuela, no teníamos que enfrentarnos a las duras realidades de ser de origen mexicano en Texas. Esa es una de las razones por las que digo que fui afortunado. Pero tan pronto dejábamos esa protección nos volvíamos vulnerables a lo que para mí fueron algunas de las peores humillaciones que jamás he sufrido. Por ello, aunque mis reflexiones son de gran esperanza, lo son sobre el trasfondo de mis tristes experiencias como inmigrante -- experiencias como la de ser echado de un establecimiento público que se negaba a servir a mexicanos, y la de percatarme de que la Iglesia Presbiteriana a que me había unido escondía su rostro del dolor y se desentendía de tales sucesos con la resignada promesa de que "las cosas cambiarán". A causa de esa resignación, decidí que mientras viviera me dedicaría a destruir las causas, y no sólo los síntomas, de tales situaciones.

Antes, cuando yo era todavía un mozuelo en México, sin idea alguna de los conflictos raciales, fue hecho "blanco" por decreto legislativo en el estado de Texas. La guerra había causado gran escasez de mano de obra, y los agricultores texanos se veían en peligro de perder sus cosechas si no importaban obreros. Puesto que el gobierno de México ponía obstáculos debido al modo en que los mexicanos eran tratados en Texas, la legislatura texana, en sesión conjunta de emergencia en 1943, declaró que, en todo lo referente a las facilidades públicas, las personas de origen mexicano serían consideradas blancas. Así fue que yo vine a ser blanco.

Esto indica las ambigüedades bajo las cuales vivimos los que venimos de México, o lucimos mexicanos. Si hemos de ser sinceros y auténticos, nuestra relación con este país tiene que llevar el sello de esa ambigüedad.

Sicológica y espiritualmente, los inmigrantes somos como los conversos. Tenemos que darle legitimidad a nuestro abandono del pasado como malo, y tenemos que darles legitimidad al presente y al futuro como buenos y prometedores. Los conversos toman muy serio las bases de identidad de la comunidad a que se unen. Lo mismo es cierto de los inmigrantes. En mi propio caso, pasé por dos conversiones: de católico a presbiteriano (un cambio rápido y feliz en la década de los 40) y, mucho después, de mexicano a ciudadano norteamericano. La justificación de esa segunda conversión tomó veinte años.

Como inmigrante, me he visto obligado a estudiar los mitos sobre el origen de los Estados Unidos. Estoy persuadido de que la ambigüedad hacia los inmigrantes --de hospitalidad y hostilidad-- se relaciona con el constante conflicto en la sociedad norteamericana entre el ideal de una nueva nación que les daría la bienvenida a todos los rechazados por otras sociedades, por una parte, y la reacción nativista que apareció desde muy temprano contra los inmigrantes, particularmente los que no procedían de los países del norte de Europa que le dieron origen a lo que yo llamo la comunidad norteamericana primordial. En cuanto se es diferente de esa comunidad primordial, queda uno excluido de los mitos de origen, y por tanto vulnerable. Para los mexicanos, no basta con ser hechos "blancos" por acción legislativa en Texas. A eso hay que añadirle las credenciales que esta sociedad requiere para considerarlo a uno verdaderamente humano. Tengo que agradecerle a la Iglesia Presbiteriana el haberme dado las "tarjetas de sindicalización" necesarias para participar de esta sociedad. También tuve la fortuna, aunque entonces no lo sabía, de que la iglesia a que me uní (protestante) puede reclamar mayor continuidad con las comunidades primordiales que la iglesia de la cual yo provenía (católica). Las instituciones de esta sociedad no fueron diseñadas para los inmigrantes, sino para la comunidad primordial, y fue así, a través de las instituciones presbiterianas, que yo pude relacionarme con la comunidad primordial. Esa ventaja de los protestantes por encima de los católicos existe todavía, y tiene gran importancia porque la inmensa mayoría de los inmigrantes latinoamericanos son católicos.

Desde sus mismos inicios este país se vio cautivado por la idea de que se estaba estableciendo a este lado del Atlántico una nación que sería ejemplo para el resto del mundo, y que era Dios quien impulsaba a las gentes a venir a estas tierras para construir una sociedad que de algún modo se sproximara a los requisitos del Reino de Dios. Los dos lemas del sello nacional resumen esa visión: *E pluribus unum* (de muchos, uno) y *Novus ordo saeculorum* (el nuevo orden de las edades). El presidente Jefferson llegó a sugerir que en el sello nacional se representara a Moisés guiando a Israel a través del Mar Rojo.

Por tanto, desde el principio se dio por sentado que habría una renovación permamente de la sociedad, porque esta nación había entrado en un pacto con Dios, y ese pacto requeriría una constante conversión y reconversión. Sin entender esto sobre el subconsciente norteamericano, creo sinceramente que es imposible mostrar la bendición que los inmigrantes pueden seguir siendo. Esa ha de ser mi orientación, tanto en teología como en otros campos. Quisiera volver a convencer a los norteamericanos de que cada vez que un inmigrante llega a esta nación, el sueño del nacimiento de una sociedad ejemplar cobra nuevas fuerzas. El elemento más noble en la vida nacional recibe nuevos bríos cada vez que tiene lugar esa acción de darles la bienvenida, como dijo Emma Lazarus, a "the tired, the poor, the huddled masses yearning to be free, the wretched refuse of the teaming shores". Otros autores, como Ralph Waldo Emerson, Herman Melville y Walt Whitman, han contribuido a mantener viva esa tradición. Todos ellos han enaltecido el ideal de las muchas naciones que se vuelven una. En 1817, Jefferson, en un discurso famoso, se refirió a "la puerta abierta a los oprimidos, un santuario para quienes necesitan empezar de nuevo, y que por tanto pueden ser bienvenidos a esta 'nueva Canaán' llamada los Estados Unidos de América".

Pero hay un gran problema al tratar de repetir esa nota de la identidad norteamericana a base de las imágenes del Exodo. Si se usa la imagen de dejar el cautiverio de Egipto, específicamente en el caso de los mexicanos, se llega a la afirmación de la nueva tierra pagando el precio de negar el país de origen. Luego no podemos unirnos a la comunidad primordial sin ambigüedades en este punto. Ciertamente no podemos hacerlo los que venimos de México y nunca dejamos de ser mexicanos --de igual modo que los protestantes que nunca dejamos de ser católicos.

Otro problema con la imagen del Exodo es que puede fácilmente reforzar el orgullo de los Estados Unidos, de considerarse a sí mismos, sin crítica alguna, como la mejor esperanza para todo el resto del mundo. Como otros han señalado, no es por pura coincidencia que muchos de los inmigrantes nos vemos obligados a tomar posturas críticas frente a las prácticas económicas de nuestro nuevo país, y a entender el patriotismo de modo distinto al de la comunidad primordial.

El otro peligro es que al usar esa imagen bíblica confrontemos a un pueblo que vive ya en agonía sicológica y espiritual con otra contradicción entre lo que predica y lo que practica en lo que se refiere a su relación con los nuevos inmigrantes. Los norteamericanos sufren de un exceso de culpa. Por tantos años han tenido dudas acerca de sí mismos, que solamente una gran tragedia puede avivar la moral de un pueblo que ha perdido su sentido de identidad nacional y su confianza en el futuro.

Pero a pesar de todos esos problemas, me atrevo a seguir hablando del tema del Exodo porque hay otros corolarios que se siguen de él. Esta sociedad, más que cualquiera otra, todavía se ve a sí misma como una tierra de nuevos comienzos, de reforma perpetua. Eso es parte de lo que se incluye en la frase "the American dream". La frase misma indica que la peregrinación del país todavía está inconclusa, que su búsqueda de fidelidad a los comienzos continúa hacia el futuro. En gran medida, tales nuevos comienzos tienen lugar. Todavía hay reformas en los EE. UU. con menos violencia y más propósito que en cualquier otro país del mundo. Nuestra presencia aquí como inmigrantes es confirmación de ello, y los millones que quieren entrar al país indican que en el resto del mundo cree en ello. No hay grandes multitudes tratando de colocarse bajo regímenes autoritarios. Nosotros los inmigrantes tenemos la obligación de ayudar a los nativos a ser fieles a los ideales que sus antepasados inmigrantes tomaron del Exodo.

La ambigüedad de la historia de nuestro país como a la vez hostil y hospitalario hacia los inmigrantes y refugiados nos recuerda la imagen bíblica del pueblo de Dios como pueblo peregrino. Los inmigrantes de hoy, como los precursores bíblicos, se vieron forzados al exilio por la opresión política, racial o económica, o por la promesa de una tierra de nuevos comienzos. Abraham y los suyos tomaron el riesgo de dejarlo todo detrás, confiando en un Dios co-peregrino, a fin de aprender a vivir por la promesa, a no llevar demasiada carga, y a encontrar su propósito en llegar a ser bendición para todas las naciones de la tierra. Tras su llegada a la tierra prometida, el llamado, la protección y la liberación de Dios se repetirían una y otra vez en el recuerdo de sus orígenes: "Un arameo a punto de perecer fue mi padre..." (Dt 26:5). Después, cuando se legisló el orden de sus vidas, se hizo provisión para los pobres, los extranjeros y los peregrinos, inclusive la devolución del uso de la tierra a quienes hubieran sido desposeídos de ella por su condición económica (Lv 25).

En el Nuevo Testamento, y especialmente en el libro de Hebreos, estas verdades de la fe encuentran eco frecuente. Una gran nube de testigos es la imagen y forma de la comunidad peregrina de Dios, siempre de camino y exiliada. La ciudad perdurable se ha de encontrar donde Jesús sufrió y redimió al mundo: fuera de las puertas, donde viven los que no cuentan (Heb 13:7-16). En esa epístola encontramos también el conocido texto de la hospitalidad cristiana: "Permanezca el amor fraternal. No os olvidéis de la hospitalidad, porque por ella algunos, sin saberlo, hospedaron ángeles" (13:1-2).

Cuando nosotros pensamos acerca de los ángeles, difícilmente esperamos encontrarlos entre los disidentes políticos o extranjeros perseguidos. Pero, según la Biblia, es allí donde es más probable que los encontremos. Y no sólo a los ángeles, sino a Cristo mismo. Porque aun el Cristo niño y sus padres no encontraron lugar en el mesón, en tierra extraña, y así comenzó la vida peregrina del Dios-humanado.

Cristo resumió toda su misión diciendo que consistía en predicar buenas nuevas a los pobres, proclamar libertad a los cautivos, restaurar la visión a los ciegos, y liberar a los oprimidos (Lc 4:18-19). Y al concluir su ministerio, Jesús unió su suerte y futuro a los hambrientos, los sedientos, los extranjeros, los desnudos, los enfermos y los presos, de modo que cuando nosotros ayudamos a una de tales personas le ayudamos a él (Mt 25).

Como cristianos norteamericanos, y como inmigrantes en los Estados Unidos, nuestra responsabilidad no deja lugar a dudas.

Summary

This reflection is truly auto-biographical. The author, an immigrant himself, came to the U.S. through the work of the Presbyterian Church. Although that church functioned as both shield and shelter from the harsh realities of being of Mexican extraction in Texas, the same community resigned itself to allow the all-too-common immigrant experiences of indignity, oppression and pain to continue in their midst in hope that in time that will change.

The psychological and spiritual experience of the immigrant is similar in scope to that of a convert. Legitimation has to be offered to consider the past in a negative vein and also to legitimate the present and the future as promising. Just as converts take very seriously the sources of identity of the community they join, an immigrant is forced to look deeply into the myths of origin of the host country. In the case of the U.S., the ambiguity toward immigrants --of hospitality on the one hand and hostility on the other-- has to do with a perennial societal conflict between the ideal of a new nation, which would be the welcoming place for rejects of other societies on the one hand; and on the other, the early nativist reaction against the immigrant, particularly those who did not come from the countries of northern Europe that established the primordial American community. Insofar as you are different from that primordial community there lies your liability.

The institutions of this society are not designed for the immigrants, and this holds true of religious institutions as well. For example, if an immigrant is not Protestant --as is the case of most Latin American immigrants-- that person quickly finds out that, that in itself is one of the greatest liabilities a person can suffer in this nation. And things could be better or worse for immigrants depending on how one interprets the fact that, from the very beginning, this country has been dominated by the idea that there was being established on this side of the Atlantic a nation that would be an example to the rest of the world, with a sense that it was God who impelled these people to come and build a society that would approximate the demands of the Reign of God. A case could be made, however, that immigrants were and continue to be a blessing in our midst. Americans need to be re-convinced that for every immigrant who comes to this nation the dream of the birth of an exemplary society is revitalized.

Theologically speaking, the image of the Exodus --which is one of the founding mythical images of this country-- has at least two negative connotations when related to the experience of Mexican immigrants. First, one is led to an affirmation of the new land at the expense of a profound negation of the country one left. Secondly, use of this imagery can easily reinforce the self-righteousness of parts of the U.S. society which uncritically consider this nation the best hope yet for all the nations of the world. On the other hand, the fact that this society still regards itself more than any other as a land of new beginnings --one of the many symbolic nuances conveyed in the phrase the American Dream-- *is an admission that the nation's pilgrimage is still unfinished, that its search of consonance with its beginnings will yet be fulfilled in the future. The fulfillment of this journey is closely linked to the immigrants in this land. Immigrants owe it to the natives to help them be true to the Exodus ideals of their own immigrant forebears.*

The ambiguity of our country's history as hospitable and hostile to immigrants and refugees reminds us of the biblical accounts of the people of God as a pilgrim people. As Christians we are reminded that time and again in the Hebrew Scriptures, the people are praised or judged by whether the stranger within the gate is welcomed or rejected. Even in the New Testament these truths of faith are frequently re-echoed. This is particularly true of the Epistle to the Hebrews. Since Christ fused his lot and future with the hungry, the thirsty, the stranger, the naked, the sick and the prisoner, as American Christians our calling on this issue is clear.

91

Towards a Theology of Mission in the U.S. Puerto Rican Migrant Community: From Captivity to Liberation

David Traverzo

The purpose of this article is to suggest some critical parameters in the formulation of a theology of mission within Hispanic American reality and the Puerto Rican migrant community in particular. We will first address the existential plight of the people that will offer a context from which to do theology and mission. When examining the life situation of the Puerto Rican people, we will identify the U.S. mainline experience represented in an urban center as New York City. The Island background will also be identified in order to provide a backdrop for the fact that 2/5 of a nation has been uprooted from its homeland.

We will submit that the process for social transformation is fundamentally within a paradigm of neocolonial captivity. A new faith orientation amid a context of exile in the U.S. will be proposed in order to respond to the context and its challenges.

The Puerto Rican Plight in North American Society

The Hispanic American community in this country has been identified as one of the fastest-growing populations in the U.S. Approximately 20 million Hispanic Americans are expected to have a significant impact upon the life and destiny of this nation.[1] It is claimed that one out of twenty persons in the U.S. today is Hispanic.[2] It has been noted that the U.S. contains the fourth largest Spanish-speaking enclave in the world. In contrast to this population boom is another side of reality: the desolating effects of poverty. Succinctly, in this country Hispanic people in general are substantially poorer than the U.S. population as a whole. Of all the constituent Hispanic groups in the country, the Puerto Rican population in particular suffers the highest indices of impoverishment and social misery.[3] It remains a grievous fact that the Puerto Rican community in the U.S. is at the bottom rung of the nation's socioeconomic ladder.[4]

The city of New York perhaps represents the quintessence of this dilemma. In an urban center like this, poverty, social alienation and despair are manifested as symptoms of a greater evil --the contradiction of neocolonial

---

1. "It's Your Turn in the Sun," *Time* (October 16, 1978), p. 5. Hereafter *Time*.

2. U.S. Commission on Civil Rights, *Puerto Ricans in the Continental United States: An Uncertain Future* (October, 1975), p. 5. Hereafter *Uncertain Future*.

3. *Ibid.*, pp. 8-9.

4. This refers to the comparative figures of medium income levels, below low-income levels and formal educational achievements. Cf. especially note number three in *Uncertain Future.*

subjugation. In essence, these manifestations range from youth drug trafficking and addiction, child abuse, prostitution, alcoholism, juvenile delinquency, to rat-infested apartments, exploitative landlords, inferior schooling and violent crimes, both in the streets and in the homes. Although these problems are not unique to an urban environment, nevertheless, the overtness and dramatic effects of their intensity are extremely visible in the city.[5] The context of the "ghetto" or the "inner-city" is an area where we find extreme conditions of poverty and oppression. In a city such as New York, numbers of people experience and learn to internalize a sense of powerlessness and alienation. The people become noted for their absence of significant political participation and economic access to the means of production and the basic goods and services. The people in the city may thus be characterized for their poverty participation. In sum, they are cut off rom the centers of power.[6]

Within such a scenario we may situate the Puerto Rican migrant community in New York City. As one of the largest national ethnic groups in New York, this migrant community represents over 10% of the city population where Puerto Rican children constitute approximately 23% of the public school system.[7] In spite of such a numerical presence, the Puerto Rican community in the city is still identified as representing "the largest --and most beleaguered-- national group among the estimated 2.6 million Hispanics in and near New York City."[8]

In terms of median income, it has been shown that Hispanic families in the U.S. are substantially poorer than the overall population. Puerto Rican families qualify to be the poorest among all Hispanic groups.[9] Over 38% of Puerto Rican families in the U.S. live below the poverty level. This is close to $6,000 for a family of four, and may be compared to Spanish origin families (23.1%) and non-Spanish origin families (8.7%).[10] While such median income levels reflect a situation of deprivation, the estimated income for Puerto Rican families rose from $3,811 to $7,669 (1959-1976). In contrast, the white family income ($15,176) is twice as high as the figures for Puerto Rican families.[11] When comparing such median family income in New York City, the income rate has been reported as low as $3,460 for Puerto Rican migrant families in Manhattan.[12]

---

5. Craig Ellison, "Cities, Needs and Christians," Craig Ellison (ed.), *The Urban Mission* (Grand Rapids: Eerdmans, 1974), p. 12.

6. Cf. Ellison, *op. cit.*, p. 12 for a definition of "inner" or "central-city" and Gaylord Noyce, *Survival and Mission for the City Church* (Philadelphia: Westminster Press, 1975).

7. *Uncertain Future*, p. 5.

8. *Time*.

9. *Uncertain Future*, p. 44.

10. Frank Bonilla and Ricardo Campos, "A Wealth of Poor: Puerto Ricans in the New Economic Order," *Daedalus* (Spring, 1981), p. 160. Hereafter *Daedalus*.

11. *Ibid.*

12. Ruby R. Leavitt, *Puerto Ricans, Culture Change and Language Deviance* (Tucson: University of Arizona Press, 1974), p. 173.

The income level disparity is also closely similar to the unemployment conditions. Labor participation rates for Puerto Ricans in the work force are lower than those of U.S. workers as a whole,[13] while unemployment rates appear to be higher among Puerto Rican youth, women, and men beginning work careers.[14]

Official unemployment records, however, do not reflect those that have abandoned the work force: the growing number of persons who have stopped looking for work, for they have lost hope of finding it. This escapes the census bureau statistics so that the conservative figures given by the government may be understood as a "relatively superficial index of the degree of labor market maladjustment that exists in a community."[15]

In the realm of formal education, the Puerto Rican migrant community suffers drop-out and delayed schooling rates that are among the highest for any social group in the U.S.[16] In New York City, Boston, and Chicago, such a condition has risen as high as 55%, 80% and 70% respectively.[17] In higher education, the national statistics represented a 5% college completion for Puerto Rican students in contrast to 28% for whites and 11% for Blacks. This phenomenon stands out in spite of the increased Puerto Rican enrollment throughout the country.[18] The aforementioned areas of income, unemployment, and educational inequality all point toward an experience in the U.S. that reflects a situation of powerlessness and social alienation.[19]

To understand better the present situation of the Puerto Rican migrant community, we might ask what are the root causes behind the poverty and the oppression. A brief historical sketch may help to unmask some of the forces that have uprooted and propelled approximately 2/5 of a nation.

The Migration Dilemma

The origins of Puerto Rican migration to the U.S. mainland may be traced as far back as the early 1800's. It is claimed that his migration began with "a slow trickle of craftsmen and merchants in the early part of the nineteenth century."[20] It is estimated that by the 1920's the Puerto Rican population in New York City had gone from 8,500 to over 45,000.[21] By 1930,

---

13. *Daedalus*, p. 157.

14. *Ibid.*

15. *Uncertain Future*, p. 48.

16. *Daedalus*, p. 162.

17. *Ibid.*

18. *Ibid.*, p. 163.

19. *Uncertain Future*, p. 123.

20. Puerto Rican Forum, *The Puerto Rican Community Development Project* (New York: Arno Press, 1975), p. 13.

21. The History Task Force: Centro de Estudios Puertorriqueños, *Labor Migration Under Capitalism: The Puerto Rican Experience* (N.Y.: Monthly Review, 1979), pp. 96-112. Hereafter *CEPR*; C.A. Iglesias, ed., *Memorias de Bernardo Vega* (Rio Piedras: Ed. Huracán, 1980).

it was reported that there were Puerto Rican migrants in all forty-eight states.[22]

The most dramatic shift occurred after World War II, and is often referred to as the era of the "big wave." Although between 1909 and 1940 the total volume of migrants that moved between Puerto Rico and U.S. was close to one million, nevertheless, the total number that remained in the U.S. was approximately 71,000.[23] In 1946 alone, an estimated 49,911 migrants were reported entering the U.S.[24] In just one decade 1/4 of a million persons migrated to the U.S. and by 1970 "some 615,000 persons emigrated to the mainland so that today two-fifths of the Puerto Rican population --nearly 2 million people-- live abroad."[25]

The question remains: why did such a massive population movement occur and how could we best understand its historical development? The field of Puerto Rican migration studies has attempted to confront this with a variety of answers that range from "poverty" and "population density" to "push-pull" factors and even suggesting that this is a migration "like any other."[26] Out of such studies has emerged what may be considered a "highly positive vision" of the origins and dynamics of the migration. The Puerto Rican migration is thus viewed by an influential sector of North American social scientists in light of social progress and job opportunities obtained --based on the promises of a liberal democratic capitalist order.

As opposed to the above perspective, there is another approach. The migration is hence interpreted as a manifestation of the decaying, hapless and contradictory economic order in Puerto Rican society. As Mortimer Arias has succinctly observed, the Puerto Rican "showcase of democracy" has resulted in the example of *the development of underdevelopment*. This is similar to what Eduardo Galeano has identified as five centuries of the pillage of a continent: *The Open Veins of Latin America.*[27] Poverty and wealth are understood as conflicting forces and the results have been that while power and might overcome, the weak and the powerless succumb. Poverty therefore thrives on account of intentional wealth and accumulation. Wealth proliferates due to the spoliation and plunder of the earth and its people.

---

22. *CEPR*, p. 146.

23. *Ibid.* Cf. table 4.6, p. 109.

24. Oscar Handlin, *The Newcomers: Negroes and Puerto Ricans in a Changing Metropolis* (Cambridge: Harvard University Press, 1959), and also Federico Ribes Tovar, *Handbook of the Puerto Rican Community* (New York: Plus Ultra Educational Publishers, 1970), p. 277.

25. *Puerto Rico: A People Challenging Colonialism --A People's Primer* EPICA Task Force, (Washington, D.C.: EPICA Task Force, 1976), pp. 21, 49. Hereafter EPICA.

26. C. Wright Mills, Clarence Senior, Rose Kohn Goldsen, *The Puerto Rican Journey: New York's Newest Migrant* (New York: Russell & Russell, 1950); Joseph Fitzpatrick, *Puerto Rican Americans: The Meaning of Migration to the Mainland* (Englewood Cliffs, NJ: Prentice Hall, 1971); Clara Rodríguez, *The Ethnic Queue in the United States: The Case of Puerto Ricans* (San Francisco: R & E Research Associates, 1974) and *CEPR*, pp. 15-31.

27. Eduardo Galeano, *Open Veins of Latin America: Five Centuries of the Pillage of a Continent* (New York: Monthly Review Press, 1973).

Capitalist development in Puerto Rican society has reached the level of heightened contradiction of which massive unemployment and abject poverty are the symptoms. U.S. expansion on the island, along with its corporate interests, have reaped enormous profits while the labor force, students, and the majority of the poor have experienced the social consequences of these political and economic forces. Historically, what has resulted is essentially:

1) The Consolidation of U.S. economic hegemony in Puerto Rico;

2) The justification of U.S. colonization through federal, executive and legislative actions;

3) The imposition of ultimate power expressed by economic and political control via U.S. military force.

To explain more in detail the quandaries of a continual level of unemployment in the last three decades, or the highest proportion of "idleness" in the world, or why there is a lower per capita income in Puerto Rico than in the poorest state in the Union, one must point to the real obstacles at work --a faltering economic order.[28] As the pattern of U.S. capital concentration rises or falls, so have unemployment and poverty conditions in Puerto Rican life.[29] This is clearly demonstrated within the rising unemployment rates from 250,000 in 1970 to 400,000 in 1974 and over 600,000 in 1976. In the last decade, this has about doubled. The rate of unemployment along with underemployment thus amounts to approximately 50% of the available labor force of Puerto Rico --a number close to 1 million or so, or one out of every two persons.[30]

Consequently, instead of experiencing a well-stabilized or functional economy, Puerto Rican society has encountered an industrialization program that has beset the Island with accompanying atmospheric pollution, water contamination, land destruction, a national debt that manages "to pay the interest on loans by additional borrowing"; and a local economic structure that "today finds itself in serious crisis."[31] It is out of such a societal crisis that 2/5 of an entire nation has been dispersed outside its own homeland, and scattered to the corners of the U.S.

The once hoped for "showcase of democracy" has been shattered as the Puerto Rican experience reflects the *development of underdevelopment.* The biblical paradigm of captivity by a foreign imperial power may serve to illumine the plight of such a form of imperialistic domination in the life of the Puerto Rican people.

---

28. *CEPR*, pp. 223-24.

29. *Daedalus*, p. 135.

30. EPICA, p. 47; *CEPR*, p. 139.

31. EPICA, pp. 45-46.

A Faith Response

In terms of the Christian Church and its mission within the existential reality of the Puerto Rican migrant community in the U.S., how can we attempt to understand the phenomena of captivity? In attempting to address the issue of captivity, Mortimer Arias says that:[32]

> The last decade has been hard on our people south of the Rio Grande, in political frustrations, economic exploitation, social oppression and military and police repression. We have been living in captivity in our own land! As in biblical times, a new theology has been born from our exile and out of our captivity --the theology of liberation. We have been rediscovering the God of Exodus, the Liberating God. Out of the depths of oppression and repression we may have something to share with Christians of the North, something of what the Lord has been saying to us through this dreadful experience.

The exile itself may be understood as one of the most traumatic experiences that occurred in the history of the people of God. It was a forced migration under Babylonian imperial domination. Deportations to a foreign land evoked feelings of abandonment and despair. An overall state of crisis engulfed the political, economic, and religious life of the people. Both State and Temple were overrun as the Empire wreaked havoc on the promises of God's protection from the enemy. The national theology and political hopes fro freedom were devastated by the oppressive forces of the Empire.[33]

At the same time, the exile period could also be considered a creative epoch in the history of the world.[34] The international struggle for power[35] forced the people of God to come to grips with the meaning of faith and history. From within the bowels of the Empire, human calamity came face to face with the revelation of God's liberating activity in history. From the grave of national annihilation, new hope was promised. The dry bones of political frustration, economic domination, social oppression, and religious idolatry would all be raised to new life as the Spirit of God would transform the state of siege into a new day of hope. The liberative power of the God of history declared to the people that a *new thing* was going to happen amid the state of national and spiritual chaos.

The Puerto Rican migrant community and the plight of Puerto Rican society may appear to be as problematic as the dry bones of the exile. At present, the apparently omnipotent grasp of the Empire continues to suffocate the historical realization of nationhood of hundreds of thousands of Puerto

---

32. *Ibid.*, p. ix.

33. John Bright, *A History of Israel*, (Philadelphia: Westminster Press, 1972), pp. 331ff.

34. Peter Ackroyd, *Exile and Restoration: A Study of Hebrew Thought of the Sixth Century B.C.* (Philadelphia: Westminster Press, 1968), p. 7.

35. Roland K. Harrison, *Introduction to the Old Testament* (Grand Rapids: Eerdmans, 1969), p. 806.

Ricans here in exile and abroad. A state of crisis is apparent as the foundations of faith and praxis bow down to the external forces of imperial domination and internal capitulation. Today, political opportunism, internal dissension, betrayal of a greater vision, and idolatry, (as in the case of Jehoiakim, Jehoichin, and Zedekiah during the sixth century B.C.E.) threaten to attack both our church and community when authentic liberation is sold for a bowl of porridge or substituted for specious activism.

In New York City alone, school district leaders, congressional and other political representatives, principals, teachers, and church leaders as a whole, appear impotent to offer prophetic direction for gong beyond survival and on towards meaningful hope and liberation.[36] There is evident a type of ideological enslavement to the patterns and practices of the civilizational ethos of the Empire. Where is the meaning of hope among many of our youth in their lifestyles of widespread teenage pregnancy, and as "crack" threatens to swallow up the community? Is our prophetic faithfulness as a people of faith confused with traditional religiosity? What is the path for authentic liberation amid a context of captivity?

It was Orlando E. Costas who once declared that we the Hispanic Church must go beyond psychological, cultural, and social survival and identity formation, and move onto integral liberation. Costas further reverberated that in the church, temporal powers are relativized and the ultimate meaning of human history is grasped. In the church we "cease to be intimidated by the powers of this world --whether political or economic, social or cultural. [We] are set free . . . and where the spirit of the Lord is, there is freedom --freedom from the ambiguity and predicament of history, freedom for the God who transcends all human lords and human thought, and for the world which God has promised in Christ, beyond injustice, oppression, and death."[37]

Consequently, this freedom and courage to be is a militant response to a situation of captivity. It rejects the acceptance of the religion of the conquerors and the temptation to return to traditional cults and practices of old.[38] Rather, this new faith orientation accepts the prophetic interpretation that the divine word and the activity of God in history are validated as the paths of hope are carved out of the bedrock of impossibilities. The gods of the Empire do not have the last word.[39] Out of the disaster of imperial invasion, domination, and dehumanization, the God of the Exodus brings into being new life-giving possibilities that blossom in the deserts of hopelessness and oppression.

The plight of the Puerto Rican migrant community calls for a new commitment from a "new breed of Christians" who can redefine the nature

---

36. Orlando E. Costas, "Survival, Hope, and Liberation in the Other American Church: An Hispanic Case Study," in Ruy O. Costa, ed. *One Faith, Many Cultures: Inculturation, Indigenization, and Contextualization* (Maryknoll, NY: Orbis, 1988).

37. *Ibid.*, p. 144.

38. Ackroyd, *op. cit.*, p. 39f.

39. *Ibid.*, p. 41.

and mission of the church in the world.[40] This would consist of "a new presence of the Church." A few outstanding themes and characteristics of this new orientation would suggest that:

1) The Church fulfills a prophetic role of denunciation of social injustices in Latin American society.

2) There is an urgent need for a conscienticizing evangelization. Such a redefinition of evangelization "will free, humanize, and better [humanity] and will be nourished by the recovery of a living faith committed to human society.

3) "There arises . . . the urgent need for a profound renewal of the present ecclesial structures." This also includes "the need to change the current *lifestyle* of the clergy." This is in tune with "their commitment to the creation of a new society."

4) Lastly, "there is a new attitude --ever more lucid and demanding-- suggestive of a qualitatively different society and of basically new forms of the Church's presence in it."[41]

The crisis of neocolonial captivity suggests that a new faith orientation is imperative in order to break with the history of enslavement to the powers and principalities that dominate the structures, institutions and ideological formation of both the religious and national community. In the Puerto Rican migrant community, the role of the church can be no other than to serve as a liberating agent where deep-seated idolatry has replaced authentic worship and faith in the God of history. The proclamation of the Gospel requires a living faith that is set free to denounce injustice at all levels of social existence, and to pronounce new models and new meaning for ecclesial and community life. In response to the God who liberates from enslavement, the church is constrained to be an agent of social and spiritual transformation "to pluck up and to break down, to destroy and to overthrow, to build and to plant" (Jer 1:10). Out of the exile emerges the formation of a new community with a new heart and a new spirit. Freedom for the future irrupts out of the chaos. This new faith orientation will attempt to break the yoke of the death sentence that engulfs both State and Temple. A new Exodus points the way toward a new day of integral salvation.

Such an agenda for reconstruction and restoration will be rooted in what Costas refers to as "an ecclesiology of liberation." One that frees the church from "introversion, other-worldliness and churchism."[42] If indeed we

---

40. José Míguez Bonino, *Doing Theology in a Revolutionary Situation* (Philadelphia: Fortress Press, 1975), pp. xxi-xxviii; 1-83.

41. Gustavo Gutiérrez, *A Theology of Liberation* (Maryknoll: Orbis, 1973), pp. 114-119.

42. Costas, *op. cit.*, p. 144.

proclaim a faith that witnesses to the God of history, then even today, the God of Jesus the Christ is engaged in a historical project of doing *a new thing* as a new breed of Christian announces a new day of prophetic ministry amid a context of neocolonial captivity. At times this new faith orientation will be highly strident and even conflictual. It could be no other if it is to be faithful to the God of the prophets.

In the Puerto Rican migrant community, the prophetic role of the church is to denounce the very systems and spurious leadership that benefit from and perpetuate the state of captivity. This new faith is oriented toward the construction of a new social order where justice and fraternity exist.[43] A theology of mission in a context of such captivity announces a new presence of the church in solidarity with the aspirations for a day of national reconstruction and integral liberation. As Orlando Costas reminds us,[44] this is a vocation to fulfill as agents of hope and liberation.

> Therefore let us not be co-opted by the structures of Christendom but . . .
> let us be prophets of hope in a world of disillusionment and false dreams,
> pressing forward to a city of God --the world of true justice and real
> peace, of unfeigned love and authentic freedom . . .

Within the contextual reality of Hispanic American life and the impending forces of imperial power, let us strive to be in tune with the liberating spirit of God. Out task will be to discern not only the sign of the times but the moment of God as we are led out of captivity into the promise of authentic freedom and integral faith. In this we may trust and await hope.

---

43. "Los cristianos y la acción política: declaración de Jarabacoa," *Misión* 2 (Diciembre, 1983), pp. 38-43.

44. Orlando E. Costas, *Christ Outside the Gate: Mission Beyond Christendom* (Maryknoll, NY: Orbis Books, 1982), p. 194.

Nuclear Apocalypse and Metánoia: Christian Theology in the Light of Hiroshima and Nagasaki[1]

Luis N. Rivera Pagán

A New Idolatry

After the Second World War, several Jewish thinkers have stressed the need to restructure the theological discourse in the light of the crucial and tragic community suffering events of Auschwitz and Dachau.[2] According to Marc H. Ellis, the holocaust as an "experience of dislocation and death has provoked a crisis of faith, to the point where the language of transcendence seems irrelevant to many."[3]

It is perplexing that a similar "crisis of faith" did not occur in Christian theology: What does it mean to speak about God and divine love in the perspective of Hiroshima and Nagasaki as parables of the probable destiny of humanity? Maybe such a crisis did not take place because the atomic weapon was considered, as a reader wrote to the *Christian Century* editor, "a miracle of God" chastising Sodom and Gomorrah.[4] It was a weapon in the hands of Christians, used against infidels.

> Ever hear[d] of Sodom and Gomorrah? . . . God is no pink-tea grandmother. If men were to turn blind to destiny and prove too cowardly or too soft to defy piracy and hell, the Almighty himself would have to take a hand and wipe out earth's demons in order to salvage such civilization as we have. The atomic bomb was in truth God's --and man's-- miracle.

A theological analysis, not only political or economic, of the nuclear weaponry system is imperative for one fundamental reason: such a system is the most important contribution of the twentieth century to the history of idolatry. It is the modern fetish. It threatens not only to enslave, but to destroy humankind, to erase divine creation. It is *thánatos* with the diabolical claim of universal deadly hegemony. The cause for its resilience, despite the many criticisms it receives, lies in its mythical/demonological character. It constitutes an ominous idolatry, a technocratic fetishism. Truly an idol with technologically awful cosmicide potentialities. Its essence is best described by

---

1. Paper presented to the "Pastoral Theology and Psychology Conference: Resources for Justice-Based Peacemaking," June 19-23, 1989, Teplice, Czechoslovakia.

2. Richard Rubenstein, *After Auschwitz* (Indianapolis: Bobbs-Merril, 1966); Emil Fackenheim, *God's Presence in History* (New York: New York University Press, 1970); Irving Greenberg, "Cloud of Smoke, Pillar of Fire: Judaism, Christianity, and Modernity After the Holocaust," in Eva Fleischner (ed.), *Auschwitz: Beginning of A New Era?* (New York: KTAV, 1977); Marc H. Ellis, "Notes Towards a Jewish Theology of Liberation," *Liaisons Internationales* (Centre Oecuménique de Liaisons Internationales), No. 44, Winter 1987-88, pp. 13-23.

3. "Notes Towards a Jewish Theology of Liberation," p. 17.

4. Thomas F. Opie, letter to the editor, *The Christian Century*, March 27, 1946, p. 400.

an absurd paradox: it promises absolute redemption by threatening absolute destruction. As such it partakes of the nature of holiness as ascertained by Rudolf Otto: *mysterium tremendum, mysterium fascinans.*[5]

Robert Jay Lifton, the noted Yale University psychiatrist and author of one of the best books on the fate of the Hiroshima *hibakusha,*[6] describes very eloquently the idolatrous and religious nature of the nuclear military system:[7]

> Nuclearism is a secular religion, a total ideology in which "grace" and "salvation" --the mastery of death and evil-- are achieved through the power of a new technological deity. The deity is seen as capable not only of apocalyptic destruction but also of unlimited creation. And the nuclear believer . . . allies himself with that power and feels compelled to expound on the virtues of his deity. He may come to depend on weapons to keep the world going.

Nuclear Theology

The religious/idolatrous character of nuclear weapons posed a significant challenge to the Church. This was specially critical in the United States, the nation first to develop them. Paul Boyer, after studying the 1945-1950 reactions of North American ecclesiastical authorities to nuclear weapons, comes to this critical judgement:[8]

> It is surely not without significance that at the dawn of the atomic era, when values and attitudes were still in a formative stage, the nation's religious leaders, while clearly deeply troubled by the ethical implications of atomic weapons, failed to render a clear and unequivocal no to these new instruments of mass destruction.

This hesitancy, however, was changed into embracement after "Joe I", the first Soviet atomic explosion in 1949, and the bankruptcy of the illusions of nuclear monopoly. The religious character of the dependence upon nuclear weapons became evident in the active effort to legitimate theologically its possession and even possible military employment. There were two North American theologians who played an important role in this effort: the Protestant Reinhold Niebuhr and the Catholic John Courtney Murray, S.J. In the decisive first decades of nuclear deterrence, both criticized pacifism for its alleged inability to acknowledge human sinfulness, and promoted nuclear strength as a bastion against the aggressiveness of Adam's children, specially of his illegitimate offspring, the communists.

---

5. See Ira Chernus' illuminating book, *Dr. Strangegod: On the Symbolic Meaning of Nuclear Weapons* (Columbia, South Carolina: University of South Carolina Press, 1986).

6. *Death in Life: Survivors of Hiroshima* (New York: Random House, 1967).

7. *The Broken Connection: On Death and the Continuity of Life* (New York: Simon and Schuster, 1979), p. 369.

8. *By the Bomb's Early Light: American Thought and Culture at the Dawn of the Atomic Age* (New York: Pantheon, 1985), p. 229.

Niebuhr criticizes the "illusions" of pacifists and promoters of world government (among them Albert Einstein), and the "one world" movement. They, in his opinion, are unable to acknowledge that in the dispute between the United States and the Soviet Union:[9]

> The primary differences arise from a civil war in the heart of Western civilization, in which a fanatical creed has been pitted against a libertarian one . . . The immediate political situation requires that we seek not only peace, but also the preservation of a civilization which we hold preferable to the universal tyranny with which Soviet aggression threatens us . . . We may have pity upon, but can have no sympathy with, those who flee to the illusory security of the impossible from the insecurities and ambiguities of the possible.

The nuclear weapons in the hands of the United States, the only nation then with an atomic arsenal, are thus transfigured into a providential shield against the "universal tyranny" of the communist "fanatical creed." Certainly, the preservation of peace is an immediate goal. But it is predicated upon the primacy of "a civilization which we hold preferable," the Western Christian civilization. To the fulfillment of that task, nuclear weapons are consubstantial. Those who preach world government or nuclear disarmament are fleeing "to the illusory security of the impossible from the insecurities and ambiguities of the possible." They lack the sense of historical reality, the courage to face human sinfulness, the awareness of the unavoidable historical tragedy.

Niebuhr, maybe the most politically influential theologian in the history of the United States, wrote in the popular magazine *Life* an article significantly entitled "For Peace We Must Risk War," a resounding call to military strength. In it there are loud and clear resonances of Vegetius' strategic dictum *si vis pacem para bellum* ("if you want peace, prepare for war").[10]

The Jesuit theologian John Courtney Murray is even more explicitly anti-communist in his political theology. He promotes not only nuclear deterrence, but also the need to design strategies of nuclear "limited" wars.[11]

> The essential fact here is that Communism, as an ideology and as a power-system, constitutes the gravest possible menace to the moral and civilizational values that form the basis of "the West", understanding the term to designate . . . an order of temporal life that has been the product of valid human dynamisms tempered by the spirit of the Gospel . . .

The superiority of the West as a human civilization is based upon the fact that it is a culture infused by "valid human dynamisms" which, more to

---

9. "The Illusion of World Government," *Foreign Affairs*, Vol. 27, No. 4, April 1949, pp. 379-388.

10. "For Peace We Must Risk War," *Life*, September 20, 1948, pp. 38ff. The historian Walter LaFeber considers Niebuhr the theologian of the cold war. *America, Russia, and the Cold War, 1945-1966* (New York: John Wiley, 1967), pp. 40-43.

11. "Morality and Modern War," in William Clancy (ed.), *The Moral Dilemma of Nuclear Weapons* (New York: The Council on Religion and International Affairs, 1961), pp. 7-16.

the point from the perspective of a theologian, has been "tempered by the spirit of the Gospel." It might be thus called a "Christian" humanitarian civilization. Even if Murray might acknowledge that its relationship with other nations could be best described as imperial, it would nevertheless be a "Christian" empire. The defense of the West becomes thus a moral imperative. Against pacifism he stresses: "The problem is to refute the false antinomy between war and morality . . . War is still the possibility, not to be exorcised by prayer and fasting."[12]

History repeats itself. Murray's argument is similar to Augustine's justification of war against the barbarians in defense of the Roman Christian empire. War ceases to be contrary to the Sermon of the Mount. It becomes an unavoidable means to protect the imperial historical synthesis between the Christian symbols and the Western political institutions. This aggressive defense of Christian and humanist civilization, *mutatis mutandis*, is what Murray promotes, in the historically different context of the nuclear age.

The basic idea is not original. It is rather an attempt to restate the validity of the doctrine of just war in the atomic age.[13]

> Th[at] doctrine asserts, in principle and in fact, that force is still the *ultima ratio* in human affairs, and that its use in extreme circumstances may be morally obligatory *ad repellendam injuriam*. The facts assert that today this *ultima ratio* takes the form of nuclear force.

"Christian realism" must face the uncomfortable fact that "force is still the *ultima ratio* in human affairs." The Christian nations use force only when all other means are exhausted, only as *ultima ratio*, and only as a response to repel unjust aggressors --*ad repellendam injuriam*. Thus things happen, at least in the illusory history of the political theologian Murray, who never considers the possibility of an aggressive, unjust, colonialist Christian West. Not a word about the history of slavery and colonialism, or the misuse of Christian symbols for national expansion. Yet another forward step is taken by the Jesuit political theologian.[14]

> The facts assert that today this *ultima ratio* takes the form of nuclear force . . . The problem today is limited war . . . Since nuclear war may be a necessity, it must be made a possibility. Its possibility must be created.

The doctrine of the just war in the atomic age poses acutely the possibility, nay, even the necessity of using nuclear weapons. In 1949, when Niebuhr wrote the essay above analyzed, only the United State had nuclear weapons. Niebuhr could thus be confident in the doctrine of nuclear deterrence. A decade afterwards, the nuclear club had expanded. Murray thus has to face the ominous possibility of a nuclear war. He clearly perceives the contradiction between the indiscriminate destructive power os such weapons

---

12. *Ibid.*, pp. 12, 14.

13. *Ibid.*, p. 14.

14. *Ibid.*, pp. 14-15.

(it was the time of the huge multi-megatonic thermonuclear bombs), and the principles of discrimination and proportionality intrinsic to the doctrine of just war. But he refuses to accept the two apparently obvious implications: a) That the tradition of just war has become obsolete and the only alternative is "no war or total war." b) That the only possible rationality of nuclear weapons is to threaten with them, never to use them (the doctrine of deterrence as it evolved under the stress of the balance of terror).

On the contrary, Murray asserts the imperative to develop types of nuclear weapons and design strategies for their limited use. "Since nuclear war may be a necessity, it must be made a possibility. Its possibility must be created." Only if we can answer the *quaestio facti* --the viability of limited nuclear wars-- could we then proceed to solve the moral issue of the *quaestio iuris* --its legitimacy. This is the path in which the political theologian becomes a promoter of limited nuclear warfare.[15]

By treading that path, asserted the Jewish theologian Steven S. Schwarzschild, in a poignant answer to Murray:[16]

> The Church is deeper in the business of justifying war than ever in history. In the past, religious institutions have demanded that war be waged and blessed it while it was taking place, but now more is asked, nuclear war must be made a possibility by, among other things, education under the direction of a moral imperative and the construction of model limited wars in terms of --presumably theological-- conceptual analysis. The next step might be the formation of an Institute for the Theological Formulation of Atomic Military Strategy, known as ITFMS. Such an Institute would be the logical *reductio ad absurdum* of most contemporary theologizing on the problem of war.

This politico-theological linkage was of decisive significance for the ideological legitimation of the possession of nuclear weapons. This uncritical acceptance of the doctrine of nuclear deterrence in religious and ecclesiastical circles was facilitated by the historical coincidence of an intense critique to the naive anthropological optimism of theological liberalism, the grotesque demonstration of human evil and sinfulness, the Second World War, and the emergence of nuclear weaponry in the hands of a nation apparently moved by a "manifest destiny" to uphold the values and mores of Christian Western civilization. Once again, the doctrine of just war was put into the service of a Christian empire, predicated on the need for overwhelming power to moderate and neutralize the violence of the city of sin.

It is noteworthy, however, that Karl Barth, the most important protagonist in the so-called neo-orthodox theology, and the foremost critic of theological liberalism, refused to engage in this kind of atomic theological

---

15. A similar enterprise is propounded by another Catholic political theologian, a prominent student of the tradition of "just war." James Turner Johnson, *Can Modern War Be Just?* (New Haven: Yale University Press, 1984). For example, he is in favor of the "neutron" bomb, for its alleged tactical "usability."

16. "Theologians and the Bomb," in William Clancy (ed.), *The Moral Dilemma of Nuclear Weapons*, p. 24.

legitimation. In 1959, he sent a message to the European Congress for Outlawing Atomic Weapons, which met in London, in which he stated that:

> The intelligentsia in particular, along with a large group of church leaders, willingly devoted themselves to profound philosophical and theological discussions about such problems as the tragic dimension of man's existence in the atomic age, but they stubbornly avoid making any specific decision against atomic weapons.

Barth clearly perceived the intense anti-communism at the root of this paralysis of the prophetic spirit.[17]

> The reason for this inner contradiction is found in the fear of a supposedly greater threat aimed by the enemy of all that is most sacred . . . This threat, it is held, can be forestalled only by the recourse to the counter threat of atomic weapons.
> Unless the anxiety created by the ideological opposition between the West and the East is overcome, the result will be fateful and ominous: "the blasphemous and deadly development of atomic weapons."

The most important expression of this "nuclear theology" is the report prepared in 1950 by a commission of the Federal Council of Churches of Christ in America: "The Christian Conscience and Weapons of Mass Destruction." It was drafted in 1950, a time in which both the United States and the Soviet Union where rushing to the possible development of a thermonuclear bomb, a radical progress in the establishment of a universal destruction machinery. It was also a moment in which there was strong debate in the United States with respect to the desirability or morality of such a lethal device.[18] Known as "Dun Report," the commission was chaired by Bishop Angus Dun. It is the result of the deliberation of some of the most important Protestant theologians in the United States. Among its signers were theologians of the intellectual stature of Reinhold Niebuhr, John C. Bennett, and Paul Tillich.[19] The Report asserts,[20] in one of its crucial passages:

> For the United States to abandon its atomic weapons, or to give the impression that they would not be used, would leave the non-communist world with totally inadequate defense. For Christians to advocate such a policy would be for them to share responsibility for the world-wide tyranny that might result. We believe that American military strength, which must include atomic weapons as long as any other nation may possess them, is

---

17. Reproduced in Georges Casalis, *Portrait of Karl Barth* (Garden City, New York: Doubleday, 1967), p. 45.

18. On the thermonuclear weapon debate, Herbert York, *The Advisors: Oppenheimer, Teller and the Superbomb* (San Francisco: Freeman, 1976).

19. "The Christian Conscience and Weapons of Mass Destruction," A Report of the Special Commission appointed by the Federal Council of Churches of Christ in America, 1950. It is reproduced in *Christianity and Crisis*, Vol. 10, No. 21, December 11, 1950, pp. 161-168. Long quotations appeared also in *The Christian Century*, Vol. 67, No. 50, December 13, 1950, pp. 1489ff.

20. *Christianity and Crisis*, p. 165.

an essential factor in the possibility of preventing both world war and tyranny. If atomic weapons or other weapons of parallel destructiveness are used against us or our friends in Europe or Asia, we believe that it could be justifiable for our government to use them in retaliation with all possible restraint. We come to this conclusion with troubled spirits.

Nuclear weapons acquire providential meaning. They are technological effective means to avoid either of two evils; "world war and tyranny." Hopefully they can fulfill that function by means of the terror produced by their destructive potentialities. However, there is the ever-present possibility that deterrence might "fail." In that case it would be morally justifiable to retaliate with nuclear weapons, "with all possible restraint." The commission did not try to solve this last problem, how to retaliate with "restraint" by means of indiscriminate instruments of mass destruction.[21] Neither did it contemplate the possibility of a Western aggression.

The language of the Report is the Manichean discourse typical of the cold war. It calls the citizens of the United States to a crusade against Communism, for "Communism, is more than the tyranny and imperial ambitions of the Soviet rulers. It is also a political religion . . ." As a travesty of true religion, it is a formidable spiritual adversary. Thus, the need for "self-discipline and resolution and a tightening of our belts such as we have never achieved,"[22] for the nuclear weapons needed to maintain atomic hegemony will be anything but cheap. Christians, however, should be ready to sacrifice their individual comfort for the sake of the nuclear fortress. This challenge cannot be avoided, for "since we believe that peace in the world must be sustained by power, we believe that peace in our world can be preserved only by the strength of the free world."[23]

Though not quoted directly, there are clear reminiscences in the Dun Report of the famous address read by Winston Churchill, on March 5, 1946, in Fulton, Missouri.[24] In that speech, spiced by Churchill's classical eloquence, the world is divided in two antagonical blocks: the East of oppression and aggression and the West of civil liberties (guaranteed by the Magna Carta and the American Bill of Rights, the English common law and the Declaration of Independence) and peace. Churchill defined the task in the precise way the Dun Report would: to avoid both tyranny and war. Fortunately, God has provided the United States with the talisman to exorcise both demons: nuclear

---

21. Two of the nineteen members of the commission refused to sign the Report. Robert L. Calhoun, of Yale University Divinity School, wrote a note arguing that the theory of a "just nuclear retaliation" cannot be considered Christian and criticizing the subordination that, in his opinion, the Report made of theological reasoning to criteria of military victory. The only woman of the commission, Georgia Harkness, lamented the lack of specific Christian moral orientation of the Report. *The Christian Century*, p. 1491.

22. *Christianity and Crisis*, p. 166.

23. *Ibid.*, p. 167.

24. Reproduced in Joseph Morray, *From Yalta to Disarmament: Cold War Debate* (New York: Monthly Review Press, 1961), pp. 43-50.

weapons. Churchill was speaking some years before the development of the Soviet nuclear arsenal ("God has willed that this shall not be").[25]

A Theological Critique

Only late in the nuclear age have atomic weapons been the object of critical theological debate. The efforts are still few and not very impressive. The importance of such theological critique, however, has been stressed by one of the founders of moderns peace studies, Johan Galtung, who, in an essay published while visiting lecturer at the Institute of Global Conflict and Cooperation of the University of California, studies the theological archetypes sustaining the foreign and military policies of the United States, and insists on the decisive significance of "changing the very conceptualization of God . . . If theology is the underpinning of aggressive foreign policy, then theology may also be its undoing."[26] A new theological perspective on the nuclear challenge is, according to Galtung, extremely relevant for both theological and political reasons.

The complexity of the task proposed by Galtung is formidable. The hegemony that nuclear deterrence, with its mythical symbolism and technological idolatry, has enjoyed during four decades reveals how deeply rooted it has become in the minds and spirits of the Christian West. Many would support the following devout statement of faith, as expressed by a nuclear deterrence believer:[27]

> We live in the age of deterrence. It is deterrence that constitutes the limiting condition of all our lives. And it is deterrence that forms the object of faith by which we have come to live. For we are nearly all believers in deterrence, though we may express a common faith in different ways . . . It is only a faith in deterrence that preserves continuity with a familiar past.

Gordon Kaufman is one of the few theologians who with imagination and courage has faced the challenges posed by the nuclear threat, in 1984, in a series of lectures to the University of Manchester, United Kingdom.[28]

Kaufman's view that the new human condition, characterized by the technological viability of extinction, demands a rethinking of traditional theological concepts and rationality. "We live now in a radically new historical period . . . It is necessary, therefore, for us to think through our religious symbolism afresh, in face of the horrific possibilities that confront us . . ."[29] This rethinking leads him to question the authoritarianism and heteronomy --deity as absolute power-- underlying Western theology. In a nuclear

---

25. *Ibid.*, p. 45. That *will of God* lasted only three more years.

26. *United States Foreign Policy: As Manifest Destiny* (University of California Institute on Global Conflict and Cooperation, 1987), p. 20.

27. Rovert W. Tucker, "Morality and Deterrence," in Russell Hardin, et. al., *Nuclear Deterrence: Ethics and Strategy* (Chicago: The University of Chicago Press, 1985), p. 53.

28. *Theology for a Nuclear Age* (Manchester, UK: Manchester University Press, 1985).

29. *Ibid.*, p. 53.

technocratic age the doctrine of divine sovereignty has to be recasted, for it has historically led to the conception of the *imago dei* as holder of absolute power, which in a perverse way, is expressed not as potentiality of *creatio ex nihilo*, but as *potestas annihilationis mundi*.

Kaufman's recasting of theological concepts has been considered too radical by more conservative authors.[30] Yet, his is the merit of seriously stressing that the nuclear predicament demands a new reflection on the meaning of the most fundamental Christian symbols and concepts. Apart, however, from the judgement merited by his different specific conceptual proposals, such as his reformulation of theological methodology as "imaginative construction" or "creative activity of the human imagination,"[31] his emphasis on the nuclear threat as a *religious* and *theological* issue, not to be reduced to political an economic terms, is a fair and proper statement.

As the future of *homo sapiens* is radically put in doubt, by means of a technological system with the capability drastically and globally to menace the *imago dei*, the perennial human condition, its tragedy and sinfulness, is revealed from a new perspective, which poses us the demand to think, to act and to be in new ways. Radical challenges to human existence and its ultimate destiny are also, and even primarily, theological problems.

Kaufman stresses the imperative urgency of a radical and global transformation or our thinking and acting, what the New Testament calls *metánoia*.[32]

> A dramatic and full transformation --a *metánoia*-- of our major social, political and economic institutions, of our ways of thinking and acting, of the very structures of our selves, is required. Devotion to God, loyalty to God . . . demands reflection on and action to bring about a *metánoia* in human life as a whole . . . since we humans now have the power to destroy human life on earth completely, what we do can have disastrous consequences for the divine life itself.

If Kaufman, from the perspective of academic theology, rediscovers the need for a radical and full *metánoia*, a similar perception came to Richard Barnet, when as a bright and promising young scholar he began working as consultant on national security affairs.

Barnet, author of several critical works about national security,[33] has written a brief memoir of his experiences as defense analyst for the Kennedy government.[34] After hearing an Air Force general speaking enthusiastically about a new "early warning system" that would give the United States

---

30. Cf. G. Clarke Chapman, *Facing the Nuclear Heresy: A Call to Reformation* (Elgin, Illinois: Brethren Press, 1986).

31. *Theology for a Nuclear Age*, pp. 20-28.

32. *Ibid.*, pp. 45ff. According to Kaufman, God's destiny is indissolubly linked with ours.

33. See, for example, *Real Security* (New York: Simon & Schuster, 1981).

34. "Of Cables and Crises," *Sojourners*, Vol. 12, No. 2, February 16, 1983, pp. 16-18.

President "an extra seven minutes" to decide whether to launch the missiles and bombers of the Strategic Air Command, Barnet realized:[35]

> That he was offering illusion instead of security. The biblical language of idolatry made far more sense as a description of what was happening than the language of nuclear strategy. There was no way out of the race to destruction except somehow to transcend it.

Faced with the awful power of nuclear idolatry, Barnet rediscovers the validity of the biblical symbols and concepts, and the requirement to rethink their historical relevance, as a basic conviction in the resistance against the hegemony of nuclear deterrence.[36]

> The Christian faith was becoming important in my life. The foolishness of God --that men and women could live in the world without destroying or threatening to destroy one another, that security could never be found in planning for mass murders-- was a surer anchor than the "realism" that seemed to lead only to more fear and eventual annihilation. I began to see that the way of the national security managers was not only irrational but blasphemous. Ignorant men were taking delight in playing God . . . I began to see war games, war plans, and all the paraphernalia, of bureaucratic homicide as symptoms of a profound spiritual sickness.

Barnet discerns in the nuclear discourse the human quest for absolute security, the magic formula for total power, which always degrades itself into illusory idolatry. Humanity worships its new technological idols in a necrological religiosity, abdicating on the altar of global death its liberty and spiritual autonomy. On the basis of this perception, Barnet finds in the struggle against idolatry by Old Testament prophets the hermeneutical key for the proper understanding of the deep spiritual roots of nuclear deterrence.

Barnet rediscovers thus the contemporaneity of the prophetic battle against the cult of Moloch, with its never-ending demands for human sacrifices. The prophets call the people to repentance, what the New Testament would conceptualize as *metánoia*, to abandon the illusion of idolatry and to trust only in the God that created the heavens and the earth. Barnet was thus envisioning something similar to what the Old Testament scholar Norman K. Gottwald was writing about also in the period of the Kennedy government:[37]

> The Christian nuclear pacifist stands in the prophetic tradition of ancient Israel; he says "Turn!" [*metánoia*]. . . He does not believe that the way will be found or the burdens shouldered unless man gains the courage to cast away the fear-producing and fear-incarnation instruments of mass death --false gods which he clutches in superstitious compulsion.

---

35. *Ibid.*, p. 18.

36. *Ibid.*

37. Horman K. Gottwald, "Nuclear Realism or Nuclear Pacifism?," in Donald Keys (ed.), *God and the H-Bomb* (New York: Bellmeadows Press, 1961), p. 72.

Barnet stresses the need for an integral liberation from the bondage of nuclear idolatry. The required task is not to make some superficial rearrangements (e.g., the INF treaty). The demand is for a genuine transformation, a true *metánoia*, a radical and full spiritual and existential turning around. Barnet, political scientist and national security analyst, attempts a religious and theological interpretation of the famous Albert Einstein dictum about new ways of thinking.[38]

> Within the hermetic system of nuclear rationality there were no solutions. Every good idea or disarmament had its own equally plausible objection. We need a change of heart as a people . . . The idea of *metánoia* became much more important in my thinking . . . When Einstein said at the dawn of the atomic age that everything had changed but our ways of thinking, he was posing an essentially religious challenge.

Only a transformation of such a profundity and radicality can save us from the shadows of Armageddon.[39]

38. "Of Cables and Crises," p. 18.

39. For space limitations, I leave out of consideration the fertile theme of the possible relationships, convergences and divergences between the biblical concept of *metánoia* and the now popular Soviet idea of *perestroika*.

Una perspectiva bíblico-teológica sobre la mujer en el ministerio ordenado

Minerva Garza Carcaño

A pesar de que al presente la Iglesia Metodista Unida tiene tres mujeres en el episcopado, casi 30 superintendentas de Distrito y alrededor de 2,000 mujeres en el ministerio ordenado, todavía hay en mi denominación quien se sorprende cuando se habla de mujeres en el ministerio. Estamos acostumbrados a un clero masculino. Además de la sorpresa, nuestra respuesta a tal "fenómeno" toma varias caras: en ocasiones la curiosidad nos lleva a preguntar sobre la fuente de inspiración del llamado de nuestras hermanas que se dedican al ministerio: "Y Ud. hermana, por qué entró al ministerio?" --se oye preguntar con cierta indredulidad y cierto prejuicio.

Algunos de nosotros y nosotras nos alegramos y afirmamos que la presencia de Dios sí se manifiesta a través de mujeres en el ministerio. Para otros esto es más difícil. La noticia de que recibirán una "pastora" en el nuevo año conferencial ha causado enojo, tristeza, rechazo y algunas otras emociones en iglesias no muy lejanas. Triste es la situación que causa tal reacción, porque la realidad es que la mujer siempre ha sido parte del ministerio de la comunidad de fe. Dios ha llamado, está llamando, y seguirá llamando a mujeres a su Santo Ministerio. ¡Ay de nosotras quienes oigamos el llamado y no respondamos! ¡Ay de nosotros quienes seamos obstáculos al llamado del prójimo, sea mujer u hombre!

Muchas veces usamos la falta de ejemplos femeninos en la Biblia como razón por la cual no afirmar la mujer en el ministerio. Si los líderes del pueblo escogido y de la iglesia primitiva como se relata en le historia bíblica, eran principalmente hombres, entonces: el ministerio es para el hombre.

Sí, es cierto que en comparación al lugar que se le da al hombre en la Biblia la mujer recibe poca atención. Pero la razón de esto no es la falta de la participación de la mujer en el ministerio, como el menosprecio que la cultura en la cual se escribió la Biblia y la interpretación bíblica cerradamente masculina han dado al papel de la mujer. Puesto de otra manera: hemos preferido afirmar, recordar, escribir, y predicar sobre la historia de hombres (varones) de fe. A pesar de esto, la historia de la mujer de fe se proclama por medio de las Escrituras.

En compañía de los profetas y de los líderes del pueblo de Israel encontramos a la profetisa Miriam; proclamadora de la liberación de Dios: "Y Miriam la profetisa, hermana de Aarón, tomó un pandero en su mano, y todas las mujeres salieron en pos de ella con panderos y danzas. Y Miriam les respondía: Cantad a Jehová, porque en extremo se ha engrandecido; ha echado en el mar al caballo y al jinete" (Ex 15:20-21). Miriam fue líder entre los grandes. Yavé mismo afirma el ministerio de Miriam al hablar con Israel: "... yo (Yavé) te hice subir de la tierra de Egipto, y de la casa de servidumbre te redimí; y envié delante de ti a Moisés, a Aarón y a Miriam" (Miq 6:4). Entre los sabios recordamos a Débora cuya sabiduría era dada por Dios y reconocida por el pueblo: "En aquel tiempo, Débora, una profetisa, mujer de Lappidot, era juez en Israel... y los Israelitas subían donde ella para resolver sus pleitos" (Jue 4:4-6).

Veinte años había sufrido el pueblo de Débora bajo la cruel opresión de los cananeos. Los Israelitas clamaban a Yavé porque el enemigo "tenía novecientos carros de hierro" (Jue 4:3). Yavé escuchó el clamor de los suyos y por medio de Débora los dirigió a la plena libertad. Un hombre llamado Barac acompañó a Débora a la cabeza de las fuerzas armadas de Israel pero al fin, fueron dos mujeres, Débora y Jael (Jue 4-5), a quienes Dios usó para vencer la opresión del pueblo escogido.

En el Nuevo Testamento nos damos cuenta de que la mujer también puede predicar efectivamente. Jn 4:39 nos dice que "muchos samaritanos de aquella ciudad creyeron en él (Jesús el Cristo) por las palabras de la mujer que daba testimonio". La mujer es la samaritana a quien Cristo ofreció "del agua que brota para vida eterna" (Jn 4:14). Los discípulos se sorprendieron de que el Maestro hablara con una mujer (Jn 4:27), pero Jesús la salva y le ordena, no sólo que escuche sino que también predique.

Más adelante, hagamos memoria de Priscila. En la Epístola a los Romanos, el apóstol Pablo da reconocimiento a esta mujer de fe: "Saludad a Prisca y Aquila, colaboradores míos en Cristo Jesús. Ellos expusieron sus cabezas para salvarme. Y no soy yo sólo en agradecérselos, sino también todas las iglesias de la gentilidad; saludad también a la Iglesia que se reúne en su casa" (Ro 16:3-5). En los Hch de los Apostoles, Romanos, I Co, y II Timoteo, encontramos la historia de Priscila o "Prisca", como es llamada con afecto. Descubrimos que era una evangelista, predicadora, maestra de las escrituras, colaboradora de Pablo. En ningún momento le dice Pablo a Priscila que oiga la instrucción en silencio, en sumisión o que no le permite enseñar. Al contrario, la afirma por su valor y su consagración al ministerio del Evangelio de Dios.

Y, ¿qué de Sara, Rebeca, Rut, Ana, Julda, Tamar, María, Marta, Lidia, y Dorcas? La lista no termina aquí. Incluye a todas las mujeres de fe que por palabra y acción han dado testimonio de la grandeza y poder de nuestro Dios y que han sido llamadas y han recibido poder para servir en el ministerio del Reino de Dios. ¿Cuándo fue la última vez que en nuestras iglesias se predicó un sermón o se tuvo un estudio bíblico en el cual se hizo mención de una mujer de fe? Si no nos acordamos o si hace mucho tiempo, nosotros y la iglesia estamos recibiendo sólo parte de la historia de la fe.

Veamos un poco más de este asunto de que nos ha llegado solamente parte de la historia bíblica. ¿Por qué ha sucedido? ¿Por qué es que solamente parte de la historia ha recibido énfasis? y ¿por qué es que es la historia masculina? La misma historia cultural y religiosa del mundo bíblico nos ayuda a encontrar respuesta.

En la cultura del tiempo bíblico la mujer era considerada persona sin derechos, inferior al varón, e importante sobre todo por su habilidad de tener y procrear hijos varones. Aunque hay lugares en la Biblia donde la mujer es presentada por su inteligencia y sabiduría, por lo general el valor de la mujer se medía por la ayuda que le rendía al hombre... padre, esposo, hijo. La cultura era patriarcal --en otras palabras, el poder y la autoridad se encontraban en las manos del padre, el patriarca.

La mujer era persona sin derechos, viviendo siempre bajo la autoridad de un hombre u otro. Mientras soltera la autoridad de su vida era su padre. Cuando se casaba la autoridad pasaba a su esposo. Si enviudaba y tenía hijos varones, esos hijos llegaban a tener autoridad sobre ella, y si no tenía hijos varones entonces su vida era transferida a manos del pariente varón más cercano; y en la ausencia de parientes varones quedaba a la misericordia de los varones de la comunidad. Sharon Neufer Emsweiler muy perceptivamente menciona en su libro de estudio *The Ongoing Journey: Women and the Bible* que "la mujer seguía siendo por toda su vida una menor legal sin la posibilidad de jamás asumir responsabilidad por sí misma o su familia" (pág. 21). Aunque la mujer no era esclava en términos técnicos, sí era considerada propiedad a lo menos en los casos de esposa y esposo siendo en esa relación, propiedad de su esposo (Ex 20:17). Si era maltratada por padre o esposo la mujer no tenía absolutamente ningún recurso de defensa o protección (Gn 19:8; Jue 19:1-30; II S 13:1-22).

Dentro del cuadro religioso del pueblo de fe, la mujer se encontraba a las orillas dando apoyo a la participación de los varones en su vida. Para comenzar, el pertenecer a la comunidad del pacto requería circuncisión, algo limitado a los varones. El sacerdocio estaba compuesto netamente por varones los cuales determinaban los rituales y las leyes. Aun Dios era presentado en términos masculinos.

Rituales de pureza como los presentados en Lv 12 también mantenían a la mujer al margen de la comunidad y sus actividades. En la menstruación y en el parto, la mujer era considerada inmunda. Durante estos días y los subsecuentes días requeridos para su purificación a la mujer no se le permitía participar en las actividades de la comunidad de fe. El capítulo 15 de Lv nos da a saber que había momentos en la vida del varón cuando su condición también se consideraba inmunda. Lo particular que se menciona en Lv 15 es el flujo de semen. Cuando había flujo de semen el hombre se encontraba inmundo. Lo interesante es la diferencia en los requisitos de purificación. En el caso del hombre, el período de purificación era "hasta la noche" (Lv 15:5). En el caso de una mujer en menstruación su período de purificación era siete días. En el parto si tenía un varón, la mujer era inmunda siete días y necesitaba 33 días para su purificación, *pero*, si daba a luz una hembra, la mujer era inmunda 14 días y su purificación tomaba 66 días. Durante todos estos días de inmundicia y purificación la comunidad se justificaba en la exclusión de la participación de la mujer así quitándole oportunidades de expresión y crecimiento espiritual y social.

La mujer era vista principalmente por su habilidad de parir niños masculinos, así continuando el linaje de la familia del esposo, y por dar apoyo al elemento masculino de la sociedad. En cuanto a la cultura y las estructuras de fe del pueblo escogido la mujer tenía un papel secundario e inferior al hombre y siendo así, no era importante afirmarla o recordarla como se daba

114

afirmación y se tenía memoria de los varones. Era un mundo masculino. Hasta Dios era representado en forma de varón.

Ahora, por un momento, examinemos el contexto mayor --la religiosidad de los pueblos paganos en cuya presencia y bajo cuya influencia se encontraba Israel. Estudios y excavaciones de las religiones del mundo antiguo tan temprano como el año 25,000 antes de Cristo, nos dan a saber que las primeras imágenes del ser divino eran imágenes femeninas. Leonard Swidler en su libro *Biblical Affirmations of Women* comenta que "Todas las áreas del Mundo Antiguo donde se encontraban civilizaciones mayores (es decir sociedades complejas donde se desarrollan pueblos y ciudades, acompañados por el desarrollo de diferentes culturas) demuestran fuerte evidencia de haber sido inicialmente adoradoras de diosas" (pág. 22). Entre estas civilizaciones se encuentran las civilizaciones de la región del Mediterráneo donde viene a nacer y crecer la comunidad del Antiguo Testamento.

Hay varias razones para la imagen femenina de la presencia divina, pero la mayor entre ellas parece ser el aspecto de la fertilidad asociado con el sexo femenino, fertilidad de la cual toda vida depende. Todo esto en un tiempo cuando la humanidad dependía principalmente de la tierra y sus frutos. Por miles de años las diosas reinaron con completo dominio. No es hasta el desarrollo de la ganadería donde surge como importante el papel de la paternidad que el mundo comienza a reevaluar las representaciones de sus dioses. James Cult en su obra *Cult of the Mother Goddess* nos dice que: El papel del dios (masculino) avanzó a uno de igualdad y en ciertos casos, de superioridad a aquel de la diosa bajo el impacto de olas de ataques Indo-Europeos que dependían de la ganadería y cuyas culturas por su manera de vivir habían llegado a expresarse en formas patriarcales y adoptado una imagen masculina para sus dioses". Esto alrededor del año 2.000 A.C. Sin embargo, a pesar de la imposición de dioses masculinos, la diosa persiste como figura divina.

Durante los tiempos del Antiguo Testamento nos damos cuenta de que la lucha constante era la de mantener la fidelidad del pueblo escogido para con el Dios de Israel. Una de las atracciones o distracciones era el dios Baal; pero fuerte también era la influencia de diosas, entre ellas las diosas Astoret y Asera. Los hebreos por largos años tuvieron que luchar contra la influencia de dioses paganos y muy especialmente la influencia de la adoración de diosas. En I R 11:5 encontramos que "...Salomón siguió a Astoret, diosa de los sidonios". Como consecuencia de esto, Dios manda mensaje de juicio a Israel por medio del profeta Ajías (I R 11:31-33). En otro momento el profeta Isaías proclama que Israel será castigado y su mirada quitada "...de los altares que hicieron sus manos, y no mirar a lo que hicieron sus dedos, no a los símbolos de la (diosa) Asera, ni a las imágenes del sol" (Is 17:8). Jeremías le reclama a Judá que su "pecado escrito está con cincel de hierro y con punta de diamante; esculpido está en la tabla de su corazón y en los cuernos de sus altares, mientras sus hijos se acuerdan de sus altares y de sus imágenes de Asera", y que sus "tesoros serán entregados al pillaje por su pecado". En II R 17:10-11 leemos que Israel "levantó estatuas e imágenes de Asera en todo collado alto y debajo de todo árbol frondoso... y quemaron incienso... e hicieron cosas muy malas para provocar a ira a Jehová". I y II de Reyes e Isaías están llenos de referencias a las diosas paganas; pero también encontramos tales referencias en Ez, II de Cr, Os y como ya hemos mencionado, en Jer.

Quisiera sugerir que por la cultura patriarcal y machista y la lucha contra las religiones paganas que tendían a enfocarse en diosas e imágenes femeninas, la comunidad de fe se enfocó en lo masculino de Dios y da su apoyo y atención al elemento varonil del carácter de Dios en el desarrollo de su historia y en la memoria de ella. Sin embargo, y a pesar de una historia cultural y religiosa que presenta el sexo femenino en forma negativa y a lo menos inferior, las Sagradas Escrituras afirman lo femenino como algo bueno e importante en el entendimiento de Dios y en el propósito divino.

Comenzando con Gn 1:27 se nos dice que "Dios creó al ser humano a su imagen, a imagen de Dios lo creó; varón y hembra los creó". Tanto el varón como la hembra son criaturas de Dios hechos a su imagen y semejanza. Implícita en la obra creativa está una bendición de igualdad para el varón y la hembra. Dios no establece jerarquía de preferencia o poder al crear a los seres humanos, hembra y varón, sino que elige manifestarse en la naturaleza de ambos.

En otras expresiones de la presencia de lo divino, Dios es presentado como poderoso guerrero, como esposo, rey, señor --definiciones masculinas, y definiciones comúnmente usadas para describir a Dios aun hoy día. *Pero* la Biblia también habla de Dios como una mujer poderosa. Is 42:14-16 dice que Dios "dará voces como la que está de parto; asolará y devorará juntamente, convertirá en soledad montes y collados... y guiará a los ciegos, por camino que no sabían".

En Dt 32:18, en el cántico de Moisés, la imagen de Dios es de una madre que da a luz hijos e hijas: "De la Roca que te creó (parió) te olvidaste; te has olvidado de Dios tu Creador". El Salmo 22:9 presenta a Dios como partera: "pero tú eres el que me sacó del vientre; El que me hizo estar confiado desde que estaba a los pechos de mi madre". En Gn 3:21 Dios es una costurera para su creación: "Y Jehová Dios hizo al hombre y la mujer túnicas de pieles y los visitió". Y en el Salmo 123:2 Dios es tanto señora como señor: "He aquí como los ojos de los siervos miran a la mano de sus señores, y como los ojos de la sierva a la mano de su señora, así nuestros ojos miran a Jehová nuestro Dios, hasta que tenga miserircordia de nosotros".

Todo esto no quiere decir que Dios pueda ser caracterizado por completo con atributos femeninos y/o masculinos. Dios es también luz, amor, y como el águila. Lo que sí quiere decir es que Dios no puede ser limitado a una imagen masculina y que si Dios mismo escoge revelarse en imágenes femeninas, entonces tampoco puede ponerse a la mujer en una papel secundario al del hombre.

La memoria bíblica ha sido muy selectiva pero ni logra eliminar la afirmación que Dios mismo da a la imagen femenina o la parte que Dios da para la participación de la mujer en la sociedad humana en general o en las cosas de Dios en lo particular. Y no hay mejor afirmación de esta verdad que el testimonio que recibimos de la perfecta revelación de Dios --Jesús mismo.

Jesús promovía la igualdad entre mujeres y hombres; su trato con la mujer era basado primeramente en el hecho de que ella era un ser humano; y estaba dispuesto a quebrantar las costumbres sociales para actuar a base de sus convicciones.

Los evangelios jamás cuentan de algún momento en el cual Jesús haya tratado a la mujer como un ser inferior al varón. Aun más, cuando recordamos lo restrictivo que eran los tiempos y la cultura del judaísmo palestino de los días de Jesús, el hecho de que Jesús no haya asumido la actitud de la superioridad masculina es extraordinario.

A la mujer, por ejemplo, no se le permitía estudiar las Escrituras, la Torá. Un rabí del primer siglo se expresó de la siguiente manera: "Las obras de la Torá deben ser quemadas antes de ser encomendadas a una mujer. Quien enseñe a su hija Torá es como aquel quien le enseña lascivia". La mujer no era incluída en la adoración, y no se le permitía dar testimonio. Un buen hombre no hablaba con una mujer en público. Un rabí no le dirigía la palabra ni aun a su esposa o hija si se encontraba caminando por la calle.

Sin embargo, Jesús públicamente rechazó estas costumbres opresivas. Aun siendo rabí, Jesús en un buen número de ocasiones se encuentra en público hablando con mujeres, aun mujeres de mala fama. Y hablaba con ellas no como objetos inferiores sino que como personas de valor. Tenemos como ejemplos sus encuentros con la samaritana quien entre sus fracasos tenía la triste historia de haber sido casada y divorciada repetidas veces. Tenemos también el relato de la mujer tomada en adulterio y la historia de María Magdalena.

Jesús también rechazó la prohibición judía en contra de que las mujeres dieran testimonio. Por ejemplo, su primera apariencia después de su resurreción fue a mujeres a quienes comisionó para dar testimonio a los once.

De semejante manera Jesús públicamente tomó una posición contraria al antiguo tabú del flujo de sangre. Esto vemos claramente en su respuesta a la mujer que había sufrido de un flujo de sangre por 12 largos años. Jesús la sana pero no queda satisfecho con sanarla. Usa la oportunidad para llamar la atención de todos al hecho de que ella lo había tocado, y que a pesar del dictamen del ritual que al ser tocado por ella él quedaba inmundo, él la había sanado y ponía en alto su fe. La implicación de las acciones de Jesús era entonces que él rechazaba la idea de que una mujer era inmunda por tener un flujo de sangre regularmente.

Otra idea que Jesús rechaza es la idea de que las actividades intelectuales son reservadas para el varón y que el lugar de la mujer se encuentra solamente en el hogar. Esto lo vemos en la visita de Jesús al hogar de Marta y María. Marta asume el papel típico de ama de casa y se entrega a los muchos quehaceres. Al otro lado María asume el papel identificado como el papel masculino: "se sentó a los pies del Señor y recibió sus enseñanzas". Marta aparentemente asume que María no ha tomado un papel apropiado y se queja con Jesús. Jesús no acepta el papel tradicional de la mujer que la limita a quehaceres y afirma el derecho de María de escoger dar su tiempo a las actividades intelectuales y espirituales. Jesús dice: "María ha escogido la mejor parte", y firmemente añade, "no será tomada de ella".

Así que aun más allá de las afirmaciones de los tiempos veterotestamentarios, con lo que hace y dice Jesús, no hay manera o lugar para el menosprecio de la mujer, no hay justificación para relegarla a un papel sedundario, y no hay razón por la cual quitarle el privilegio de servir a Dios, ya sea como predicadora o de otra manera.

¿Por qué es entonces que casi 2,000 años después de Jesús seguimos enfretando discrimación en contra de la mujer y viendo grandes obstáculos ante ella, muy especialmente cuando escoge servir a Dios en el ministerio ordenado?

Creo que hay varias razones, pero para nuestra consideración quisiera que enfocáramos nuestra atención en una en particular. Y la razón que quisiera presentar es la razón de interpretaciones teológicas erróneas y problemáticas en cuanto a la naturaleza y papel de la mujer. Teologías desarrolladas en el movimiento de la historia cristiana.

Así como los escritores y primeros intérpretes de la Biblia fueron muy selectivos, prejuiciosos y gobernados por sus experiencias culturales y sociales, así también encontramos a teólogos en la historia cristiana que en muchos casos han presentado teologías muy pintadas por sus propias experiencias dentro de marcos culturales y sociales que ellos apoyan. Entre la teología de algunos teólogos y las sociedades de sus tiempos encontramos mucho apoyo mutuo. Por ejemplo, cuando Tertuliano dice que la mujer es la puerta del diablo, la sociedad se siente respaldada en oponerse a la mujer para que no llegue a asumir ningún papel de autoridad o influencia, siendo que ella es nada menos que instrumento del diablo. Cuando alguien como Agustín dice que la mujer no es hecha a la imagen de Dios, se afirma para todo el mundo que el varón es superior, la mujer inferior, y merecedora de un trato inferior. Y, ¿que se hace con el comentario de Tomás Aquino de que la mujer es un "varón mal parido"? La mujer es vista como pobre imitación del varón.

Llegando más cerca a nuestro tiempo, tomamos un momento para examinar la teología de Karl Barth. Fundamental en el pensamiento teológico de Barth es la revelación de Dios por medio de la "Palabra de Dios". Es el mecanismo por medio del cual Dios da una señal, dándose a conocer y así permitiéndole la oportunidad de conocer a Dios y a sí mismo por medio de El, quién es Dios. El énfasis cae sobre la idea de que Dios es el iniciador; es Dios quien obra. Dios y sólo Dios es el sujeto. El ser humano es el objeto. Establecida esta relación del sujeto divino y el objeto humano, entonces Dios obra y la humanidad simplemente recibe la acción divina. Este pensamiento teológico se expresa al nivel de relaciones humanas a lo menos en dos formas que definitivamente han influenciado la apertura o falta de apertura a la mujer en el ministerio ordenado.

En primer lugar vemos una influencia negativa por medio de la imagen que se ha establecido alrededor de la predicación. De acuerdo a Barth, Dios habla por medio de la palabra escrita, la palabra revelada en Jesucristo y la palabra predicada o proclamada. Pero es en la predicación, así como la concibe Barth, que vemos un efecto muy interesante que afecta la relación entre el hombre y la mujer. Durante la predicación el predicador asume el papel de sujeto mientras la congregación toma el papel del objeto. Hasta cierto punto se duplica esa relación de Dios como Señor sobre el ser humano, entre el predicador y la congregación, a lo menos en el evento de la predicación. En la persona del predicador se proyecta una imagen masculina de Dios y una relación de señorío sobre la congregación, la cual se ve en imagen femenina y como pasiva y dependiente. Una vez más podemos ver el control de lo que es posible conocer y la acción ya no solamente entre la relación divino-humana sino que esa relación de sujeto-objeto se transfiere a la relación entre varón y hembra. A partir de esto podemos comenzar a entender por qué aun nuestras abuelas hasta la fecha se escandalizan con la idea de que una mujer tome el púlpito y asuma la responsabilidad de ser portavoz de Dios. Si la mujer es objeto sin ninguna parte o manera dentro de sus capacidades para llegar al conocimiento de Dios, imposible le es ser representante de Dios.

¿De dónde toma Barth la idea de que es el varón quien ha sido escogido como predicador de Dios con exclusividad? Creo que de las selecciones y exclusiones de las generaciones bíblicas afirmadas por los prejuicios de su propio tiempo y cultura. Barth ha adoptado como norma la perspectiva patriarcal de la sociedad en la cual se escriben y por primera vez se predican las Buenas Nuevas. El prejuicio cultural es adoptado como parte de la autoridad teológica.

Una segunda influencia de la teología de Barth que afecta negativamente a la mujer y al hombre es la posición de Barth en cuanto a la distinción sexual entre el hombre y la mujer. La perspectiva de Barth es que la diferencia entre los sexos es algo natural y básico a la existencia humana. Aun más toma la postura de que el tratar de sobrepasar esta situación es entrar a una especie de "gnosis", una espiritualidad falsa. En lo superficial la postura de Barth no es nada radical. Sin embargo, cuando esto se pone en el contexto de lo anterior, del entendimiento de la relación de sujeto y objeto, este segundo punto de Barth hace nada menos que afirmar una relación en la cual el hombre es activo y la mujer pasiva.

Barth habla de orden. En su concepto de orden la relación entre el hombre y la mujer es una reflexión de la relación entre el hombre y Dios. El hombre inicia y la mujer responde. Hay entonces una super-ordenación del hombre y una sub-ordenación de la mujer. Bajo este esquema, el hombre tiene su lugar y la mujer el suyo, y el lugar de la mujer nunca es de iniciar en el orden de las relaciones. Siendo así, el púlpito es por definición lugar cerrado para la mujer. Una vez más vemos no un ordenamiento divino sino una simplificación de relaciones establecidas a partir de una perspectiva masculina.

Sirva como conclusión el decir que si nos compenetramos en las distintas etapas culturales humanas, las cuales son imperfectas y cambiantes, en nuestro escudriñar en la Biblia y en nuestros esfuerzos de, con la ayuda de Dios, entender el movimiento del Espíritu de Dios, encontraremos que Dios no discrimina, ni en contra del varón ni de la mujer. Que derrama su amor sobre ambos por igual, dotando a ambos sexos con dones y capacidades cuyo uso Dios llama para la bendición de su creación y la edificación de su Reino; llamando tanto a hombres como a mujeres a diferentes tareas incluyendo la tarea del ministerio ordenado.

Sigue ante nosotras el trabajo de escudriñar, de analizar, de pensar para vencer todo aquello que nos separa de Dios y su propósito para nuestras vidas. Hay que re-examinar la Biblia, las teologías que han llegado a nosotras, continuar nuestra contribución teológica, pero sobre todo, ser fieles a nuestro Creador y Redentor.

Summary

Women have always been part of the ministry of the community of faith. God has called, is calling, and will continue to call women into God's Holy Ministry.

We often use the lack of examples of women in the Bible as a reason not to affirm women in the ministry. It is true that, in comparison to the place that is given to men in the Bible, women receive little attention. But the reason for this is not so much the lack of participation of women in the ministry, as it is the way in which the culture in which the Bile was written, and the exclusively male interpretation of the Bible, have scorned the role of women.

In spite of this, the story of women of faith is proclaimed through the Scriptures. Sarah, Rebekah, Miriam, Deborah, Ruth, Hannah, Huldah, Tamar, Martha, the Samaritan woman, Priscilla, Lydia and Dorcas are among the women of faith who through word and action have witnessed to the greatness and power of our God.

Why is it that only part of the story has been emphasized? And why is it the male story? The cultural and religious history of the biblical world helps us to find the answer.

In the culture of biblical times women were considered persons without rights, inferior to men, and important only for their ability to have male children. On the religious scene, the woman was found on the periphery giving support to the participation of the men in her life. In the first place, belonging to the covenant community required circumcision, something limited to males. The priesthood was composed exclusively of men, who determined the rituals and laws. Even God was presented in masculine terms. Purity rituals such as those presented in Lev 12 also kept women at the margin of the community and its activities.

The greater context was the religious life of the pagan peoples in whose presence and under whose influence Israel found itself. Studies and excavations reveal to us that the first images of the divine being were female images. There are several reasons for the feminine image of the divine presence, but the greatest of them seems to be the aspect of fertility associated with the female sex, fertility on which all life depends. This was in a time when humanity depended mostly on the land and its fruits. It is not until the development of cattle raising, where the role of paternity becomes important, that the world begins to reevaluate the representations of its gods.

During Old Testament times the constant struggle was to maintain the faithfulness of the chosen people to the God of Israel. The Hebrews for many years had to fight against the influence of pagan gods and especially the worship of goddesses.

I would like to suggest that because of the patriarchal, male-centered culture and the constant struggle against pagan religions which tended to focus on goddesses and female images, the community of faith focused on the maleness of God. The biblical memory has been very selective but does not succeed in eliminating the affirmation that God gives to the feminine image or to the part that God give to the participation of women in human society in general or in the things of God in particular. There is no better affirmation of this truth than the testimony of Jesus.

Why is it the, that almost 2,000 years after Jesus, we continue to face discrimination against women and to see great obstacles before the, especially when they choose to serve God in the ordained ministry? I think that there are several reasons, but for our consideration I would like for us to focus our attention on one in particular: erroneous and problematic theological interpretations regarding the nature and role of women.

Just as the writers and first interpreters of the Holy Scriptures were very selective, prejudiced and governed by their cultural and social experiences, so also we find theologians in Christian history who have presented theologies colored very much by their own experiences within cultural and social frameworks which they support.

One example is Karl Barth. Fundamental in his thought is the revelation of God through the "Word of God." The emphasis is on the idea that God is the initiator. God is the subject; the human being is the object. In preaching, the preacher assumes the role of subject while the congregation plays the role of the object. This subject-object relationship is transferred to the relationship between man and woman. Barth has adopted the patriarchal perspective as normative. In his concept of order the relationship between man and woman is a reflection of the relationship between man and God. Man initiates and woman responds. This being the case, the pulpit is by definition closed to women. Once more we see, not a divine ordering, but a simplification of relationships that has been established from a male perspective.

In conclusion, God does not discriminate, either against man or against woman. God pours out love on both in equal form, giving both sexes gifts and abilities whose use God calls for, calling women as well as men to various tasks including the task of the ordained ministry.

La iglesia como comunidad hermenéutica

Cecilio Arrastía

Este artículo se escribe a raíz de un experimento realizado en una clase de homilética avanzada en el Seminario Evangélico de Puerto Rico. Esta información se ofrece, a manera de introducción, para subrayar el hecho de que el resto del artículo no descansa en una teoría sin prueba, sino que obedece a algo probado.

El experimento consistió sencillamente en convertir toda una clase en una comunidad de reflexión bíblica --comunidad hermenéutica-- para involucrarse en un proceso de reflexión como antesala a la preparación de sermones por los miembros del grupo. A diferentes grupos pequeños se les asignó un texto bíblico común, y se pidió a sus miembros que "bombearan" los pasajes en grupo, anotando posibilidades homiléticas. Hecho esto, y con este material como "la masa homilética" que horneada produciría el sermón, cada alumno, con su contexto en mente, y girando contra los fondos de su cultura y aplicación al estudio, produjo el sermón.

A la luz de ese ensayo, proponemos en estas líneas la tesis siguiente: que con miras a renovar y a redefinir la tarea homilética, la iglesia local se convierta, por medio de un grupo representativo de la misma, en una comunidad hermenéutica que participe en la labor de reflexión previa a la predicación semanal del pastor. Dicho de otro modo, la iglesia ha sido llamada "comunidad de fe", "de gracia', "que adora", "de esperanza". Nosotros proponemos que, sin descartar esas hermosas caracterizaciones, se añada funcionalmente una más, y que sea llamada "comunidad hermenéutica".

De modo continuo me acompaña la convicción de que el púlpito hispano sufre de una crisis innegable. Esto puede ser reflejo de la crisis vocacional que sufre la iglesia. Pero ello no disminuye la fuerza deprimente de la realidad. En general, la predicación es superficial, ahistórica, ateológica; se desvincula del pasado rompiendo con tradiciones teológicas vitales, y no hace matrimonio con una escatología que tenga integridad. Resultado: el pastor se columpia sobre una tierra de nadie, sin tocar el aire ni desentrañar el mañana y, por lo tanto, sin afectar el presente. Entretiene pero no edifica; insulta pero no desafía; enajena y divide, negando así el espíritu de suma y de reconciliación de Aquel gran predicador itinerante cuyos púlpitos fueron las montañas, playas y plazas de su tierra, y cuyo mensaje se resume en una palabra: amor.

A la luz de esto, reiteramos nuestra tesis: un posible camino de salida sería una redefinición del proceso homilético, que implicaría una redefinición del papel de la iglesia local en este proceso.

En predicación --como en toda reflexión válida-- hay dos componentes: metodología y contenido; proceso y sustancia. Claro, el primero no garantiza de modo automático la existencia del otro. Y el método que proponemos trata de combinar ambos elementos de manera funcional. Un buen cocido no se da por accidente: allí se unen la ciencia y la paciencia del cocinero; el tiempo y el fuego: elementos dados y elementos ganados por la disciplina y la reflexión. Y así es el sermón. La crisis actual señala a una realidad cierta: la ciencia y la paciencia se han limitado a las del pastor como individuo, y pocas veces se han tomado en cuenta las de la congregación como comunidad pensante. Mas si tenemos comités que planifican las tareas de educación cristiana, evangelismo, mayordomía, acción social y trabajo con la juventud, ¿por qué no pensar en la posibilidad de tener personas que, trayendo en forma encarnada las preocupaciones y aspiraciones de distintas edades, sexos, formación cultural y trabajo secular, ayuden al pastor en su labor de planificar y producir sus sermones dominicales?

Más adelante elaboraremos el concepto señalando sus ventajas. Por ahora, quedémonos con la semilla sembrada y pasemos a fundamentar nuestra tesis en un vistazo a la historia.

Una mirada a la historia

La imagen del predicador como un "lobo solitario" no corresponde a lo que la historia bíblica y la historia de la predicación revelan. La forma en que se construyen los púlpitos en nuestros templos --altos y apartados del pueblo-- contribuye a reforzar la imagen del pastor como una figura solitaria, ancha y ajena. El individualismo caudillista, por otro lado, también subraya esta percepción falsa. Mil dedos torcidos señalan al predicador como una persona que, por estar tan cerca de Dios, tiene que estar lejos de la humanidad, y cuya voz --que muchas veces clama en el desierto-- es la de un ente elegido y distinto, consagrado y distante.

Es con la Reforma Protestante que tal presuposición parece demolerse. Pero sólo "parece". La doctrina del sacerdocio universal del creyente pudo ser el factor que afectara la ecuación homilética en forma positiva. En la práctica, la doctrina no pasó de ser eso: doctrina. Sus aristas homiléticas nunca fueron consideradas seriamente. Se individulizó, se hizo base para reclamos conducentes al evangelismo personal, pero el predicador siguió hablando *al* pueblo, y no *con* el pueblo. El elemento dialógico de la predicación, sin el cual no hay buena predicación, no cristalizó. Tal vez el creyente sería sacerdote, pero el pastor seguía siendo el *profeta* por antonomasia.

La toga, que tanto contribuye a la solemnidad del culto, acentuó --allá por los siglos XVII y XVIII-- la imagen del pastor como alguien separado y distinto. En cierta forma, la doctrina del sacerdocio universal se asfixia y muere en los pliegues de la toga pastoral. La toga negra es sudario de la doctrina. El púlpito alto y arquitectónicamente separado del pueblo establece distancia, no sólo física sino emocional y cultural entre el predicador y el pueblo. (Para un modelo elocuente, visite el lector la Primera Iglesia Presbiteriana de Nueva York, escenario de parte del ministerio de Harry Emerson Fosdick). Aquel personaje críptico, escondido en su negra toga y tocando con su cabeza los contornos de la bóveda celeste, era el único conocedor de la Palabra de Dios.

La realidad innegable es una: en la tradición bíblica la comunidad valida la predicación. La interacción de estos dos factores no puede quebrarse sin que se rompa algo esencial en la vida de la iglesia cristiana. Tal cosa obedece a realidades que señalamos ahora.

En primer lugar, de modo expreso o tácito, la predicación ha sido tarea de la comunidad y no del individuo. Este habla, pero su voz es la comunal. Debe recoger los anhelos, sueños, frustraciones, confesiones y acciones de gracias del pueblo. El testimonio de las Escrituras nace, se interpreta y se escribe en el seno de una comunidad de creyentes. Los pactos --tanto el Antiguo como el Nuevo-- son eventos comunitarios. Los poderosos actos salvíficos --liberación de Egipto, conquista de Canaán, experiencias con el Resucitado, Pentecostés-- fueron actos ocurridos en el seno de la comunidad. La tradición es realidad que la comunidad atesora y transmite. Los profetas del Antiguo Testamento levantan sus voces en la aparente soledad de sus rebeldías; pero lo hacen desde una comunidad y para una comunidad. Jesucristo mismo, "Hijo del Hombre", realiza su ministerio alrededor de una comunidad de seguidores. Se rodea de doce que son representativos de aquella comunidad que es Israel. Todo sermón auténticamente inspirado se produce en el seno de la comunidad. Es un regalo triple: de Dios a la comunidad, de ésta al predicador, y de éste al pueblo que celebra. El sermón que no es "encarnado" es una realidad docética que repite la herejía gnóstica; y de sermones gnósticos "está empedrado el camino al infierno".

El proceso apunta la sustancia de que éste debe brotar: la Palabra --que se habla a la comunidad de fe-- se oye y analiza por la comunidad hermenéutica. La fe, que sólo viene por el oir, y el culto, que debe ser racional, motivan y comprometen a la iglesia local en esta tarea acústica y reflexiva. La estampa que de la iglesia apostólica nos ofrece el Libro de Hechos es la de una comunidad que se reúne para estudiar la Palabra, "porque eran asiduos a la enseñanza de los apostoles" (Hch 2:42). Clyde Reid lo expresa de manera clara cuando dice que "la renovación del ministerio de la predicación está en el redescubrimiento de su carácter comunal".[1]

Las analogías paulinas de la iglesia como cuerpo refuerzan nuestra tesis. Como cuerpo, la función de la iglesia es de coordinación, y esta coordinación es totalizadora. No se trata de la coordinación de un aspecto de su función --la pietista, la evangelizadora, la social-- sino de su tarea total. Y en el centro de esta tarea total aparece la de la predicación, fuente de motivación e iluminación para la comunidad que sirve. El clérigo --kleros-- es parte de un todo, y separar la parte del todo mutila sus posibilidades y produce suididio profesional. La reflexión del profeta de Dios se ubica en el marco de las demandas y expectaciones de la comunidad. Estas expectaciones llegan a oídos del profeta en formas muy variadas, pero una de ellas, que es de valor innegable, es la del diálogo reflexivo. Tal diálogo producirá una predicación dialógica, al estilo de Cristo. El tomó las preguntas planteadas por

---

1. Clyde Reid, *The Empty Pulpit* (New York: Harper and Row, 1967).

el pueblo y las convirtió en tema de sus mensajes. Tal modelo sigue siendo válido. Paul Tillich lo recomienda en su método de correlación. La vigencia del mensaje y su pertinencia crucial dependen de la antena del profeta para captar las preguntas que el pueblo sugiere. Pero, ¿cómo oirá el profeta si no se dispone a oir?

Un modelo de la tarea de la iglesia

Esta segunda sección de nuestro trabajo trata de explicar una forma de poner a funcionar la tesis antes expuesta.

La idea se reduce a lo siguiente: seleccionar un grupo de personas que representen todas las aspiraciones e inquietudes de la iglesia. Profesionales y obreros; jóvenes y adultos; hombres y mujeres; conservadores y liberales; miembros nuevos y veteranos del Evangelio. Este grupo se constituirá en un equipo o comité de reflexión y retroalimentación. Su tarea específica sería, en reuniones previamente programadas, reunirse con el pastor y, leyendo en varias versiones de la Biblia los textos que servirán de base a futuros sermones, reaccionar, reflexionar, discutir las implicaciones de esta Palabra en sus propios contextos naturales. El pastor tomará nota y usando discreción y criterio selectivo incorporará a su predicación lo que de sustancia este grupo produzca. Esta reunión es sólo la primera fase de un proceso que culmina en el púlpito. La fase intermedia es la del pastor, cerrado en su estudio, luchando con raíces griegas y hebreas, con comentarios bíblicos y con crítica literaria e histórica, buscando en su semillero personal de ideas, ilustraciones, citas, relatos de novelas y leyendas mitológicas.

La reacción de los miembros de este grupo vendrá en los distintos niveles en que cada uno de ellos sirve y piensa. Pero será reacción de entraña: no se pretende la refinada reacción del erudito bíblico o del teólogo profesional. La teología bíblica es teología del pueblo, de obreros, de pescadores, de hombres y mujeres con raíz comunitaria. Y este grupo hará la oferta de su "reacción primitiva" al texto seleccionado. Que habrá aberraciones y disparates, nadie lo niega. Pero la emisión de estas expresiones fuera de órbita le brinda al pastor en su tarea docente la oportunidad de rectificar y enderezar los entuertos teológicos y bíblicos que el pueblo ha cultivado por años. El disparate que emite un miembro del grupo puede ser la misma aberración sobre la cual vive toda la comunidad.

La segunda tarea de este equipo reflexivo será la de ofrecer retroalimentación al predicador, una vez que el sermón se haya predicado. El cuerpo frío de la pieza homilética se coloca sobre la mesa de disección, y el pastor contempla al grupo discerniendo las partes del sermón, "leyendo" lo que el pastor ha dicho. Será un instrumento métrico que capacite al profeta de Dios para calcular su capacidad para comunicar, no sólo con caridad, sino con claridad, el mensaje de reconciliación que de Dios ha recibido para el pueblo.

No podemos ni debemos continuar sin antes hacer una rotunda observación: este tipo de experimento reclama, en la primera reunión del grupo, una explicación clara de las funciones de este equipo de trabajo. Se debe proveer tiempo para una amplia discusión. Hecho esto, el pastor debe llegar a un "contrato" con su equipo de reflexión. Las partes del contrato se discuten y deciden por consenso. Pero dos componentes no pueden faltar. *Uno*, un voto mutuo de total confidencialidad: el pastor no lleva al púlpito "secretos de confesión"; los miembros del grupo no cuentan a otros lo que en la hermandad del grupo se comente "como cosa personal que no deseo salga de este cuarto". *Dos*, entre el pastor y este equipo debe haber el entendimiento de que el sermón en su forma final es responsabilidad del pastor, y que éste no se compromete a incluir en su sermón *todo* lo que *todos* los miembros del grupo opinen o contribuyan a la conversación.

Las reuniones de este comité deben realizarse en un marco de bien definida piedad y espíritu de oración. La responsabilidad del equipo de reflexión es grande, y un sentido de "temor y temblor" debe presidir todo el proceso. En ningún momento un orgullo farisaico debe invadir a este grupo. Al cumplir su tarea, están en verdad ante la zarza ardiendo de la Palabra de Dios, que quema y no se consume, y todos deben quitar sus sandalias para acometer con el trémulo del futuro liberador, la tarea de quebrar la piedra de la Palabra para que de ella brote "el agua que salta para vida eterna".

En su formato tradicional, el sermón parece una camisa de fuerza: rígido, almidonado, con temas limitados y enfoques dignos de siglos pasados. El predicador vive tropezando, en su ejercicio homilético, con las paredes de una estructura tradicional inoperante. La predicación debe reflejar frescura, novedad, fluidez. Es "río de agua viva" y no estanque de agua corrompida y fétida. La novedad del mensaje no es algo artificial producido sólo por la activa imaginación del predicador. Debe brotar del choque iluminador de la eterna verdad del Evangelio con las penúltimas realidades del ser humano. Es en el choque de estos dos pedernales que brotará la chispa de lo nuevo, de lo liberador, que es lo viejo de todas las edades: la gracia de Dios hecha persona en Cristo Jesús.

Summary

The Christian preacher is not a lone ranger *or a* lone wolf. *Preaching is the task of the whole community of faith. As a way out of the crisis in preaching --shallow, soporific, ahistorical, non-biblical, humanistic preaching-- the local preacher must involve the congregation in the process leading to the building of the Sunday sermon.*

History presents proclamation as part of the witness of the community of faith. As it was yesterday, it must be today. The Protestant claim in relation to the basic role of the lay people in the ministry of the church, applies also to this area. But, how to involve lay leaders in this weekly and challenging task?

The answer asks for some planning. An advisory group, representing all the concerns of the church and the natural community, *could be appointed to meet on a regular basis (weekly, bi-weekly, monthly, quarterly) with the pastor to* pump, *to* squeeze *the texts that will be the foundation of the sermons. The Lectionary would be a great help. These lay people will react to the Bible lessons. It will be a* gut level *reaction. Biblical theology is* popular theology: *it is not formulated by professional theologians; but by* common people. *In these meetings the pastor will write down everything that is said by his or her* reflection task force. *These notes will be part of the* homiletical dough *used by the preacher in the preparation of the Sunday sermon.*

In is important to draft some kind of agreement or covenant with the task force. One, *there must be a vow of confidence among the participants in the conversation: nothing said in the group will be proclaimed outside if it is some personal testimony or experience.* Two, *the preacher will use this information, only if the persons who gave it agree and allow the pastor to use it, naming or not those involved in the experience related.* Three, *the preacher must be very specific and frank and make clear to the members of the group that not everything they shared will be used in the sermon. The last word --the editorial word-- belongs to the pastor who is responsible for the drafting and the preaching of the sermon.* Four, *feed-back and evaluation of the sermons must be part of the agenda of the next advisory meeting.*

The Best Administrator Is a Poet: Towards a Theology of Administration

Ignacio Castuera

The issue of theology and administration surfaced with intensity for me after my appointment to the Superintendency in the United Methodist Church in July of 1980. I had been an administrator before but I had not pondered the basic question which I now address. For me the issue is simply this: how can I administer the Los Angeles District in a manner that is congruent with my theological convictions?

The question may appear too narrow and parochial, but generalizations must spring forth from very particular settings. What I share with the readers of this paper is the tentative answer I have received and a bibliographical collage of the sources that have informed my thinking.

The question of this paper was inspired by what originally was meant as a derogatory remark made by a Chicano colleague about another Hispanic Presbyterian administrator. In derision this friend stated that among Hispanic administrators "the best is a poet." The remark stayed with me and soon I began to see the positive aspects of a poetry of administration or, better yet, administration as poetry. The poet organizes, arranges, brings together elements which on the surface appear to be contradictory, raises people's sights above the ordinary, invests the common things with extraordinary qualities, and above all inspires. It is now possible to see why indeed the best administrator is a poet.

I must indicate before going any further that my theological convictions are informed by process thought and the theology which emanates from taking seriously the liberation struggles of peoples in this nation and around the world. The administrative style that I wish to develop should be consistent with process and liberation theology.

The appeal to poetry is consistent with both of the theological sources that inform me. Whitehead's use of poetry in his philosophy and his concern with esthetics is well known. In particular his preference for the works of Wordsworth is often noted. Liberation theologians also have pointed out the revolutionary value of the artists who through esthetics inspire the imaginations of the oppressed to envision and struggle for a world better than the one they experience in the present. Gustavo Gutiérrez frequently quotes artists who use different media to convey a message of liberation. José María Argueda, the Peruvian poet/novelist, and the surrealist film make Luis Buñuel provide Gutiérrez with innumerable illustrations which he uses creatively in his theological essays. James Cone, the Black theologian of liberation, has consistently pointed out the liberation power present in the musical and poetic works from the Black culture from the Negro Spiritual to the Blues.

128

The Theology Implicit in Traditional Models of Administration

One of the significant contributions of the feminist movement has been the unmasking of the pyramidal, hierarchical nature of enterprises, both secular and religious. The traditional manner of administering has a person (or a small elite) usually male and white, at the top. This person gives orders to people who are assumed to be only fit to follow and who must be constantly watched and forced to do the assigned tasks. This traditional model of administration has been labelled the X model or theory ever since Douglas McGregor characterized it in this manner in his work *The Human Side of Enterprise*.

The theological foundations (stated or implicit) in the theory X of administration are deeply ingrained in the Christian tradition. This mode of management is only a slight variation of the "divine right of kings." The "divine right of administrators" presupposes a hierarchical arrangement of the world with an omnipotent omniscient Lord at the top. Administrators (like the kings in the past) dimly reflect the omniscience and omnipotence of the traditional theistic God.

There is a second long held belief that informs and underpins X styles of administration. This is the doctrine of the Fall. Since human beings are utterly depraved as a result of the Fall of Adam and Eve, they will follow their base desires rather than fulfill company objectives. Therefore people must constantly be watched and forced to complete their appointed work. In this model people cannot be trusted. Administrators who subscribe to this kind of administration must constantly crack the whip making sure that order is observed and laziness curtailed.

There is some obvious exaggeration and generalization in the picture painted in the preceding paragraph. Unfortunately there is also a great deal of truth. This is specially true of operations overseas. Some companies which manage under one more mundane model in the North Atlantic shift to X theory management in Third World countries on the assumption that the natives (not being so civilized) bear more clearly the effects of the Fall.

From different perspectives and with different tools process theologians and liberation theologians have rejected or modified the two doctrines which underlie X theory of management. God is definitely not seen as omnipotent and omniscient in the same sense in which traditional theistic theology has depicted the deity. Human nature is also not seen as fixed or as depraved as traditional theologians would have us believe. It follows quite naturally that an administrative style congruent with process and liberation theology must reject vehemently the traditional X theory of management. In addition someone seeking to be faithful to process and liberation theology in management practices must enunciate, even if only in a tentative manner, some characteristics of an administrative style consistent with the theology and anthropology of process and liberation. To the latter task I turn next.

A Bibliographical Collage

It is obvious that in developing a theology of administration theologians should draw on the work of those who have addressed the issue from what one might call a more progressive perspective. In the following pages I shall summarize the positions of four theoreticians who, in my opinion, have addressed the issue of administration in a novel way and from a significantly different perspective. These authors' proposals seem to me to be congruent with the theological perspectives that sees God "managing" the world in a mode different from the way in which traditional theology saw God "ruling" the world. The authors whose positions I shall summarize are Douglas McGregor, who writes from the perspective of an academician charged with the responsibility of training future managers; William Ouchi, also an academician but enriched with a cross-cultural background; Abraham Maslow, the well known psychologist who presents us with enticing theories to pursue and verify; and finally, from the field of sociology and sociology of religion, Andrew Greely presents a "job description" which I feel is very much in keeping with what a "poet" administrator ought to be.

Theory Y

For over twenty years Douglas McGregor's *The Human Side of Enterprise* (McGraw Hill: New York, 1960) has been a handbook for progressive managers. Earlier in this paper I mentioned theory X, and it is in contrast to that management theory that McGregor developed his Y theory of management.

Five basic tenets constitute the foundational scaffolding for theory Y. I present them in a list without chronological order or priority.

1. Under the proper conditions work is as natural as play.

2. Sometimes self-control is indispensable in order to achieve organizational goals.

3. The capacity for creativity to solve organizational problems is widely distributed in the population.

4. In order to motivate people one must appeal to one or more of these levels:
        a) security level,
        b) physiological level,
        c) self-actualization level,
        d) social esteem level.

5. When properly motivated most people can be self directed and creative at work.

This is indeed a contrast to theory X. Instead of forcing, manipulating, and suspecting, the function of management is primarily that of convincing, sharing, empowering, and inspiring. The central task of an administrator is finding out how to motivate properly the persons working in the company, church, diocese, or district.

McGregor was greatly influenced by Maslow's work in the field of psychology, and understood well that the principal task of an administrator is the development of people. Production, company goals, the enterprise's survival, etc., flow out of the basic empowerment of people. Five years after McGregor, Maslow himself wrote a book which chronicles his encounter with the field of management. But it was McGregor who first applied Maslow's concepts in the business world. (Independent of all this work Peter Drucker suggested similar directions in 1954. Unfortunately my knowledge of Drucker is limited to second-hand quotes and references to his monumental work *The Practice of Management.*)

Those familiar with process and liberation theologies will undoubtedly see the congruence and harmony between McGregor's proposals and these theologies. The administrator is not a dim reflector of the divine king, but instead tries to use the very same power which process theology proposes that God uses: persuasion. The best administrator is the one who continually is looking for more effective ways to "properly motivate." Manipulation and force are proscribed and, keeping in mind the theme of this essay, the main task of the administrator is akin to that of the poet: to inspire.

Theory Z

William Ouchi's indebtedness to McGregor should be obvious from the title of his work: *Theory Z: How American Business Can Meet the Japanese Challenge* (Addison-Wesley Publishing House: Massachusetts, 1980). However, the title also conveys the impression that Ouchi intends to go beyond McGregor. And indeed he does so in several significant ways.

The most important improvement by Ouchi stems from the fact that the author of theory Z did a cross-cultural study of Japanese companies and of American companies which according to many academicians are well managed. In these *in situ* studies Ouchi looked for common denominators of good management as well as transplantable concepts from Japanese models. Ouchi acknowledges his indebtedness to Hewlett-Packard, IBM, Eli Lilly and Dayton Hudson. From the Japanese side Sony Corporation and the Japan Productivity Center are specially referred to. All to these companies provided Ouchi with very valuable data and practical applications of theoretical models.

Much of what Ouchi identifies in the Japanese companies as elements of importance in the success of Japanese companies presupposes cultural upbringing in Japan. However three concepts remain translatable and applicable across culture: trust, subtlety and intimacy. I was immediately attracted to the book when (after a tip by the Rev. Peter Chen from San Jose, Ca.) I found this paragraph in the early pages of Ouchi's work:

> Above all, this book recognizes that steel-pushing or fashion jeans-selling companies, mysterious hospitals, and bureaucratic post offices are social beings. This book, therefore, is about trust, subtlety and intimacy. Without them, no social being can be successful. I learned about trust from my first pastor, Allen Hackett, who permitted his congregation to grow as individuals because he trusted in them. I learned about subtlety from my mother, my sister, and above all my father, who guided my development

in unobtrusive ways. I learned about intimacy from my wife, who has shown me that through closeness both trust and subtlety develop (p. ix).

A significant portion of the book is dedicated to comparisons and contrasts between American and Japanese companies. Still another important section of the book deals with techniques or steps needed to change a company from whatever mode of management into a Z company. The theoretical part of Ouchi's work is for our purposes the most instructive and important.

Trust, subtlety and intimacy are extremely important concepts to us in the West. Subtlety, however, is less so than the other two. These three are interlocking and interdependent concepts in theory Z; they are the tripod that makes theory Z stand. They are not presented in chronological order nor in order of importance by Ouchi. They seem to emerge slowly, simultaneously, but certainly not "mysteriously."

In a Japanese company trust, subtlety and intimacy arise more easily given a more homogeneous culture and shared cultural presuppositions. Once the employee has been accepted into a company she or he can trust the company and all co-workers. (The fierce form of competition which one observes in Western companies is mirrored in the schooling of Japanese but seldom in company life.) The hiring of a person constitutes proof of the trust the company has in the person hired.

Subtlety is more carefully and --should one say-- more subtly cultivated in the Orient. Subtlety is all around. People are trained from birth to recognize the most delicate movements, the slightest changes of body language, the quiet ways of culture and nature. Japanese art can be characterized as "subtle." Social interactions abound with subtlety. In contrast, in the West subtlety is much more difficult to cultivate. There are not enough positive reinforcements for subtlety. The "macho" world in which we live usually sees subtlety as "feminine" and therefore less valuable. Ouchi is very much aware of this problem for American companies and yet he wishes to stress the need for us to learn this virtue and incorporate it into our administrative practices.

Intimacy is not often seen as a foundation or a goal for business enterprises. Schools of psychology recognize the value of intimacy for persons but not for factories or even universities and churches. (Pastors seldom have intimate friendships with parishioners and the role of Superintendent is in constant tension with the role of friend or pastor according to many church administrators.) This is what makes Ouchi significant and important. For him there is no radical discontinuity between biological beings and social beings. Ouchi emphasizes the continuities; he sees factories, stores and churches in an organic fashion.

The role of the administrator who wishes to be in harmony with theory Z is to optimize conditions to enhance trust, subtlety and intimacy. Administrators must be more concerned with relationships between persons than with "production." Optimal production is the result, the important by-product of the promotion of trust, subtlety and intimacy. Little wonder then that in many Japanese companies workers are willing to forego raises and even to take salary cuts when the companies are threatened. They trust the company. They trust that the company has a "memory" and will remember the sacrifices of workers during hard times rewarding them in periods of bounty.

From a process theology perspective this theory abounds with parallels and congruences. Power is derived from relations rather than simply from position. Differences enrich rather than impoverish the company. Intimacy promotes trust and subtlety. A good manager is like a poet subtly bringing together elements which appear to be disparate, paralleling God's action, God's management of the universe. The give and take which trust, subtlety and intimacy require (and almost paradoxically create) echoes the way in which all actual occasions relate to each other and to God. The "boss" in a company run by Z principles varies from other workers only in that he or she has a larger number of interactions; but ideally the mode of interaction remains the same. No divine right, no (or minimum) top to bottom decision making, a mutual accountability, and minimal hierarchy.

From a liberation theology perspective a problem arises. Trust, subtlety and intimacy are indeed worthwhile goals for persons, institutions and societies to pursue; but, are they achievable in a country where a capitalist mode of production prevails? Ouchi appears to be aware of this problem.

> The first lesson of Theory Z is trust. Productivity and trust go hand in hand, strange as it may seem. To understand that assertion observe the development of the British economy during this century. It is a history of mutual distrust between union, government, and management, a distrust that has paralysed the economy and lowered the English standard of living to a dismal level. Karl Marx foresaw this distrust as the inevitable product of capitalism and the force that, in his view, would bring about the ultimate failure of capitalism (p. 5).

Ouchi goes on to say that capitalism and trust need not be mutually exclusive. The data he offers to counter the argument is very skimpy, however. In fact, the subtitle of his book already betrays the spirit of Theory Z: "How American Business can Meet the Japanese Challenge." The dog-eat-dog nature of the capitalist system creeps in through the back door. In several other places Ouchi shows that there are too many problems within the system.

> The other important lesson that theory Z translates from Japanese practice into American ways is subtlety. Relationships between people are always complex and changing. A foreman who knows his (sic) workers well can pinpoint personalities, decide who works well with whom, and thus put together a team of maximal effectiveness. These subtleties can never be captured explicitly, and any bureaucratic rule will do violence to them. If the foreman is forced, either by a bureaucratic management or by an equally inflexible union contract, to assign work teams strictly on the basis of seniority, then that subtlety is lost and productivity declines (p. 7).

"Bureaucratic management . . .inflexible union contracts"-- these are the daily realities of a capitalist mode of production and neither Ouchi nor theologians can afford to ignore them.

In managing ecclesiastical institutions one can learn much from Ouchi. Authority (exousia) must be derived not from rank or position but from being and relating. The best administrator is the one that trusts and can be trusted, one who cares and who subtly convinces and encourages.

In managing ecclesiastical institutions one can learn much from Ouchi. Of special interest to us should be the idea that trust may develop better when evaluations are less frequent and promotions proceed at a slower pace. Being in the middle of United Methodist Charge Conferences which occur annually and having just returned from a consultation on evaluation makes me painfully aware of how slowly trust develops between churches, pastors and denominational executives.

Ouchi supports the idea expressed in the title of this paper when he states that "Management is *too much of an art* and too little of a science to submit to . . . regularity of description . . . The objective is to achieve commitment of employees to the development of a less selfish, more cooperative approach to work" (p. 98, emphasis mine).

Maslow's Eupsychia

As stated earlier Maslow, who inspired McGregor, eventually wrote notes on management. These notes were made during the course of a summer visit to a company; an event which Maslow described as a "sort of Visiting Fellow at the Non-Linear Systems Inc. plant in Del Mar, Ca."

These journal notes were edited into the book which bears the unlikely name of *Eupsychian Management*. The book makes constant reference to Drucker's *Principles of Management* and (to complete the cycle) to *Human Side of Enterprise*.

Eupsychia is Maslow's utopia: a theoretically possible society generated by 1000 self-actualizing people in some sheltered island where they could live and work without outside interference. Eupsychian management is the ideal kind of management by self-actualized persons with the purpose of self-actualizing all employees.

The greatest value of *Eupsychian Management* is in the question it raises and the problems it presents for people like Drucker, McGregor, Ouchi, and their followers. Trust, subtlety, intimacy, self-actualization, etc. are great components of good management. But in addition to the social block, to such type management (see preceding section for instance) Maslow forces us to recognize the intra-psychic forces that militate against enlightened management. These forces are not, however, the result of the Fall; nor are they inevitable. They are there to be reckoned with and eventually transformed, channeled or overcome. How to "properly motivate" (in McGregor's terminology) presupposes realizing the ego needs of employees by managers.

A most important principle of eupsychian management is that people are improvable. This is something which we as religious need to believe and actualize in our management and in the way we view all of society. We emphasize (as noted earlier) too much the fallen nature of humanity without equally emphasizing the improvability of persons. This from the perspective of liberation theology is not accidental, but is rather an ideological necessity. If in practice we do not "verify" (make true) our belief that individuals can improve, that they can and will respond to "proper" motivation, then --our thinking goes-- enterprises and systems cannot improve either. It takes very little effort to move from this position to the logical consequence of "why try?" Why try to replace this or that system? Why experiment with an economic system other than capitalism? Anything that fallen humans produce will eventually be plagued with problems but only magnified. Evolution is favored over revolution if only because it can hide the changes much better and is therefore less threatening to the comfortable.

In Wesleyan thinking we have emphasized sanctification at the theoretical level. This is the theological equivalent of Maslow's concept of improvability of human beings. However, at the practical level we keep on acting as if we really did not believe that persons, institutions, systems or societies can indeed change.

The poet believes in change. The poet insists on the fact that if one can imagine a better society then a better society is in fact possible. The manager as poet empowers colleagues and subordinates. The poet/manager provides supervision as *super* vision (lifting people's horizons, helping them to see beyond) and not merely "snooper vision" (as Paul Dietterich often characterizes management practices). Eupsychia, Z companies, even non-capitalist novel possibilities, are realizable to poet/managers.

A Sociological Job Description for Enlightened Managers

Andrew Greeley's *The Making of the Popes 1978* might seem a most unlikely place to find a theory of management. However, this book which reads like a mystery novel also includes something which is informative for those of us struggling to find an administrative style congruent with process/liberation theology. This "something" is a job description for a pope. With only slight modifications I wish to submit this job description as illustrative of the kind of person a process/liberation theologian can be as an administrator.

> An effective administrator must be able to communicate with many people with radically different concerns. This person must understand the aspirations, needs and longings of the human race and be able to respond, not necessarily with clarity and preciseness, but with warm sympathetic and hopeful answers.
>
> It is not necessary that a good administrator be a saint, but "holiness" would help. The personal life of an effective administrator must reflect the deep convictions that guide her/him. Poverty, lack of ambition, political naivete, etc., are not requirements, but the effective administration must be free of the slightest taint of financial and organizational wheeling and dealing.
>
> In addition to being a "holy" hopeful person, a good administrator must also smile. Must be the kind of person whose faith and convictions make him/her happy and whose hope makes her/him joyful. A grim, stern, pessimistic, solemn faced leader will not appeal to any one as someone possessed by the mission he/she wishes to fulfill. The more a leader laughs, the more effective that leader will be.

Since no one person can possibly make all decisions which affect organizations today, an effective administrator must be shrewd in selecting colleagues and subordinates and must preside over her/his team in such a way as to release rather than inhibit the best of their talents.

A leader must have an instinct for the strategically important problems that should occupy his/her time and energy, and the ability to focus on those problems and to delegate responsibilities for other problems to subordinates.

An effective administrator must trust others: staff, colleagues, other administrators, scholars, etc.

Hope, holiness, self-confidence, maturity, trust, the ability to delegate power and responsibility, personal security. These are qualities of a good leader and they are dictated by a purely sociological analysis of the role of leadership in institutions (Adapted from pp. 88-89 of Greeley's *The Making of the Popes 1978*).

Artists and Artisans: Almost a Postscript

In any organization effective managers need to surround themselves by people who are better than them in areas where the administrators do not excel. Middle management is extremely important in any organization. These persons are to the poet/administrator what artisans are to artists. They carry out the details of the larger vision of the artist. The selection of associates and assistants in churches or any other enterprise is an important index of the kind of leadership one has steering the organization.

Three management axioms are worthwhile to keep in mind when talking about middle management. a) Middle management can seldom (if ever) be held responsible for the failure of an organization. b) Failure in middle management is tantamount to failure in top management. c) Administrators usually hire the help they deserve.

While the top/bottom imagery in the preceding sentences must be transcended, generally the content of those premises holds water. The translation that is needed for this essay is into the aesthetic language of artists and artisans.

The administrator as poet/artist must surround herself or himself with artisans who can execute well in those areas in which they are best trained. In addition the administrator must release (as noted in the preceding section) these artisans, trust their own initiative and empower them through delegation to release their creativity. The artist/administrator then is released to provide the "super-vision" which is influenced and informed by the "artisans" and which in turn is shared with the total organization. When the administrator can provide the institution being administered with a super-vision which members of the organization at all levels can "consciously hold and vividly apprehend," then that administrator and that institution will be functioning in a manner harmonious with what process and liberation theologies attempt to achieve in practice.

Double Dutch: Reflections of an Hispanic North American on Multicultural Religious Education

Robert W. Pazmiño

I am an Hispanic-North American, a new breed Hispanic. My ethnic roots are Ecuadorian in my father's lineage and Dutch and German from Pennsylvania in my mother's lineage. Given the fact that persons from German lineage in Pennsylvania are called Pennsylvania Dutch, my three and half year old daughter names this strand of our family heritage from my mother's roots "Double Dutch." It is an appropriate naming because double dutch is also the term for a rope game played with two jump ropes which are turned in tandem. My active daughter, Rebekah, observes and practices this rope game which requires a unique combination of jumping and coordination to balance one's position successfully between two ropes rotating in opposite directions and converging on the person whose turn it is to jump. This image of jumping double dutch is appropriate for considering the status of minority persons in public and religious education in the United States within a dominant Anglo middle class ethos.

A person who is "Hispanic-North American" is conscious of being at a point represented by the position of the hyphen in that term, the position of navigating and balancing the convergence of two cultures which rotate in distinct orbits and require careful coordination and balance. In our pluralistic society with various cultures converging, the image of jumping between two ropes provides insights for negotiating the interaction of elements in multicultural education. Yet this image is particularly helpful for the new breed Hispanic population which Virgilio Elizondo describes as *mestizaje*, the origination of a new people from two ethnically disparate parent people.[1]

Like the rope game of double dutch, my life represents the tandem play of two cultures because I grew up in close association with my father's extended family and cultural roots due to a distancing and disassociation from my mother's family. Yet these extended family ties were immersed in the world of an Anglo dominant local community and culture.

Elizondo vividly describes my status and that of others in relation to the experience of persons with mixed blood, not unlike the status of being a Galilean in first century Palestine. Like Galileans, new breed or new generation Hispanics are looked down on both by Latin Americans for their cultural impurity, and by Anglos for their ethnic ties. New breed Hispanics are Hispanic in their approach to life, but their first and dominant language is

---

1. Virgilio Elizondo, *Galilean Journey: The Mexican-American Promise* (Maryknoll, N.Y.: Orbis Books, 1983).

either English or "Spanglish," which is a mixture of English and Spanish. In most cases they are not at home in Anglo society and struggle with the status of being modern day Galileans.[2]

Galilee at its best was a crossroads of cultures and peoples with an openness to each other, not unlike some small communities and associations in the city of my origin, New York. But Galilee at its worst resulted in the exclusion and division of those who were different, not unlike the experience of a vast majority of minority persons in the United States and a number of cultural groups in New York City. This experience of exclusion was heightened for me through my marriage to a woman of pure Puerto Rican descent. I feel Puerto Rican as an adopted member of my wife's extended family and as a result of six years of ministry in a predominantly Puerto Rican church in East Harlem, New York. Being Puerto Rican and being Hispanic in that context requires nurture through a constant effort to re-own one's cultural heritage within a dominant culture that has generally sought to squelch it and assign it to an inferior status.

For those of new breed status who are second, third, and fourth generation Hispanics in the United States, the distinct challenge is to recover those aspects of Hispanic language and culture which were decimated through decades of racist and discriminatory practices, components of which are ever present in individual and corporate life. This recovery must occur while actively participating in a wider society which devalues this very renewal of Hispanic culture as evidenced through, for one example, the increased opposition to bilingual education. Such recovery is subject to numerous factors which must be addressed. One factor is the potential danger of further ghettoization where the maintenance of an ethnic enclave results in alienation from the wider society and an inability to impact upon that society in constructive ways. A second factor is the unwarranted perception by those in the wider society that the affirmation of one's ethnic identity inherently represents an immature longing for one's home group with the attending feelings of security and connection. A third factor is the complex of shifts in a multicultural global existence which necessitate interaction and dialogue on a daily basis across ethnic and cultural divisions. Additional factors can be cited, but the challenge remains to broaden our understanding for addressing such realities. One source for understanding is embodied in the promise of Galilee as Elizondo has prophetically suggested.

The Promise of Galilee

The promise of Galilee at its best can be discerned through exploring some of its history. Galilee, literally denoting a ring or circle, referred to a region comprised of Gentiles and foreigners, of persons from various nations. It was a region that was constantly experiencing infiltration and migration. At various times in its history, Galilee was controlled by Babylon, Persia,

---

2. Orlando Costas, "Evangelizing An Awakening Giant: Hispanics in the U.S.," in *Signs of the Kingdom in the Secular City*, comps. David J. Frenchak and Clinton E. Stockwell, ed. Helen Ujvarosy (Chicago: Covenant Press, 1984), p. 57.

Macedonia, Egypt, Syria, and Assyria. In the first century, Galilee with a population of approximately 350,000 persons had a large slave element and about 100,000 Jews who were largely Hellenized. The primary language at this time was Koine Greek, although Jews spoke Aramaic. Thus the Galilean Jews represented a bilingual community. Galilean Jews were lax in the matter of personal attendance at the Temple in Jerusalem, in part for the obvious reason of distance, and this attitude was symbolic of the modified orthodoxy of Jews in Galilee of the Gentiles.

It is significant that much of the teaching of Jesus, directed primarily to those living in this context, was not acceptable to the orthodox interpreters of Judea, for he gained a reputation for unusual and controversial interpretation. Jesus manifested a freshness and independence of mind as to the meaning and application of the Law, consonant with the religious spirit of Galilee. This region was occupied by a mixed population and had a reputation for racial variety and mixture in and around its borders.[3]

It was in this very context of Galilee that God chose to be incarnate in the person of Jesus of Nazareth. Yet it is the very nature of this multicultural context which is so often ignored in considering Christian religious education today. Nevertheless promise is realized for educators who take heed to the nature of Galilee which is inclusive of ethnic and cultural diversity. The existence of this region assumes that some form of boundaries were set to define this space and/or the persons occupying this space. By focusing on the question of boundaries which is ever present in human interactions, the religious educator can explore dimensions of ethnicity and religious faith, particularized in this case from the perspective of the Christian faith.

Anya Peterson Royce points out that the maintenance of ethnic identity involves the use of symbolic boundaries from within a group to distinguish it from other groups. Those groups maintaining these boundaries celebrate their differences among peoples as distinctive and affirm the place of beauty in their culture and ethnic heritage. But at the same time other boundaries are imposed by external groups upon and ethnic group, thus reinforcing distinctions. These distinctions too readily become a source of trouble for ethnic groups, fostering ethnic stereotyping, discrimination, and racism. These secondary boundaries isolate differences among peoples as deficits as compared with the positive distinctives maintained by the groups themselves. Thus there often exist double boundaries or two ropes with which ethnic groups must contend.[4] Ethnic groups that have developed boundaries to define themselves, often in response to a hostile context, can find that additional boundaries have been set which divide them from others. The struggle then becomes how to maintain one's identity and integrity as a

---

3. K.W. Clark, "Galilee," in *The Interpreter's Dictionary of the Bible*, ed. George A. Buttrick (Nashville: Abingdon Press, 1962), pp. 344-347.

4. Anya Peterson Royce, *Ethnic Identity: Strategies of Diversity* (Bloomington: Indiana University Press, 1982), pp. 18-19.

member of a minority group and yet fully participate in the larger society both across defining boundaries and dividing boundaries imposed by that larger society. Those dividing boundaries perpetuate oppression and injustice with a host of complicating factors for ethnic minorities. The struggle becomes how to play double dutch in being both Hispanic and North American and wanting to play in a way that affirms the significance and integrity of both realities. This conflict is not unique to Hispanic-North Americans because similar issues can be posed for those who seek to be Black and American, Asian and American, or even Christian and North American. Yet the current historical context of the United States and the corresponding emphases upon global and multicultural education provide a unique setting in which to consider the emergence of a new people, new breed Hispanic-North Americans who have experienced the joys and pains of emergence. This emergence offers the opportunity for dialogue and interaction across various cultures in addressing the need for religious education which seeks to be multicultural. Both the historical and sociological studies of general and religious education have revealed various models of education which have functionally emerged and have been perpetuated in education. Each of these models of education, formulated in relation to ethnic and cultural differences, have primarily patterned themselves after the larger communal contexts of which they are a part.

Models of Education

The various models of ethnic or cultural education are manifest more at the level of the hidden or null curriculum than that of the explicit curriculum.[5] An investigation of the explicit written curriculum of religious education, as helpfully undertaken by Charles Foster, reveals a progression of models which increasingly favors multiethnic and multicultural pluralism.[6] On the basis of this history of the actual written materials used in religious education, one could conclude that significant progress is being made in the area of addressing ethnocentrism in religious education. But if a researcher explores the actual experiences of minority persons and considers what areas of ethnic studies are being forgotten in terms of the null curriculum, a very different impression is gained. Whereas the explicit curriculum may affirm a multicultural education, the hidden and null curricula may operate effectively to undermine that emphasis. This is too common an experience for ethnic groups who experience the wide gap between what Lawrence Cremin has termed the stated intentions of the explicit curriculum and the revealed preferences of the hidden and null curricula.[7] Such is an inevitable

---

5. Elliott Eisner makes these distinctions in *The Educational Imagination: On the Design and Evaluation of School Programs*, 2nd ed. (New York: Macmillan Publishing Co., 1979), pp. 87-108.

6. Charles Foster, "Double Messages: Ethnocentrism in the Education of the Church," *Religious Education*, 82 (Summer 1987), pop. 447-467.

7. Lawrence Cremin, *Public Education* (New York: Basic Books, Inc., 1976), p. 50.

consequence of life within a society which does not consistently address the existence of institutional racism in its educational efforts.

The works of both Ricardo García in general education and Charles Foster in the history of church education suggest the following four models which currently operate despite a national commitment in the United States to integration and the elimination of some of the effects of racism.[8]

1. Anglo Conformity Model

This model maintains that some persons are inferior and marginal because of their cultural, racial, and/or ethnic origin. Such a model perpetuates racial and social exclusion either intentionally or unintentionally and devalues the heritage, identity, and experience of persons who do not belong to favored ethnic groups. Whereas the vast majority of educational efforts in the United States do not intentionally emphasize conformity at the explicit or stated level, the hidden and null curricula reveal contradictory evidence.

A few examples from personal experience will suffice to illustrate the presence of this model which operates functionally for minority persons. My family and I lived in a New England small town community with such a small percentage of minority persons and a parochial ethos that it essentially functioned from an Anglo conformity model. The educational experience for our son in the local middle school was typified by the comment of its principal as to why only French was being taught to the exclusion of Spanish in the school's curriculum, the explicit curriculum. The principal's response was that Spanish was only needed to use at a local chain restaurant to order Mexican food. One can imagine the extent to which Latin American heritage gains access in this school at the levels of the hidden and null curricula. A similar experience awaited the family in a local church where our daughter was often neglected in her nursery and Sunday School class in overt preference to children with Anglo heritage. The differential treatment extended to the point where our daughter was actually once physically struck to deal with her crying. Upon confronting the teacher with our daughter's account, she initially denied the incident. No Anglo children in this class received such treatment. These examples could proliferate to illustrate the subtle and not so subtle messages that persons of ethnic differences received. We were not welcome in the public and religious education programs in this community.

Richard de Lone's work, *Small Futures*, describes the functional caste system in the United States which isolates Blacks, native American peoples, Mexican-Americans, and Puerto Rican Americans.[9] My family and I experienced the realities of casting in terms of the hidden and null curricula

---

8. See Ricardo García, *Teaching in a Pluralistic Society: Concepts, Models, Strategies* (New York: Harper & Row, 1982), pp. 37-57; and Charles R. Foster, "Double Messages: Ethnocentrism in the Education of the Church," (Nashville: Scarrit Graduate School, 1986).

9. Richard H. de Lone, *Small Futures: Children, Inequality and the Limits of Liberal Reform* (New York: Harcourt Brace Jovanovich, 1979), pp. 153-160.

of the public and religious education offerings in this locale sufficiently to warrant the presence of an Anglo model.

2. Melting Pot Model

Historically this model characterized the educational rationale in the United States prior to the 1960's. As García indicates the melting pot model began to show signs of collapse in the 1960's when Nathan Glazer and Daniel Moynihan published the book *Beyond the Melting Pot*. By 1975, the melting pot model had become intellectually outmoded, but not functionally inoperative.[10] A melting pot or ethnic synthesis model maintains that all cultures melt down to a common denominator which in the case of the United States has been Anglo dominant and English speaking.

The melting pot functions very selectively and can be illustrated by the comments of a Black seminary student who shared with me about the number of well intentioned peers who said to him that they no longer saw him as Black, but as a Christian brother. The place of *koinonia* or community is to be affirmed, but not at the loss of recognition of persons as they have been created by God. Ian Malcolm, an Australian religious educator, has appropriately identified the drive to cultural or ethnic uniformity in the melting pot model as rooted in human pride and arrogance. From his perspective ethnic diversity reflects an appropriate relationship between a transcendent God and a finite humanity.[11]

The melting pot works to eliminate ethnic distinctives in the effort to develop a unified identity. It does so not to the extremes of the Anglo conformity model, nevertheless distinctives are merged in a way that inevitably favors the dominant culture. From the perspective of the minority person this model might best be compared with a melt down of a nuclear reactor in terms of the destruction of that which is to be preserved in an ethnic heritage. Whereas the Anglo community model seeks to deny and/or obliterate ethnic distinctives that are not Anglo, the melting pot model serves to diminish seriously these distinctives in relation to the perceived higher good of unity. Whereas the Anglo conformity model stresses uniformity, the melting pot allows for a unity which at least at the ideational level seeks a muted and distorted diversity. These two models choose the higher value for unity over against diversity. But this unity is realized at a great cost to persons of ethnic backgrounds not viewed as the favored majority. The hidden curriculum of a major portion of the educational settings and programs in the United States affirms the values of this melting pot model.

One may not expect the revolutionary social changes initiated in the 1960's civil rights movement and resulting legislation to make significant inroads in the value system and ethos of educational institutions in the United States within such a short time. Some progress has been realized at the level

---

10. García, *Teaching in a Pluralistic Society*, pp. 37-45.

11. Ian Malcolm, "The Christian Teacher in the Multicultural Classroom," *Journal of Christian Education*, Papers 74 (July 1982), pp. 48-60.

of the explicit curriculum, but addressing the hidden and null curricula is a task of long term magnitude. Work and struggle must continue in this area, but realistic expectations must also be maintained. The recent rise of racial incidents on university (and I might add seminary) campuses are a reminder of the continued efforts which must be extended to realize a more equitable education for minority persons in the United States.

3. Cultural Pluralism Model

This third model stresses the inclusion of racial and ethnic minorities into the life of the nation, community, school, or church. It seeks to have a representative ethnicity as a means by which to pattern global or national realities. At various points in the actual practice of this model Anglo superiority emerges, but the effort is made to mute over paternalism.[12] Various ethnic heritages are recognized, but the implicit expectation is that with maturity one's ethnic heritage will no longer be emphasized. The message is that people have a right to maintain their ethnic identities, but no one must be carried away with this emphasis in the interest of genuine dialogue and affirmation of a unity which transcends the existent diversity.

This third model is a welcome alternative to the first two described, yet it still expects of minority persons the denial or submergence of one's heritage rather than its enrichment as it is offered as a gift to other peoples. A unity is sought which essentially displaces one's ethnic identity rather than a unity which coexists in the midst of one's heritage. The choice is posed between either maintaining one's ethnic identity throughout one's life or diminishing its importance in the interest of engagement with the larger cultural plurality. Such terms are not in actuality applied equitably to all ethnic groups in the United States because the heritage of some groups is maintained in the existing plurality to a much greater extent. Such a situation parallels the situation in George Orwell's description in *Animal Farm* where the position of some is more equal than that of others. The lack of emphasis upon some ethnic heritages is tantamount to their obliteration in a societal context steeped in racial and cultural domination. For example, if Armenian Americans do not emphasize their cultural heritage, then it will no longer be a gift to this nation or the world because of the genocide experience of this group.

Plurality is encouraged in this model of cultural pluralism, but within the bounds defined by the dominant culture and circumvented by the press for a maturity and a unity ill conceived. A vastly diminished particularity of ethnicity is promoted which for the Hispanic-North American represents a contradiction in terms and commitments. Educationally this model operates to welcome the participation and contributions of representative ethnic groups without addressing the long term implications of the inclusion and nurture of their ethnicity. Ethnic diversity in this perspective becomes a long term detriment in favor of a universal agenda that is too narrowly defined. For one

---

12. Foster, "Double Messages," pp. 457-458.

to project a point of maturity in which I no longer emphasize my heritage and identity is to deny my person as created by God, even within the purview of the new creation of Jesus Christ.

4. Multicultural Model

As García defines this model, it suggests a type of education committed to creating educational environments in which students from all cultural groups will experience educational equity. Multiethnic education is a specific form of multicultural education. It includes not only a study of ethnic cultures and experiences, but also making institutional changes within the school setting so that students from diverse ethnic groups have equal educational opportunities.[13] This type of educational format assumes that ethnicity is a salient and continuing part of national and personal life. In this emphasis a multiethnic or multicultural model moves beyond the model of cultural pluralism. This is the case because those who support multicultural education value the continuing significance of ethnicity throughout the maturing process. Ethnic diversity is maintained and not diminished in the interest of realizing a narrowly defined unity.

A multicultural model suggests two educational movements, the maintenance of both being essential for a proper rhythm and balance. The initial movement is that of emphasizing one's ethnic identity and definition. The complementary movement is that of seeking a common ground for community, for life in a global village grappling with the realities of ethnic and cultural plurality. This second movement involves a quest for universality, for unity, but not at the expense of diversity. The model of cultural pluralism diminishes the first movement in favor of emphasizing the second. This second movement in the multicultural model does not deny one's identity, but embodies that identity in dialogue with others from distinct ethnic backgrounds. By its very nature it includes exploring ethnic heritages other than one's own heritage and learning to appreciate them. This dialogue assumes that one has had the luxury and space for grounding one's ethnic identity. This luxury and space have not been afforded to everyone in the United States, and the securing and maintaining of that space are crucial in the context of a continuing racially divisive environment. Such racism is perpetuated on the institutional and personal levels of North American society, even with the explicit advocacy of a multicultural model.

This description of two complementary movements in multicultural education suggests the imagery of double dutch. A careful coordination of both movements is needed in order to maintain the proper balance of both diversity and unity. The other three models described have in one way or another sacrificed diversity in the interest of unity with a resulting loss of ethnic distinctives which provide an essential ground for identity. Such unity has been maintained at an unacceptable sacrifice to minority persons in the

---

13. García, _Teaching in a Pluralistic Society_, pp. 8, 105.

United States. This fourth model is a welcome alternative with the complementary emphases upon diversity and unity.

With the description of a multicultural model, there remains the question of the basis for unity amidst the vast diversity of ethnic and cultural groups encountered in our world. The Christian claim is that unity is found in Jesus Christ the Galilean. The resurrected and exalted Christ at Pentecost gifted his followers with the Holy Spirit. The experience of Pentecost points to a multiplicity of ethnic groups and tongues as the first sign of the Spirit's action in bringing healing to a divided world. Pentecost represents the reversal of the divisions of Babel with persons from diverse ethnic and language communities finding unity amidst their diversity as each person hears the gospel in their own tongue. The Spirit on that birthday of the Christian church points to a new source of human understanding and unity, a source embodying persons from every race, culture, and language. That source is the Lord Jesus Christ.[14] Personal and communal ethnic identities are not nullified or forgotten with Christian maturity, but are transcended in Jesus Christ. This transcendence does not entail the denial of the gift of ethnicity, but sharing of that gift with others while receiving the gifts of their heritages as described in a multicultural model. This is Galilee at its best present in Jerusalem.

In conclusion, one can see that a multicultural model of education is to be sought. Double dutch can be played through incorporating both movements of multicultural education which affirm one's identity and one's participation in the larger world. Double dutch is played at risk, but the risk is worth the taking if one is to be faithful in the task of educating in a pluralistic world. An image of double dutch distinct from the rope game and more in tune with the dominant North American culture is that of sharing equally the costs of one's outing with a date of friend. It is a multicultural model that assumes each contributing ethnic group can equally share its heritage and gain from those of others in a climate of mutual respect. To do otherwise is to deny the full implications of the gospel of Jesus Christ and to refuse to address the ethnocentrism resident in each of our lives.

---

14. Marina Herrera, "The Hispanic Challenge," *Religious Education*, 74 (September-October 1979), p. 458.

Pastoral Care and Counseling in a Mexican American Setting

Roberto L. Gómez

This essay is s description of the Mexican American setting, and suggestions for achieving effective pastoral care and counseling in such a setting. It seeks to provide some answers to the question of how a religious professional (minister, priest, nun) engages in pastoral care and counseling with a Mexican American person in a Mexican American setting. Are there concerns and issues to which one should be sensitive? What knowledge and expertise are most helpful in working in a Mexican American setting? These are crucial questions which need attention if one is to achieve competency in pastoral care and counseling.

In an article entitled "The Professional in the Chicano Community," Dr. George G. Meyer, a psychiatrist, writes that "Mexican Americans are so different from one another that classifications can be quite misleading."[1] This observation should be kept in mind by a person called to do counseling with a Mexican American. As Meyer notes elsewhere in his article, there is a tremendous diversity among Mexican Americans as to their socio-economic, religious, educational, language, and racial background. A Mexican American can be poverty stricken, extremely wealthy or very middle class; a nominal believer, or a committed church person; an illiterate or someone with a graduate degree; monolingual (Spanish or English) or bilingual (Spanish and English). In physical appearance and color a Mexican American may be confused for a Native American, Black, Asian, Anglo or Jew. Each Mexican American is an individual who needs to be treated as such. The pastoral counselor who forgets this and assumes that all Mexican Americans are very much alike will be unable to work effectively.

It is important to understand that the Mexican American perceives the counselor to be primarily a religious person. The pastoral counselor is not perceived as a social worker, psychologist, or therapist. The Mexican American goes to a religious professional because that person is considered to be a "person of God."

Several years ago I worked as a chaplain at a county hospital in Houston, Texas. On one occasion I was asked to officiate at the baptism of a very sick infant of a Mexican American Roman Catholic couple. The Catholic chaplain spoke no Spanish and since I did, I was asked to perform the baptism. When I met the couple, I told them I was a chaplain but not Roman Catholic and I wondered about their feelings towards me. The mother answered by saying, "It does not matter that you are not Catholic, what

---

1. George G. Meyer, "The Professional in the Chicano Community," *Psychiatric Annals* 7:12 (December, 1977), p. 11.

matters is that you are a man of God." Paul Pruyser, a psychologist, has written that problem-laden persons who seek help from a pastor do so for very deep reasons --from the desire to look at themselves in a theological perspective.[2] This is true of the Mexican American who goes to a religious person to seek help in his or her relationship to God.

The Mexican writer Samuel Ramos has written of the importance of religiosity in Mexican culture.[3] The meeting of a Mexican American with a professional for pastoral care and counseling becomes a religious event in which the use of prayer, Holy Scripture, and acceptable religious symbols are of great importance. I concur with Pruyser who has written that ministers should "reflect on their special heritage and use its theoretical foundations and practical applications to the full."[4]

Ramos has also written, in an essay entitled "Psychoanalysis of the Mexican," about the lack of trust of the Mexican. This is an initial concern for a religious person counseling a Mexican American. Ramos wrote in this essay:[5]

> The most striking aspect of Mexican character, at first sight, is distrust. This attitude underlies all contact with men and things. It is present whether or not there is motivation for it. It is not a question of distrust on principle . . . rather a matter of irrational distrust that emanates from the depths of his being. It is almost his primordial sense of life. Whether or not circumstances justify it, there is nothing in the universe which the Mexican does not see and evaluate through his distrust. The Mexican does not distrust any man or woman; he distrusts all men and women.

If Ramos is correct, and I believe he is, this means that a pastoral counselor who is meeting for the first time, or is getting better acquainted with a Mexican American who has been a casual acquaintance, will have to spend a considerable amount of time on building trust in order to allow a caring relationship to be established. Carl Rogers, a psychotherapist, is helpful here with his idea of congruence which he defines as being perceived as "trustworthy, dependable or consistent."[6]

Perhaps because of the Mexican American's sense of distrust, a study of Mexican Americans has demonstrated that they are less willing to disclose their feelings and thoughts than Anglo Americans, which suggests "that Mexican Americans may be more reserved about disclosure to a stranger, in this case, a therapist."[7] If follows that a pastoral counselor has to be very intentional in establishing a trust relationship with the Mexican American

2. Paul Pruyser, *The Minister as Diagnostician* (Philadelphia: Westminster, 1976), p. 43.

3. *Ibid.*, p. 10.

4. Samuel Ramos, *Profile of Man and Culture in Mexico* (Austin: University of Texas Press, 1962), p. 77.

5. *Ibid.*, p. 64.

6. Carl R. Rogers, *On Becoming a Person* (Boston: Houghton Mifflin, 1961), p. 50.

7. Frank Acosta, "Ethnic Variables in Psychotherapy," *Chicano Psychology*, ed. Joe L. Martínez, Jr. (New York: Academic Press, 1977), p. 225.

counselee. The advantage that persons have in a local church setting is that the trust level can be established long before the religious person is called for counseling. Indeed, such a call is based on trust!

The pastoral counselor needs to have a basic understanding of a number of other factors which are of great importance to the Mexican American. One such factor is that the Mexican American is an historical creature, with a past filled with conquest upon conquest and much violence.[8] The original Mexicans, the Aztecs, ruled by conquering surrounding Mexican tribes. Once the Aztecs fell, the Spaniards, French, and Americans took turns conquering Mexico. The story of Mexico has been one of political, economic, cultural, and religious oppression. As a third world nation, Mexico has experienced tremendous political instability and economic depression until recent years. This, coupled with the fact that Mexico exists in close proximity to the United States, a large, powerful, prosperous nation, has led to a feeling of inferiority. A by-product of this feeling is tremendous anger toward the United States.

Consequently, the recent Mexican immigrant has great emotional feelings towards the United States, perceiving it as a country which has stolen land from Mexico and embarrassed Mexico by invading it as recently as the 1930's. To the Mexican, the American citizen represents political and economic oppression. There is a saying in Mexico which sums up these feelings quite well: "Poor Mexico, so close to the United States and so far from God."

It is also important to understand the socio-economic attitude of the Mexican American. Class struggle is much more important to the Mexican American than to the Anglo American. The Aztecs had a feudal socio-economic system which was reinforced by the lord-peon class structure which the Spaniards brought with them. Even today the feudal system prevails in Mexico, which has a small but powerful upper class, a small, growing middle class, and an extremely large lower class. Status and power are centered around the father, the local politician, and the wealthy. For the Mexican American, class does make a difference, and actions depend on the class to which one belongs.

An example of this is a recent incident in which a young Mexican American physician visited in the home of a lower middle class couple to whom he is distantly related. The middle aged Mexican American couple gave their best bedroom to the doctor, while they slept on the floor in the living room and worried about what he would think of their humble home. It was a case of classism, although it occurred within an extended family!

The family is also an important factor in counseling, as the Mexican American relies greatly on the family for support and direction. A recent study by three California psychologists revealed that Mexican Americans depend more on their families as emotional support systems that do their

---

8. Octavio Paz, *The Labyrinth of Solitude* (New York: Grove Press, 1961), p. 86.

Anglo counterparts.[9] A Mexican American involved in counseling may reject a suggestion (however valid and reasonable) and discontinue counseling sessions if the family or an authority figure in it decides it is not in his or her best interest. Failure to understand this factor can easily undermine the best efforts of a pastoral counselor.

Failure to understand the language and culture of the Mexican American can also prove disastrous for a counselor. Assumptions must not be made as to what language a Mexican American will use. For the pastoral counselor, it is[10]

> necessary to recognize that Chicanos [Mexican Americans] live in a bilingual-bicultural milieu. Both languages and both cultures affect their total life style and have contributed to the formation of the Chicano culture. Mexican Americans are bilingual to a lesser or greater degree. A common definition of bilingualism is the use of two languages with varying degrees of understanding and proficiency. . .

Assuming that a pastoral counselor is bilingual, bicultural, has a grasp of Mexican American history, an understanding of the socio-economic attitude, and realizes the importance of the family, what then are the counseling issues which a Mexican American may wish to consider in coming to trust the counselor? The obvious issues are: familial relationships, work situations, loss and grief occurrences, etc. In this essay I wish to identify six issues which permeate almost everything a Mexican American does.

Reference has already been made to the deeply seated feeling of inferiority that Ramos mentions as being part of the Mexican's character.[11] Octavio Paz, another Mexican writer, further develops this underlying theme and relates it to solitude:[12]

> Our sense of inferiority --real or imagined-- might be explained at least partly by the reserve with which the Mexican faces other people and the unpredictable violence with which his repressed emotions break through his mask of impassivity. But his solitude is vaster and profounder than his sense of inferiority. A sense of inferiority may sometimes be an illusion, but solitude is a hard fact. We are truly different. And we are truly alone.

In an essay entitled "The Sons of La Malinche," Paz has written of the destructive anger within the Mexican which is aggravated by a feeling of inferiority and solitude. When Mexicans cross into the United States, they carry this heavy burden and will eventually have to deal with it in some way. Helping Mexican Americans acknowledge and verbalize this anger helps them

---

9. Susan E. Keefe, Amado M. Padilla, and Manuel L. Carlos, "Emotion Support Systems in Two Cultures: A Comparison of Mexican Americans and Anglo Americans," Los Angeles: Spanish Speaking Mental Health Research Center, UCLA, 1977 (mimeographed), p. 28.

10. Guadalupe Gibson, "Training Aspects in Working with Chicanos," *Mano a Mano*, 4:4 (Houston: The Chicano Training Center, August, 1975), pp. 2-3.

11. Ramos, p. 68.

12. Paz, p. 19.

to deal with it constructively instead of destroying themselves and others in a passionate act of violence. If they choose to go to a religious person to consider this, then it obviously becomes a pastoral care issue.

Acculturation is still another issue which Mexican Americans face. The very complex and overwhelming issue of acculturation is a daily reality for the Mexican American. Even in Mexico life is influenced by the North American culture and life style. When the Mexican comes into the United States, the influence and power of the American way of life is intensified. As conservative and as anti-North American as the Mexican American my be, one cannot escape the acculturation process, which daily, insistently, wears away at one's being.

Mexican Americans have at least three alternatives to acculturation. They may choose to ignore the process, but eventually they and their families will be overwhelmed by it. They may decide to fight it, but at best this will only slow down the process and at worst they will be overwhelmed and be left feeling embittered, even more inferior, and isolated in a "no man's land"; isolated from their Mexican roots and yet not quite a part of their new North American world. A third alternative is to recognize the power and extent of the acculturation process and to decide very intentionally to what degree and in what ways one wishes to acculturate. The counseling process can be most helpful in the third alternative.

Acculturation is not only a complex issue but one which is broad in scope. There is still another aspect of acculturation which may surface as an issue for pastoral counseling. As the Mexican American becomes acculturated, a most important aspect of the acculturation process is the issue of authority: one's own authority and the authority of those around oneself. The Mexican understanding of authority is different from that of the Anglo.

That this difference exists is found in a study by R. Díaz Guerrero and Robert F. Peck.[13] During the middle 1960's researchers asked Anglo and Mexican students to choose words that best defined the word "respect." Anglo students defined respect in the following way: "look up to with admiration; treat as an equal; give the other a chance; admire; consider other's feelings; consider other's ideas."[14] In contrast, Mexican students defined respect as: "awe; fear; love; affection; expect protection from; feel protection toward; dislike; don't trespass on rights; have to obey, like it or not; duty to obey; don't interfere in other's life."[15] The study concludes that for Anglos, the word respect means a "relatively detached, self assured equalitarism."[16] For the Mexicans, respect means "a close knit, highly emotionalized, reciprocal dependence and dutifulness, within a firmly authoritarian framework."[17]

---

13. R. Díaz-Guerrero, *Psychology of the Mexican* (Austin: University of Texas Press, 1976), pp. 78-88.

14. *Ibid.*, p. 84.

15. *Ibid.*, p. 87.

16. *Ibid.*

17. *Ibid.*

While respect is not the same as authority in the United States, in the mind and life of the Mexican American the concepts are one and the same. It seems obvious that until both the Anglo and the Mexican American understand and appreciate their conceptions of respect and authority, there will continue to be breakdowns in communication and relationships between the two groups.

When a Mexican marries an American, attends a predominantly Anglo school or church, or works in a predominantly Anglo environment, one can understand the pain the Mexican American endures in trying to survive in a world with strange and different meanings and concepts. Furthermore, if the dominant society ignores or refuses to learn in an effort to understand and to be sensitive to the Mexican American's perception of life, the element of racism becomes clearly manifested. Racism in its personal, social, and institutional forms becomes a basic issue for pastoral care.

Does the gospel of Jesus Christ offer anything to the Mexican American which can be used in pastoral care and counseling? Indeed, the gospel or our Lord Jesus has much to offer the Mexican American. If Ramos and Paz are correct in saying that the Mexican feels inferior and lives in a state of solitude and anger, then the gospel of Jesus addresses itself directly to these issues. Paul Tillich, in his sermon "You are Accepted," defines sin as separation.[18] I contend that separation is the same as solitude in the sense used by Paz. It is God's grace which overcomes one's separation from God, oneself, and others. It follows that it is God's grace which overcomes the solitude of the Mexican. And it is God's grace which transforms the inward, passive, destructive anger into an anger which can be channeled for constructive purposes, such as moving from resignation in life to worthwhile accomplishment. Furthermore, the moment that the Mexican American knows that God has spoken saying "you are accepted," then the feeling of inferiority can be dealt with. The pastoral counselor can be extremely helpful in helping the Mexican American move towards hearing God say "you are accepted."

In the gospel of Jesus Christ, the Mexican American is affirmed as a person and liberated to be the person God wants. St. Paul wrote in Rom 3:24, "by the free gift of God's grace they are all put right with him through Jesus Christ, who sets them free." Feeling affirmed and freed to be a child of God, the Mexican American is empowered to fight all racism to be encountered.

The gospel of Jesus Christ invites the Mexican American to come out of solitude and be part of the Christian fellowship in which one deals with persons from different backgrounds. "So then, you Gentiles [Mexican Americans] are not foreigners or strangers any longer; you are now fellow-citizens with God's people, and members of the family of God" (Eph 2:19). At this point, the pastoral counselor can enable the Mexican American to hear God's invitation to Holy Communion.

To summarize, it is important for the pastoral counselor to remember that each Mexican American is a unique individual. It is important to spend

---

18. Paul Tillich, *The Shaking of the Foundations* (N.Y.: Charles Scribner's Sons, 1948), p. 153.

time building trust. It is also important that the counselor understand that he or she is perceived first of all as a religious person. And understanding of the history, the socio-economic attitude, the family, the language and the culture are also important. Issues for pastoral care work with the Mexican are feelings of inferiority, solitude, and anger, the pressures related to the acculturation process, the perception of authority, and the reality of racism. Finally, the gospel of Jesus Christ helps the Mexican American move towards self acceptance, self affirmation, freedom to be the person God intends, and participation in the Christian fellowship.

La música al servicio del Reino

Carlos Rosas

En la historia del género humano, la música ha jugado un papel primordial. Los sentimientos sencillos y profundos han alcanzado en ella su máxima expresión. Muchos pueblos nos han relatado su historia a través del canto, mientras que otros han dibujado su autoretrato psicológico en el lienzo musical del pentagrama. Los aztecas, en cambio, consideraban la música como el origen de la vida. Así lo expresa Miguel León Portilla en su libro, *Los antiguos mexicanos a través de sus crónicas y cantares*:

> Bellamente se afirma en el texto indígena que todas esas ciudades comenzaban su vida, cuando se establecía en ellas la música:
> Se estableció el canto,
> se fijaron los tambores,
> se dice que así
> principiaban las ciudades
> existía en ellas la música.

La música, entonces, sirve otras muchas funciones además de simplemente proporcionar alegría y esparcimiento. Entre esas otras funciones, se podría citar las siguientes:

1) La música une a las personas

El cántico patriótico "Over There" unió al pueblo estadounidense durante la Primera Guerra Mundial. Más recientemente, cuando Irán detuvo a 53 rehenes norteamericanos durante 1980 y 1981, el pueblo los recordó con listones amarillos, y la canción de Tony Orlando, "Tie a Yellow Ribbon 'Round the Old Oak Tree," adquirió un nuevo destello de popularidad (Denisoff y Wahrman, 1979:26-28).

2) La música transmite valores sociales

En la década de 1960 hubo una canción que resonaba en todas partes transmitiendo un mensaje que era representativo de ciertos valores sociales. Los Beatles nos decían que todo lo que necesitamos es amor --"All You Need Is Love"-- y todos lo repetíamos cantando y bailando "All You Need Is Love". Luego, durante la época de la guerra en Vietnam, nos pedían que le diéramos una oportunidad a la paz --"Give Peace a Chance".

Este tipo de valores no es el único que ha sido transmitido a través de la música. Entre los más hermosos ejemplos que se pueden mencionar, están los cantares de los antiguos mexicanos. Los aztecas fueron uno de los pueblos que más abundantemente explotaron esta función de la música. Ellos mantenían la tradición de sus antepasados y pasaban, de generación en generación, las enseñanzas de los hombres sabios por medio del canto. "Fueron sus sabios --los *tlamatinime*-- quienes implantaron en los centros de educación ese sistema dirigido a fijar en la memoria de los estudiantes toda una serie de textos-comentarios de lo que estaba escrito en los códices."

(Miguel León Portilla, *Los antiguos mexicanos a través de sus crónicas y cantares*). En los anales de Cuauhtitlán se encuentra el siguiente canto que es una muestra de la transmisión de valores y enseñanzas que el pueblo aprendía de memoria:

> Se les enseñaba con esmero a hablar bien,
> se les enseñaban los cantares,
> los que decían cantares divinos,
> siguiendo los códices.
> Y se les enseñaba también con cuidado
> la cuenta de los días,
> el libro de los sueños
> y el libro de los años...

3) La música denuncia injusticias

Joan Baez, en su disco de larga duración "Canto a la vida", denuncia la injusticia cometida por unos pocos causando dolor y opresión para muchos. Dolly Parton, en su canción "Nine to Five", que sirve de tema musical a la película con el mismo título, protesta contra el maltrato sufrido por las secretarias de parte de los supervisores. En los Estados Unidos hay muchos grupos minoritarios y algunos sufren distintos grados de opresión. Sin embargo, no es necesario pertenecer a un grupo minoritario para experimentar las consecuencias de las injusticias. La mujer norteamericana, aun siendo mayoría, es una mayoría oprimida.

4) La música influye en el comportamiento humano

La influencia de la música en las personas puede darse a distintos niveles. A un nivel superficial o a un nivel profundo. A un nivel superficial se podría decir que la música es el motor que impulsa y controla los movimientos corporales de las personas. Cuando alguien está escuchando música, automática o subconscientemente sigue el ritmo. En una ocasión, un contratista relataba sus experiencias en el trabajo. Decía que una vez sus trabajadores estaban pintando una casa. En el interior de la casa se escuchaba el aparato estereofónico tocando el vals "Sobre las olas". Cuando el contratista entraba a la casa, observaba que sus pintores movían sus manos el ritmo lento del vals. Entonces apresuradamente cambió el ritmo y puso "La cucaracha". De este modo logró alterar el ritmo de los movimientos corporales de los trabajadores, acelerándolos de acuerdo al ritmo de la música, y pudo terminar su contrato a tiempo. Aun cuando esta influencia se pueda categorizar como superficial, sin embargo, para el contratista, tal influencia podría traer consecuencias desagradables.

A un nivel más profundo, se puede decir que la música influye en el comportamiento de las personas. Esta influencia puede ser positiva o negativa. Como una influencia positiva se podría citar la canción "We Are the World". Esta canto impulsó al pueblo norteamericano a compartir de sus bienes para disminuir el hambre en Etiopía. Habría que subrayar que, tal vez debido a la exposición international de esta pieza musical, las distintas naciones de la tierra participaron en este esfuerzo colectivo.

Acerca de una influencia negativa de la música en el comportamiento humano, es difícil citar casos concretos. Debido a una falta de comprobación científica, tal influencia negativa de la música en el comportamiento humano queda únicamente como hipótesis. Sin embargo, no está fuera de contexto el mencionar la preocupación que existe en muchas personas acerca del daño que la letra de algunas canciones puede causar en la juventud. Varios consejos municipales en los Estados Unidos se han reunido para dictar medidas preventivas en contra de tales canciones. Algunas ciudades llegaron a prohibir conciertos de esta música "dañina" dentro de los límites urbanos.

5) La música puede tranquilizar y adormecer; y puede despertar e impulsar a la lucha

Cuando un recién nacido llora fuertemente, su madre lo toma en sus brazos y trata de calmarlo. Para lograr su intento, le proporciona alimento y empieza a entonar un canto. Paulatinamente, el niño va dejando de llorar, mientras la madre continúa cantando suavemente. A medida que el niño va tomando su alimento y escuchando el canto suave y melodioso de su madre, se va tranquilizando hasta quedar plácidamente dormido. Una de las canciones de cuna más populares en la cultura hispana es "A la ru-ru niño".

Opuestamente al adormecedor canto de cuna, están los impulsivos cantos de guerra. Este tipo de canto logra despertar conciencia, impulsando al pueblo a levantarse en armas en defensa de su nación. Generalmente los himnos nacionales de los distintos países infunden patriotismo a la vez que estimulan a los compatriotas a dar su vida por los demás.

Las características o funciones que acabamos de señalar con respecto a la música no litúrgica pueden propiamente aplicarse a la música litúrgica. Tomando dos de estos puntos, podríamos decir que:

1) *La música litúrgica une a los creyentes*

Toda acción litúrgica va dirigida a Dios Padre, en común unión con Jesús, siguiendo el impulso del Espíritu Santo. Esta acción trinitaria debe ofrecerse en comunidad, porque la liturgia no es la celebración de una persona, sino que es celebración de la Iglesia. El cuerpo entero de creyentes, pueblo y clero, constitutye la Iglesia. La Iglesia debe ser una comunidad de creyentes, en la cual no debe existir la división ni siquiera entre "pueblo" y "clero". Si hay división, no hay común unión. Somos una familia con un Padre común. Esta relación con Dios nos hace hermanos a unos con otros. Es conveniente notar que lo importante no es tanto el llamar al otro "hermano", sino el tratarlo como hermano. Es precisamente en la interacción humana, donde se manifiesta la hermandad o comunidad.

Cuando nuestra interacción humana sea más fraternal, y por consiguiente más humanitaria y propia de hijos de Dios, realizaremos entonces la súplica de Jesús a su Padre: "Que todos sean uno como Tú, Padre, estás en Mí, y Yo en Ti. Sean también uno en nosotros: así el mundo creerá que Tú me has enviado" (Jn 17:21). Esta dualidad de la común unión, unidos unos con otros y juntos en Jesús y el Padre, es esencial en la familia de Dios.

La música litúrgica sirve la función de unirnos, cuando juntos elevamos nuestras voces. La música nos une a Jesús, porque juntos con El ofrecemos nuestra oración a Dios Padre. En esta forma, la oración alcanza expresión embellecida con armoniosos acordes musicales. Además, el aspecto comunitario de la celebración litúrgica se manifiesta más claramente al resonar las voces de los fieles en el ámbito del templo.

2) *La música litúrgica transmite valores evangélicos*

El Evangelio es la Buena Noticia. La Buena Noticia es Jesús mismo. Una de nuestras responsabilidades como cristianos es el anunciar la Buena Noticia a todos los pueblos. Es decir, que debemos de dar a conocer a Jesús en todas partes. Sin embargo, este anuncio evangélico implica la denuncia del pecado. Diciendo esto en pocas palabras, se podría decir que Jesús es Buena Noticia, pero no para todos.

En nacimiento de Jesús es anunciado a los pobres y estos se alegran. El anuncio de Jesús es Buena Noticia para los pobres, y ellos responden con alegría y espontaneidad, compartiendo su pobreza, compartiendo su ser con el recién nacido (Lc 2:8-19). Esta misma noticia es anunciada al poderoso. Los magos fueron al Rey Herodes a preguntarle dónde había nacido el Rey de los Judíos. Al escuchar Herodes la noticia del nacimiento de Jesús, tembló el rey y con él toda Jerusalén. En anuncio de Jesús es mala noticia para los poderosos. El Rey Herodes respondió con violencia y trató de eliminar a Jesús (Mt 2:1-13). Es interesante notar cómo Jesús, aun siendo niño recién nacido, hace cimbrar los cimientos y bambolear las columnas del poder.

Jesús puede ser Buena Noticia para todos si cambian de actitud. La conversión sincera y radical es indispensable. El extinto Arzobispo de San Salvador, Mons. Oscar Romero, mencionó en una de sus últimas homilías: "El rico debe convertirse al pobre y compartir con él los bienes del Reino... que pertenece a los pobres" (Mt 6:24). Esta elección entre los "dos señores" (se podría decir entre dos reinos, el Reino de Dios y el reino de Satanás) tiene que ser definitiva. Jesús nos dice: "El que no está conmigo, está contra Mí" (Lc 11:23). Finalmente, en nuestra cultura hispana existe un dicho popular que afirma la elección sincera, firme y definitiva entre los dos Reinos: "No se puede chiflar y comer pinole al mismo tiempo."

Los valores del Evangelio están en oposición con los valores del mundo. La lucha de Jesús contra Satanás que nos relatan los evangelistas se podría clasificar como una lucha de valores.

Para comprender más claramente el Reino de Dios, se podría contrastar con el reino de Satanás, sintetizándose en tres verbos opuestos entre sí: El reino de Satanás consiste en *tener, subir, y mandar.* Opuestamente, el Reino de Dios consiste en *compartir, vivir* en comunidad, y *servir.*

El *tener* consiste en monopolizar. Cuando Satanás sube a Jesús al cerro más alto y le muestra todos los reinos del mundo, le dice: *todo* te lo daré si postrándote me adoras." Pero Jesús rechaza el monopolizar, que es sinónimo de "adorar a Satanás".

El *subir* consiste en dominar con tiranía a los demás. Los evangelistas nos narran cómo Satanás lleva a Jesús a la ciudad de Jerusalén, *subiéndolo* a la parte más alta del templo, y le dijo: "Si eres Hijo de Dios, tírate abajo, porque la Escritura dice: 'Dios mandará que sus ángeles te cuiden y te protejan'." (Lc 4:9-10). Nuevamente, Jesús rechaza esta manera de ser. El mandar con tiranía a los demás, o estar por encima de todos, es como cuando alguien da una señal, y todos tienen que estar listos para servirle. Jesús, en otra ocasión, nos dice que El no vino para ser servido, sino para servir.

El *mandar*, consecuencia de "subir", consiste en hacer sentir su autoridad sobre los demás, constituyéndose en amo y señor. En Lc 4:3, leemos cómo Satanás tienta a Jesús, diciéndole: "Si eres Hijo de Dios, *manda* que esta piedra se convierta en pan." Jesús rechaza a Satanás y su manera de ser. Es interesante notar cómo termina Lucas la narración de este encuentro entre Jesús y Satanás: "Cuando ya el Diablo no encontró otra forma de poner a prueba a Jesús, se alejó de El por algún tiempo" (Lc 4:13). Esto da la idea de que el Diablo va a regresar después, para seguir tentando a Jesús. Sin embargo, los evangelistas no nos presentan otra escena de Jesús y Satanás.

No obstante, en el Evangelio hay otras escenas donde Jesús continúa luchando con Satanás, aun cuando estas escenas son distintas a la mencionada en Lc 4:1-13. En Mt 20:-20-28, encontramos esta lucha de valores entre los dos Reinos. El evangelista pone en labios de la madre de los hijos de Zebedeo las palabras de Satanás: "*Manda* que en tu Reino uno de mis hijos se siente a tu derecha y el otro a tu izquierda." Jesús le contestó: "No sabes lo que pides" (Mt 20:21-22). Jesús rehusa *mandar* y ofrece la alternativa de *servir*. Después, en Mt 20:25-28, hace un contraste entre el reino de Satanás y el Reino de Dios.

La música litúrgica estará al servicio del Reino de Dios si promulga sus valores. El asunto está en que la promulgación de los valores del Reino de Dios implica la renuncia de los valores del reino de Satanás. Cumpliendo esta misión, la música adquiere una dimensión profética, propia de la familia de Dios. Cuando la música llega a desarrollar esta doble función, *profética* y *servicial*, viene a estar más eficazmente al servicio del Reino.

Si la música no cumple esta función, viene a ser como la "canción de cuna" que tranquiliza y adormece. Una música tranquilizante y adormecedora es la que canta lo abstracto, la que no parte de la realidad vivida. Una música así, es como quienes ven la miseria del otro y no hacen nada por remediarla. En otras palabras, valiendo la expresión, sería una música "miserable".

Por otra parte, la música que tiene esa doble dimensión, *profética* y *servicial*, es como el canto de guerra que despierta e impulsa a la lucha. Hay que recordar que vivimos en una lucha de valores. Depende de nosotros si predominan los valores del mundo o los valores del Evangelio. La música litúrgica que impulsa a la lucha por el Reino de Dios, es la música que parte de la realidad vivida, iluminada por el Evangelio. Esta música invita a cambiar todo aquello que esté en contra del Reino de Dios y su justicia. Esta música, *profética* y *servicial*, es también *misericordiosa*, porque ve la miseria del otro y hace algo por remediarla.

Conclusión

Los ministros de música, músicos, cantantes y compositores deben estar conscientes de las distintas funciones de la música para utilizarla más eficazmente en el servicio del Reino de Dios. Es necesario un crecimiento en el conocimiento y experiencia vivencial del Reino. Valdría la pena preguntarse cuál de las funciones de la música utilizamos con más frecuencia; si nuestros cantos son como "la canción de cuna", o si son "himnos de guerra" por el Reino; si el contenido teológico de nuestros cantos transmite los valores del Evangelio y en qué forma influye en el comportamiento de las personas; si nuestros cantos unen a la comunidad, y para qué la unen.

No es la intención el dar una conclusión a este artículo sino, más bien, dejarlo como una inquietud o un interrogante. El estar al servicio del Reino es un constante proceso de conversión. Es un ir dejando los valores egoístas del mundo y viviendo esa dimensión liberadora del Evangelio. A medida que avancemos en el proceso, más y más irán nuestros cantos proclamando la Buena Noticia y alegrando a los pobres. Poco a poco nuestros cantos harán temblar a los ricos, no buscando su destrucción, sino su conversión y vida. Entonces nuestra música estará al servicio del Reino, haciendo de este mundo un lugar más hermoso, donde todos vivamos felices.

Summary

Music, both liturgical and non-liturgical, has a variety of functions. Several of these are considered in light of their non-liturgical role. Music can unite people, it can convey social values, denounce injustices, and influence human behavior. Among these functions, two stand out. On the one hand, music can be soothing and quieting, like a lullaby. On the other, it can rouse to action and commitment, like a national anthem. Although these functions could very well be universal when discussing music in general, they certainly perform similar roles within liturgical music. Two parallel examples would be that liturgical music unifies believers and conveys evangelical values. Yet, there are significant differences too. For example, since there is a radical contradiction between the values of the Reign and those of the world, as long as we live in this world liturgical music must not be soothing, but rather rousing to action. It must move to action on behalf of the poor, for whom the Good News is primarily. And it must also be a music that makes the rich and powerful tremble, not for their own destruction, but rather for their conversion and life.

Militarism and the Poor

Hal Recinos

The Present Situation

The church was called into being to continue the mission of Jesus in the context of a world in need of liberation. How has the church interpreted its mission within the totality of human existence? What theological perceptions have informed its practical ethics? Whose interests has it served? Have the poor had Good News preached to them? Do the lame walk? Do the blind receive sight? Have the sick been healed? Do the deaf hear or the dead rise up? Can the church present itself before the poor and oppressed claiming to have lived out the call of the human from Nazareth? The foundation upon which these questions rest is the knowledge of God. The biblical faith teaches that to know God is to do justice to the poor and the oppressed; however, the church has not always chosen the way of justice of the mission of the rejected carpenter from Galilee. The U.S. global military and monetary schemes have found support within the religious community. Capitalism is growing more pious each day.

Belief rebels in the face of the nuclear threat of extinction. Death is the ultimate form of alienation. Death is the promise of the nuclear age. North Atlantic military might has been enshrined by the latest technological magic: "the bomb." Like all idols it requires human sacrifices to give it life. The death toll even now is scandalous: political repression and war in Central America; social marginalization and wretchedness in El Barrio; death on the streets of the South Bronx that comes in the form of a policeman; Ignacio was slaughtered with American made bullets in Guatemala; Rudy was killed by *El sargento* on Avenue C. The idols of death require Latino human sacrifices; however, the judgment of God is upon all those who would sustain the present system of idol worship and its structure of oppression: "All who make idols are nothing, and the things they delight in do not profit" (Isa 44:9).

The nuclear age is the fullest expression of North Atlantic militarism. Its history reaches back in time to the European conquest of all the coasts and lands of the so-called "new world." Spain conquered and colonized the South American continent with the help of a superior military technology --the horse and gunpowder. European diseases for which the indigenous populations had not developed an immunity helped to secure the territory for the Iberian Crown and Church. European capitalism was made possible by the great wealth extracted from the "new world." The gold of Zacatecas and Ouro Preto, the silver of Potosí and the "white gold" of the Caribbean financed the economic expansion of the "old world," the American Revolutionary War, and the British war against Napoleon. The North Atlantic world ascended to power over the last five hundred years through a process of pillage and human exploitation. Indians and Africans were enslaved and made the fuel that ran the colonial system of exploitations. Today, *campesinos* in Central America and Latinos of el barrio; Blacks in South Africa and in Harlem; Indians of Guatemala and South Dakota; Asians in Korea and Flushing continue to serve as fuel for the great wealth of the North Atlantic.

The 16th century conquest and colonization of the "new world" resulted in the greatest concentration of dehumanizing labor (slave labor) which had ever been known by Western humanity; moreover, it was this system of exploitation and brutalization that produced a historically unparalleled concentration of wealth for the European western elite. On the altar of North Atlantic idolatry 70 million Indians and 40 million Africans gave their lives. Capitalism was born in their pool of blood and trail of tears. Today, the inhabitants of a single country, the richest in the north, take in income equal to that of all the inhabitants of Asia, Africa and Latin America together. The military budget of the U.S. alone exceeds the GNP of whole continents. Five hundred years of pillage have given us the global relationships which exist between the Northern and Southern hemispheres of the globe.

The church participated in this process of conquest and colonization. There have been prophets crying alone in the wilderness of time; however, the church has mostly given its blessing to the power structure. The idols of death molded in the brilliance of gold, the iciness of silver and the sweetness of sugar were the platform upon which the imperial state and church rose to a power never before imagined. The nuclear age is a symbol of the last five hundred years of North Atlantic global domination. We are on the doorstep of the 500th anniversary of the invasion of the globe by Europe. And the Chief Priests continue to cry out: "We have no King but Caesar."

The U.S. is now operating on a war economy with roughly 63% of each dollar spent on the military budget. Domestically, the trade-off in civilian-military spending could mean: the eradication of hunger in the U.S. in exchange for the C-54 aircraft program; 257 apartments in New York for the cost of just 1 Navy Intruder plane; bringing all of the poor in the States over the poverty line in exchange for the B-1 bomber program; meeting all of the urban renewal needs of Newark for the cost of 4 destroyer escorts; rebuilding blighted areas of the major urban centers in exchange for just 1 nuclear carrier and escort (McGovern, A.F., 1980). The Latino community in the U.S. has been negatively impacted by the gutting of domestic social service programs. The domestic cost to military spending is very high, but a very high international cost is also on the horizon.

The White House has committed itself to a program of rearmament through which it hopes to conserve and secure its economic and strategic interests on the global level. Reagan's foreign policy is pursuing a principle first formulated following the Second World War during the U.S. ascent to power. The U.S. believes it has the right to rob and exploit in the so-called "Third World." The American public has been enlisted to support the Reagan rearmament program through a carefully executed ideological campaign designed to create a passive and ignorant understanding of complex world issues. The political theology of "anti-communism" has been repeatedly sounded and the Soviet Union has been called the "evil empire." Third World national liberation struggles from conditions of wretchedness and North Atlantic domination are conveniently called "communist" and "subversive"; however, the simple fact is that the Reagan administration, serving the interest of a private elite, will not allow any deviation from its global framework of order.

Central America and the Caribbean have been increasingly militarized over the last several years. Over one-third of all the land area of Puerto Rico is occupied by the U.S. armed forces. In Central America, the military and police forces combined have more than doubled in size between 1981-1987. The Salvadoran military forces --police and armed forces together--grew from 16,850 in 1981 to more than 57,000 in 1986. A military advisor to the country said of the increased militia: "You can call it buying influence . . . when you get down to it, we are here to protect American national interests and we have to rely on local armies to help us do that."

What interests require the institutionalization of terror and murder? Investment in El Salvador has never been very extensive. The country is a testing ground for American power and prestige; moreover, the U.S. believes that El Salvador is of great strategic value; indeed, over a billion dollars was spent during the Reagan presidency on the Salvadoran military.

The White House argues that its aim in El Salvador is to bring "peace and stability to the country by helping the Salvadorans defend themselves against externally directed communist subversion" (McMahon, 1980). The origin of civil strife in El Salvador is not the result of communist "subversion," but instead, goes back a whole century to the establishment of a small oligarchy which has ruled over the country even since. The fourteen families live in opulence, while the majority of the Salvadoran population (over 50% of the populace) lives in extreme poverty. The system of dispossession causes belief to rebel: 77.8% of the land is in the hands of 1% of the landowners; some 2% of the population received almost half of the country's income in 1982; the general population of El Salvador is the worst nourished in Latin America; 47% of those who die of "natural causes" in rural El Salvador are children under the age of five who actually die of starvation (McMahon, 1980).

The Salvadoran army has become quite adept at carrying out indiscriminate massacres against women, children, the elderly and the handicapped. More than 200,000 persons have been brutally killed in Central America since 1978 and over 1,000,000 are refugees. The only "justification" for the U.S. intervention in El Salvador is the concern for credibility. Reagan stated: "The national security of all the Americas is at stake in Central America. If we cannot defend ourselves there, we cannot expect to prevail elsewhere. Our credibility would collapse, our alliances would crumble and the safety of our homeland would be put at jeopardy." What is ultimately at risk for the U.S. is its ability to protect and defend the interests of a private business elite that has invested heavily in the Third World. The U.S. is defending the right to rob and exploit; meanwhile, war rages in Central America and the torture, mutilation and murder of *campesinos* escalates. Refugees coming to the U.S. are greeted by an anti-immigrant climate which has finally institutionalized itself by the passing of the Simpson-Rodino Bill.

The Crisis of Theology

The whole of creation . . . groaning in travail (Rom 8:22) calls the church to historical responsibility. The North Atlantic church must confess complicity in all the events which have delivered us to the present moment of history; moreover, it must open itself up to the new reformation started by Third World Christians and the poor. First, the church must seriously examine the Greco-Roman or Platonic framework permeating its theological formulations. The hellenization of the Judeo-Christian tradition has resulted in a false dualism. The ultimate reality of human beings is not *logos* or universal reason; rather, human beings are essentially historical projects called into existence by a Liberator God to fulfill the requirements of justice, peace, freedom and love. Second, the division of history into two planes, the sacred and the secular, must be recognized to be in opposition to the Hebrew tradition. Biblical faith only recognizes the one order of history. God intervenes within history in the form of "revolutionary" activity on behalf of the poor and the oppressed. The Hebrew slaves of the Exodus tradition experienced God as savior on the terrestrial plane. Salvation or liberation was related to the political and social areas of life while "independence" was understood as a concrete expression of the "protection" of God (Croatto, 1981).

Latin America is presently writing its book of Exodus. The recovery of the Hebrew tradition or, if you will, the rediscovery of the historical character of biblical faith has resulted in a new reformation movement. Liberation has become the dominant theme of this period of history. The church in the North Atlantic must open its eyes and allow itself to be nourished by the new reformation. It must recognize that the incarnational reality of God in Jesus Christ is taking place even now in the church of the poor. It is not an accident that God becomes incarnate in the form of a poor human being from Galilee. Latino Christians of the *diaspora* community tend to be more attuned to the theological and ethical concerns of an enculturated First World church; hence, these Latino Christians are in need of experiencing the promise of rebirth implicit in the new reformation. The growing presence of the Central American community in the North American Latin church will accomplish the radical conversion to the liberating God of history.

The dualism of traditional theology contributed to a negative understanding of history. The hellenization of faith contributed the two-planes theory of history: the sacred and the secular, soul and body, natural and supernatural, spirit and matter, heaven and earth. Secular history relates to the mutable order of things and thus is inferior and negative. Sacred history relates to the world of absolutes or essences to which the "soul" of humanity is naturally drawn. The privatization of faith naturally derives from this type of theological reasoning. This perception of "theo-history" has resulted in the preoccupation for one's soul, a tendency to escape from "history" and the legitimation of an oppressive order of being. The dehistorization of the Hebrew tradition has been the church's cry for the return of Barrabas. "Listen to the sound of your brother's blood, crying out to me from the earth" (Gen

4:10). Outside of history there is no sound, no brother or sister, no blood, no crying out, no God to hear the wretched of the earth.

Solidarity and the Struggle with the Poor

The story of the Rich Young Ruler (Lk 18:18-30) turns the typical religious question --What must 'I' do to inherit eternal life?"-- over on its head. The Rich Young Ruler was interested in securing for himself the blessings of "eternal life." The privatized focus at the heart of his question is very familiar to the community called church; indeed, many within the church approach the human from Nazareth in the spirit of the Rich Young Ruler. They wish to know how they can secure for themselves "eternal life" and enjoy the religious sensuality of the "other" world. Traditional theology has encouraged this private and individual understanding of discipleship to the detriment of the larger social and corporate dimensions of scripture.

The question posed by the Rich Young Ruler has only been partially answered by the reply, "Have a personal relationship with Jesus." The question must be answered in light of its inner/outer historical dimensions.

The inner moral character of the Rich Young Ruler is not the center of the parable. Jesus reminds the Young Ruler to remember and obey the commandments handed by Moses to the reconstituted people of the Exodus-Sinai experience, Israel. These commandments were repeatedly endorsed by the prophets; indeed, doing them spelled life for all of Israel. The Young Ruler indicates to Jesus that "All these I have observed from my youth." He has fulfilled the requirements of the Law in terms of a moral observation of the ordinances of Yahweh; however, inner righteousness could not create for him the sense of "well-being" he needed. Private moral righteousness had failed to secure the conditions of "well-being" for the total community. Beyond the inner sanctum of the heart God's will must be placed into life in the form of actions leading to the shared life.

Jesus links the inner and outer life of obedience. "One thing you still lack. Sell all that you have and distribute it to the poor, and you will have treasure in heaven; and come, follow me." The center of the Rich Young Ruler's life --accumulated wealth or "Gross Private Product"-- is shown to be an obstacle for experiencing "eternal life." The Rich Young Ruler learns through Jesus that radical humanization means obedience unto death --in his case the death of private wealth. He is to take up the shared life (eternal life) in the community of the poor and outcasts which has gathered around Jesus as a sign of the messianic Kingdom of God. The wealth of the Rich Young Ruler was to be placed at the disposition of the poor who had been its victims. Eternal life is an inheritance when one lives in solidarity with the poor and human suffering and one struggles to create God's shalom within human society.

The Rich Young Ruler was being asked to transform himself through a radical rejection of the economic system that benefits the few over the many. He will be rewarded with "treasure in heaven" for having contributed to the creation of a new economic order which seeks to humanize existence by virtue of its organization around the community of the poor and oppressed. Jesus is asking the Rich Young Ruler to accept and join the struggle for radical humanization. At the heart of this invitation to discipleship is a perception of reality that we might understand in these terms: persons are suffering from the economic exploitation of humans by humans and are crying out for social justice; people are suffering from political oppression and demanding political recognition of their human dignity and human rights; people are suffering under capitalism and the structures of oppression that serve it and demanding liberation and the creation of a new life together.

The Rich Young Ruler was not prepared to give up his life and share a new life with the poor. He would continue to make wealth the center of his life and the altar of his private belief system; meanwhile, the bodies of the wretched poor would continue to barely hang on to life just outside his gates. Jesus looking at him sadly said, "How hard it is for those who have riches to enter the Kingdom of God. For it is easier for a camel to go through the eye of a needle than for a rich man to enter the Kingdom of God." It is easier to uphold the systems that suppress life than to accept the new life characterized by freedom, justice, love and peace. The Rich Young Ruler is left pondering the question: "Who can be saved?"

The Rich Young Ruler's final question has become our own. The military budget is climbing its tower of Babel in a vain attempt to reach heaven. The U.S. now has a greater peace time consumption of military equipment than even before in its short history. Social programs have been gutted; was is being waged in Central America; the Iran-Contra scandal has thrown the nation into a constitutional crisis; the Latino poor are being pushed from their sub-human apartments to the city streets; the stench of death pervades the corridors of Congress and gates leading into the church. The deficit created by the new militarism requires $140 billion in annual interest --debts of roughly two of every five dollars of all individual federal taxes or all of those taxes from west of the Mississippi!

God reveals to us the movement of history in the person of Jesus Christ. The Rich Young Ruler was being called into a new being; into a new movement of history determined by God; into a new incarnation of faith; into a new state of social relationships renewed through a restructured political economy.

The church must begin to confess moral complicity with the order of death and convert itself to the Kingdom of life. "Truly, I say to you, there is no person who has left house or wife or brothers or parents or children, for the sake of the Kingdom of God, who will not receive manifold more in this time, and in the age to come eternal life." Living beyond the limitations of the present order of things and its structure of "self-interest" implies living for the Kingdom of God through a sacramental commitment to the poor and the oppressed.

Practical Considerations

Latinos in the U.S. have been marginalized from the centers of social and political power. The bi-racial structure of North American society has contributed to the Latino experience of marginalization. The war against slavery that was fought in the last century between the North and the South has imprinted the American lenses. Why hasn't the Mexican-American war commanded a similar response? The Latino community has remained quite invisible to North Americans despite the fact that all of the territory from Colorado to California once belonged to Mexico and was occupied by Mexicans. "White Society" has slightly increased its awareness of the conditions of wretchedness pervasive in *el barrio* from its work with Central American refugees. However, by and large, the Latino experience in the U.S. continues to be omitted from the language of the progressive North American community. The concern for social justice in Central America has barely been extended into the streets of *el barrio*.

The North American Latino church has been partly responsible for the persistent invisibility of the community. The Latino church in the U.S. has not fully exercised the prophetic role assigned to it by history. The Jesus of the non-scandalous cross and the Bible of spiritualization have been preached over the Jesus that made the poor, outcast, sick, women, and oppressed the heart of his mission. Moreover, the acculturation of both the "white" and "Latino" ecclesial communities has prevented the development of a Christian social ethic which makes connections between the situation of human suffering in *el barrio* and Central America. The ten billion dollars that has been spent since 1978 in Central America on military aid have caused massive levels of human brutalization for the Latino community of the North and South. Death pervades the air of the ghetto and the village streets.

What can be done to foster a more comprehensive understanding of the Latino experience? How can we begin to dismantle the ethic of exoticism? How can an ethic of "connectionalism" emerge for the church? First, the Gospel of Jesus of Nazareth must be "de-Americanized" so it can address our present historical reality. Scripture must cease to be "comfort for the oppressor" and an "opiate for the oppressed." The North American Latino church must help both itself and the white church to incarnate the Gospel in light of the Latino poor of the "connectional" context; moreover, the Latino church of the U.S. must break with the isolation of North American "Lithuanians" and to theology "from below." Second, North American ecclesial communities must make connections between economic exploitation and oppression of people of color both in the U.S. and the Third World. The contextual reality of victimization must be examined in light of the total dynamism of political economy. Third, the local church must begin to develop a global consciousness that fully questions the U.S. presumed right to rob and exploit the Third World or *el barrio*. Fourth, Latinos, Blacks, Native Americans, Asians, women and progressive White communities must forge an alliance with each other and with the justice struggles of the global poor. Fifth, the ideology of "national security" which is at the heart of human brutalization must be dismantled in light of the liberative themes of the Gospel and its concern for justice and life in abundance for the poor and oppressed. Lastly, the war economy must be questioned and brought to a halt precisely because it stands in opposition to the entire created order that groans for liberation.

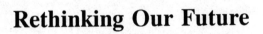

Rethinking Our Future

The Next Ten Years

Justo L. González

It was twelve years ago that a group of us sat around a table in Los Angeles, and planned and dreamed about a journal of Hispanic theology. At that point, it seemed little more than one of those "wouldn't it be nice if..." conversations. Sitting at that table, however, was Dr. Roy D. Barton, Director of the Mexican American Program at Perkins School of Theology, who took the project to heart and made it a reality. Thanks to his skill and enthusiasm, and with the collaboration of the United Methodist Publishing House and several other agencies and individuals, our first issue was published in February, 1981.

I must confess that I had serious doubts and fears as we embarked on our project. I had seen too many periodicals launched with great enthusiasm, and with more resources than we had, only to die after three or four issues. I had seen too many editors worrying about the next deadline, and too many deadlines missed. Would ours be one more in the long list of periodicals that have not survived their first year?

Now, after ten years and forty issues without missing one deadline, my fears have begun to subside. *Apuntes* has made a niche for itself among the theological journals in this country. For that, we must thank the unflagging support of the Mexican American Program at Perkins, of the United Methodist Publishing House, and of our many contributors and readers, who keep us well supplied with enthusiasm and with materials for publication.

Still, as we move towards the second decade of publication --which will end with the second millennium of the Christian era-- there are a number of challenges we must face.

First of these is the interdenominational or ecumenical challenge. Pushed by the census data, as well as by the obvious growth of the Hispanic community, more and more denominations are reconsidering their ministry among Hispanics. My own United Methodist Church has a committee to develop a national plan for Hispanic ministries. Other Protestant denominations either have such a plan, or are working on one. The Roman Catholic Church is studying the phenomenon of proselytism, whereby significant numbers of former Roman Catholics join other churches. It is significant, however, that most of these denominational efforts seek to address the needs of the Hispanic community on their own, with little or no recognition of the presence or the plans of other denominations. This leads to the ineludible suspicion that they are essentially ecclesiocentric, and that the primary needs which they seek to address are not really those of the Hispanic community, but rather those of each particular denomination.

Faced by such a situation, those of us who seek to develop a Hispanic theology must challenge that narrow ecclesiocentric denominationalism. We must certainly discuss theological issues within the context of the denominations to which we belong; but we must also build bridges to other Hispanics raising similar issues in other denominations, and we must seek to develop, throughout the Church at large, a theology and a practice that is more consonant with the needs and the experiences of Hispanic people. I see signs of this approach in a number of articles received recently, and for that we must rejoice.

A second challenge has to do with our relationships to other ethnic groups in our society. There is much in common, for instance, between what is being said by Afro-American theologians and much of what has been published in the pages of *Apuntes* in the last ten years. There is also much in common between the concerns of Hispanics and those of Native Americans. Yet, instead of normally dealing directly with each other, in most of our denominations we communicate through the channels of the denomination at large, which often have little sympathy or understanding of our issues and concerns. A case in point is the approaching date, 1992, which provides opportunity for a critical reassessment of the last five hundred years of our history, leading to repentance and to reconciliation, but which in many quarters is being promoted as the opportunity for a vacuous celebration which will leave us more divided and more deeply hurt. It is our hope that *Apuntes* will serve as a forum where all concerned will work together at the reassessment of the last five hundred years, before we embark blindly on the repetition of the same during the next five hundred.

In the next ten years, it is our hope to promote a Hispanic theology that will be in constant dialogue with and support of other theologies which are born out of similar or parallel concerns.

Thirdly, we must face the challenge of the "globalization" of Christianity --I use that word, for lack of a better one, at the same time that I question the ease and superficiality with which it is used today in many ecclesiastical and theological circles. In the specific case of Hispanics, it has traditionally been true that there are more Roman Catholic Hispanics in Latin American then in the United States. In the case of Protestants, there are now more Protestant Hispanics in Latin America than in the United States. (If present trends continue, there will soon be more Protestants in Latin America than in the United States --Hispanics or not!). We are also increasingly aware that conditions of Hispanic in the United States --good or bad-- have much to do with conditions in Latin America and in other parts of the world. While most of us are part of a Third World in the United States, we allow the media and the official interpretation of events to set us against the legitimate concerns of Latin Americans and of other people in the Third World. A Hispanic theology in the United States, one which seeks to interpret our current situation in the light of the Gospel and of God's promised shalom, must break away from such patterns of thought and of interpretation. In order to do this, a continuing dialogue with our sisters and brothers in Latin America will be necessary. It is hoped that during the coming decade the pages of *Apuntes* will be a forum for such a dialogue.

Finally, we must face the challenges of classism and elitism. Professional theology is by nature elitist and therefore classist. If in order to do theology one must know the biblical languages and several modern ones, as well as the history of theology, the contemporary theological debates, and much more, it is clear that the vast majority of our people will be excluded from such a task. No matter how much we may regret it, most of what has been published in *Apuntes* in the last ten years is elitist --indeed, most of what I have published elsewhere would fall under the same charge.

On the other hand, we claim to be speaking of things which God has hidden from the wise and understanding, and revealed to babes (Lk 10:21). That is what God has done. But we, who are so wise and understanding that we know better than God, have now managed to express them in such a way that they are hidden from any but those who have most understanding and most schooling!

This is probably the greatest and the most difficult challenge of the next decade --indeed, of the next millennium. Will we learn to listen to the wisdom of babes, of the uneducated Salvadoran refugee, of the old man who sits quietly on a pew in our church? And will we learn to translate our speech in such a way that in it the freeing Gospel of Jesus Christ may be heard by the least of God's babes? We have shown that we can do theology with the "best" and the "great"; will we be able to do it with the least and the last who are God's first?

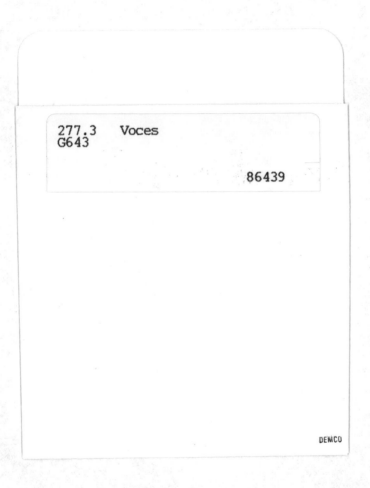